Transcendence
and the Africana
Literary Enterprise

Critical Africana Studies: African, African American, and Caribbean Interdisciplinary and Intersectional Studies

Series Editor: Reiland Rabaka, University of Colorado at Boulder

Series Editorial Board

Christel N. Temple, University of Pittsburgh; Martell Teasley, University of Texas at San Antonio; and Deborah Whaley, University of Iowa

The Critical Africana Studies book series features scholarship within the emerging field of Africana studies, which encompasses such disciplines as African studies, African diasporan studies, African American studies, Afro-American studies, Afro-Asian studies, Afro-European studies, Afro-Islamic studies, Afro-Jewish studies, Afro-Latino studies, Afro-Native American studies, Caribbean studies, Pan-African studies, Black British studies and, of course, Black studies.

The Critical Africana Studies book series directly responds to the heightened demand for monographs and edited volumes that innovatively explore Africa and its diaspora employing cutting-edge critical, interdisciplinary, and intersectional theory and methods.

Titles in the Series

Transcendence and the Africana Literary Enterprise

Christel N. Temple

LEXINGTON BOOKS
Lanham • Boulder • New York • London

Published by Lexington Books
An imprint of The Rowman & Littlefield Publishing Group, Inc.
4501 Forbes Boulevard, Suite 200, Lanham, Maryland 20706
www.rowman.com

6 Tinworth Street, London SE11 5AL, United Kingdom

British Library Cataloguing in Publication Information Available

Library of Congress Cataloging-in-Publication Data

Names: Temple, Christel N., author.
Title: Transcendence and the Africana literary enterprise / Christel N. Temple.
Description: Lanham, Maryland : Lexington Books, [2017] | Series: Critical Africana
    studies | Includes bibliographical references and index.
Identifiers: LCCN 2017038565 (print) | LCCN 2017047805 (ebook) | ISBN
    9781498545099 (Electronic) | ISBN 9781498545082 (cloth : alk. paper) | ISBN
    9781498545105 (pbk : alk. paper)
Subjects: LCSH: American literature—African American authors—History and
    criticism. | Transcendence (Philosophy) in literature. | Pan-Africanism in literature. |
    African Americans—Intellectual life. | African Americans and mass media.
Classification: LCC PS153.N5 (ebook) | LCC PS153.N5 T44 2017 (print) |
    DDC 810.9/896073—dc23
LC record available at https://lccn.loc.gov/2017038565

Contents

Foreword

At the turn of the twenty-first century there was a general sense of optimism inasmuch as the world had escaped the dismal predictions of the end-of-the-world pundits. A heightened spirit of anticipation for the innovative and the new captured the imaginations of the millennials, yet within less than a quarter into the new century a profane political discourse had emerged to bring a cultural and literary distaste to the progressive agenda found in the Age of Obama. In more than a decade of work, Christel N. Temple has championed a vision of a dynamic cultural future based upon the classical concepts found in African American life and literature. Reading *Transcendence and the Africana Literary Enterprise*, one still gets the idea that Temple believes in an optimism generated by action where knowledge and criticism marry to bring understanding.

Charles Fuller, winner of the Pulitzer Prize for drama in 1982, once said to me, "We need literary critics and philosophers who have the knowledge of African American culture to review our creative works." Temple, the head of the University of Pittsburgh's Africana Studies department, has risen to become the most emboldened theorist and critic of her day because of brilliant insights into the relationship between culture and creativity. As Charles Fuller understood, without an appreciation for the culture and social transformations in the African American community one could not write a credible review of African American literature. In my judgment Fuller is one of our special literary heroes because he understood that without literary philosophers of culture who were also critics with consciousness, the Black writer could never be properly reviewed. What this book does, as Temple has done previously, is to delineate the ground that must be cultivated before one can make the proper assessment of language, metaphor, conundrums, linguistics, meanings, and creative narratives. No one has tackled these issues more than she, in the critical landscape of contemporary Africana Studies. She is not the only theorist or critic but she is one of the best.

What makes *Transcendence and the Africana Literary Enterprise* significant is Temple's angle on literary creativity. She explores the characteristically Afrocentric issues of agency and location as markers for literature, predicting a strong disciplinary turn toward uncovering the crevices that have marked the literary criticism terrain when it comes to the study of African and African American literature. This, then, is a profoundly Africological enterprise as much as it is a project of literary criticism.

One can see in Temple's tracking of the course of literature a remarkable ability to reveal new facts, explore fictions, and suggest illusions and collusions in the cultural arena that have been long ignored by other writers. I am convinced that with her wide-ranging references to significant traditional and contemporary writers she has introduced a new language of theory and criticism.

Temple has introduced readers to literary Africology and in doing this work she has established an innovative way of viewing the Africana perspective on literature. If she had done nothing more than this, she would still be considered a revolutionary thinker in the field of critical creative theory. Where Temple is different, futuristic, and visionary happens to be in the way she reads the Black Lives Matter movement as a powerful continuation of a history of social and cultural justice. In some ways one sees that her work is a reflection on masculinity and domination, and actually this poignant recognition of gender and literature demonstrates her serious intent to re-orient the thinking of literary critics. But she is not simply taking on the bleakness one often finds in issues of gender but also the idea of human and Pan-African folk negotiation.

Most impressively Temple knows enough about our literature and criticism to be able to apply Africological sensibilities to critiques of important writings like *Iola Leroy, The Street, A Raisin in the Sun, Ma Rainey's Black Bottom*, as well as other writings in all genres. Thus, she is able to give us an insider's look into autobiography, documentaries, cultural mythology, theology, demography, eulogy, and Afrofuturism. Using concepts like Maat, womanism, text, activist genre, and hip-hop, Temple raises all of the contemporary issues in a broad and deep examination of the collusion between the right to know and the openness to cultural creativity. She gives us Toni Morrison, Lauryn Hill, and Beyoncé as well as *Hamilton* and *Aida* in a burst of creative critical theory as no other contemporary writer in any field has been able to do. What makes Temple's work different is that she reads broadly in all histories, genres of literature, and theoretical perspectives and can bring to a piece of work—whether poetry, drama, novels, short stories or lyrics—all of the power and dynamism of an Afrocentric orientation where the African persona is neither marginalized nor lost in some alien theory. This is the beauty and the strength of this work of numerous chapters of broad cultural memory.

The role of the literary critic is not merely to review works and make comments but to insure that the comments are based fundamentally on the ethical, historical, aesthetic, and artistic standards of the culture of the writing. One could, of course, attempt to apply Chinese or Indian aesthetic concepts to European writing with some novel insights but the better, more productive and profitable course of action is to discover in the culture of the writer the constituents of literary power and to use that for understanding the author's work. This takes intellectual curiosity and a broad base of knowledge. In fact, Temple's understanding of this feature of criticism is key to her advancement of the art and science of critiquing and building literary culture. Convinced that sorting through the memes of art, aesthetics, and the *asilis* of history and myths will support a powerful awakening of the literary imagination in the reader, *Transcendence* lays out a framework for the acceptance of new forms of writing.

She is methodical in speaking about the literary canon in ways that have often escaped those African and African American authors who have criticized the "Western" canon but have fallen victims to the traps of that canon without recognizing that they have become entrapped. Here is the genius of Temple at her best, that is, when she is able to deconflict the various elements of African American culture that appear to be free but are unfree in the imagination of the artist. Sorting through the junkyards of our experiences in this mine-filled culture and history there is a world of clarity to reading masculinity in *The Souls of Black Folk* and *The Living is Easy*. She is able to evoke memories and to project visions of what could be if we only examined texts from other angles. Of course, with all of our tragedies, we are, as Temple understands, a comic people; we love jokes, fun, comedy, and laughter. Out of so much pain inflicted by misunderstandings, bizarre twists of fate played by color and complexion and places of birth and social definitions, African Americans have risen without ever thinking that we could go backwards. Temple appreciates the autobiography as a text of personal construction and sees in every instance of our cultural production the light that shines through every hole in the banged-up ceiling over us. In many ways, this work of hers juts out so far into the future of African American literary thinking that it heralds a new dawning of strong Afrocentric philosophy in relationship to the agency of Black writing. Hence, in reading *Transcendence and the Africana Literary Enterprise* our minds are singing praises on every page.

Dr. Molefi Kete Asante, Professor and Chair
Department of Africology and African American Studies
Temple University
Philadelphia, PA

Molefi Kete Asante is author of the memoir *As I Run Toward Africa* and *The Dramatic Genius of Charles Fuller: An African American Playwright*

Preface

The source of my career in Africana literary studies is the discipline of Africana Studies, and regularly, I encounter students as well as emerging and elder scholars in Africana Studies spaces who celebrate with me the uniqueness and specificity of engaging with literary studies and theory from this vantage point. These encounters tend to be based on oral presentations and conversations, and it is clear that graduate and undergraduate students, and even scholars, yearn for more clarity about this Africana Studies–based enterprise from a dedicated text. In a way, I extend Toni Morrison's observations about "ways in which the presence of Afro-American literature and the awareness of its culture both resuscitate the study of literature in the United States and raise that study's standards."[1] Morrison's lecture addresses the meaning of the canon, but she also implies the role cultural studies sites such as the discipline of Africana Studies play in this resuscitating of the study of literature. Some of her references, such as Ivan Van Sertima's *They Came Before Columbus* (1976), demonstrate a broader-than-literary approach to African American culture, which is in line with priorities of the discipline's literary enterprise. From an Africana Studies perspective, the word "literature" means the function of narrative with respect to memory, storytelling craft, rhetoric and persuasion, the documentation of culture and custom, advancing a racial-culture worldview, and speculative modeling. This is in addition to explication, textual analysis, and teaching structure and form in order to inspire students who need to know literary craft toward their own aspirations as creative writers. Africana literature today is a vast repository of global ideas, experiences, migrations, and sensibilities, and texts benefit from analysis of formalist and poststructuralist approaches grounded in Africana disciplinary specificity.

I have many mentors, colleagues, and models of excellence who practice the study of African and diaspora literatures from other academic sites and who have given me their blessings and support as I strive to define a contemporary iteration of the literary world of the discipline of Africana Studies. Our collective work is strong and is in creative solidarity with one another across disciplines. In collaboration and with a shared sense of our overlapping endeavor, these scholars from other disciplinary sites in the academy support this book's focus on the distinct project of clarifying, based on a considerable engagement with the African American canon, Africana Studies approaches to literary criticism, idea formation, and using literature to advance the discipline.

The Africana literary domain is an interesting location. Scholars from many disciplinary orientations teach African and diaspora literature in the academy from myriad critical perspectives that emphasize the study of structure, form, and canon or de-emphasize these in favor of the text's thematic and artifact value as cultural production. In my orientation to the curricular Africana disciplinary craft of teaching literature, it is imperative to engage all matters of structure, theme, and function or application. This approach properly frames the discipline's literary enterprise as critically exhaustive and rigorous. The Africana disciplinary literary enterprise has had to meander through outdated assumptions that define the discipline as an unfortunate space for the total engagement of a text. However, this book and its adjacent contemporary studies seminally equip literary practitioners with a framework for advancing the discipline through its institutionalized literary enterprise.

It takes a scholar from within the discipline's literary enterprise to confirm the organic and normative impulses of the discipline's craft. This book supports and encourages an evolved training of literary scholars in doctoral Africana Studies programs and significant training at the undergraduate level. The academy seems well aware of the atmosphere of freedom enabled within the discipline. This makes departments of Africana Studies highly desirable sites for teaching and research. However, this requires some intervention. Some Cultural Studies, Diaspora Studies, Gender Studies, and Anthropology orientations to teaching within the Africana Studies literary curriculum are based on interpretations and assumptions that the discipline's literary domain gives carte blanche—that they can pursue and limit their teaching to myopic and anachronistic subjects or to personal platforms of interest. The rationale of this expectation that the Africana literary setting is a vague and undefined space is incorrect, and this book is committed to clarifying its scope and success. _Transcendence_ is what I offer to characterize the contemporary Africana disciplinary institutionalization of the literary enterprise. It is curricular, canonical, beyond canonical, innovative, exhaustive, rigorous, comparative, and disciplinary. In Africana Studies, teaching literature _is_ teaching the discipline. This book humbly suggests ways to meet this disciplinary expectation.

NOTE

1. Toni Morrison, "Unspeakable Things Unspoken: The Afro-American Presence in American Literature" In *The Norton Anthology of African American Literature*, edited by Henry Louis Gates and Nellie Y. McKay (New York: W. W. Norton & Company, 2004), 2301.

Acknowledgments

It is an honor to celebrate the many who supported this book, beginning with Reiland Rabaka, editor of the Critical Africana Studies series with Lexington Books, and Sarah Craig, Acquisitions Editor, who made my day in May 2017 when she shared, "I love this book." This book has a long history of tug-o-war and patience, as I envisioned a monograph that stabilizes the literary practices of disciplinary Africana Studies by modeling the craft for the next generation, also as I fought the impulse to publish many chapters as journal articles to disseminate the craft in a different way. James L. Conyers, Jr. has been an invaluable colleague, particularly through his challenge, years ago, that I write an essay on Africana literary historiography, which was the germination of this project. I thank scholars such as Doñela Wright of San Francisco State University, and a good handful of doctoral students from Temple University, Northwestern University, Michigan State University, and University of Maryland Baltimore County, whose enthusiasm for a comprehensive book on Afrocentric literary and cultural methodology encouraged me as I met deadlines and put the final touches on the manuscript. I send a special thanks to Inte'a DeShields who served as my graduate research assistant early in the process. I am grateful to my students who endured semesters of eureka moments as I taught many of the texts in this book and paused lectures to quickly scribble chapter topics and intriguing analyses that came to me while teaching.

I appear to work in isolation, but I am mindful of many. The camaraderie of English and Africana Studies scholars whose expertise intersects has been so helpful to my work, and I am forever grateful to Miriam DeCosta-Willis for defining this broad journey into literary criticism and the construction of theory. This book achieved an extra layer of balance and flow from the clarifying recommendations of reviewers. I thank Kameelah Martin of

The College of Charleston for organizing our panel at the South Atlantic Modern Language Association (SAMLA) with Dana A. Williams of Howard University which enabled us to confer on our collective work, and which set in motion my future SAMLA participation with Shauna Morgan Kirlew of Howard University and McKinley E. Melton of Gettysburg College on dimensions of Africana literary practice. Also, I value tremendous goodwill and a conversation about the canon from Gene Andrew Jarrett. These interactions come after many compelling and supportive encounters with the College Language Association (CLA) and its members such as Joanne V. Gabbin, Sandra Y. Govan, Yakini Kemp, Dolan Hubbard, Antonio Tillis, R. Baxter Miller, and Mbye Cham. Colleagues here at the University of Pittsburgh have been equally inspiring, namely Shalini Puri, and the team of Imani Owens and Autumn Womack (now at Princeton University), who brought brilliant new potential and critical work to our brainstorming to enhance the Africana-English joint major. Also, I thank Gloria Stephens Smith, professor emerita at Michigan State University, for inspiration for several chapters' contexts of religion and spirituality fine-tuned through opportunities to work with a series of Michigan State's African American and African Studies doctoral program's Black Religion and Spirituality (BRS) conferences.

My former colleagues at the University of Maryland Baltimore County have been amazing in so many ways. Thomas N. Robinson, Jr. gave me the freedom and funding to initiate several of these chapters at the annual conventions of the National Council for Black Studies and CLA, at the annual Cheikh Anta Diop International Conference, and internationally at the Afroeuropeans: Cultures and Identities Conference. I am especially grateful to Willie Lamousé-Smith for ongoing support and mentoring toward framing many layers of my research in innovative ways. My current and retired colleagues at the University of Pittsburgh are worthy of tremendous thanks for helping to maintain a rigorous, fast-paced, and innovative research environment of mutual support. Brenda F. Berrian is at the top of the list for modeling such savvy literary and cultural work in and out of the classroom. I thank Michele Reid-Vazquez for lending a critical ear, as well as Yolanda Covington-Ward, Felix Germain, Robin A. Brooks, Michael T. Tillotson, Oronde Sharif, and Jerome Taylor for helping to maintain a vibrant Africana Studies setting. Finally, I thank my family—my parents, Rev. and Mrs. Fernando E. Temple, Sr., and especially my son—for sharing me with my work, and I offer special gratitude to too-many-to-name, for dutiful friendship and ongoing feedback. Grounded by so much wonderful support, I have forged ahead to make this humble contribution to better defining the literary dimensions of the discipline of Africana Studies.

Introduction

The Canon and the Africana Worldview

The African American literary canon is the chronological collection of pioneering and excellent creative, oral, aesthetically successful, narrative, and written sources that are the structural models and core content of the ongoing tradition of African American literature. Anthologies help to maintain it, and credentialed practitioners keep its magic alive with a vision and constant awareness of the cyclical interplay between past creative production and the ongoing genius it inspires. The canon and its criticism are older than the discipline of Africana Studies, even though the discipline's objective is to order the comprehensive study of African-derived phenomena within the university setting and beyond, and for the benefit of people and community. The discipline has matured and evolved to stabilize itself as an innovative and expanding network of critical idea formation and new knowledge, and in its most formal organization, it is empowered by a paradigmatic approach that sustains its institutionalization. The curriculum of the discipline of Africana Studies covers many subject areas, and this book explores how it frames literary study in a distinct way.

Literary criticism plays a significant role in maintaining the canon, the tradition, and society's understanding of how literature is a prism that reflectively signifies the culture's historical, social, political, psychological, linguistic, narrative, and conceptual realities. This book orients literary criticism toward Africana disciplinary practices, which is a route toward better institutionalizing the discipline's literary practices. Most chapters explore one to two featured canonical texts framed by specifically Africana Studies–based methodologies and perspectives. The chapters reflect an African-centered worldview and Afrocentric agency-driven responses to the African American literary canon. The canon is the source of literary criticism as each generation experiences texts and literary periods to draw both similar and divergent conclusions from the texts based on the generation's unique point of view and sociohistorical reality. This can be said of disciplines as well. This book contributes to African American canonical discourse not from the perspective of a new generation, necessarily, but from the vantage point of a disciplinary generation whose critical assessment is sharpened from a precise lens that is attentive to the ways literature functions systematically within Africana Studies. This approach produces transcendence in numerous discourses that are in direct dialogue with traditional approaches to African American literature but significantly feature Africana Studies' conceptual priorities.

Aisha Blackshire-Belay's edited collection *Language and Literature in the African American Imagination* (1992) is a pioneering work that, as a volume, raised the question of what impact the Afrocentric paradigm will have on processes of African American literature. In particular, "the widespread debate over the canon in American literature, the issue of cultural diversity, and the need to have books with critical inquiry into African American cultures could make this collection suitable for scholars and students in such diverse fields as literature, linguistics, and African American studies."[1] Her collection announced an inevitable shift in African American literary studies, as English-trained scholars joined ranks with Africana Studies innovators to apply the paradigm, in concrete and recognizable Africana disciplinary language, to their African-centered orientations to criticism. The Black Arts and Black Aesthetic movements had prepared them for a new and advanced radical, culturally centered orientation that would restructure how the academy and the community approach knowledge. While some scholars quickly aligned themselves with the new tools, others chose to continue to do centered cultural work, yet without embracing terms such as Afrocentric. Over twenty-five years later, the discipline's literary enterprise has sufficiently incubated. This collection on transcendence and the Africana literary enterprise emerges for final and optimum impact as an act of institutionalizing the discipline's literary practices.

In more recent years, literary scholars have offered compelling contextualizations of the relationship between the canon and Africana Studies. In *Contemporary African American Fiction: New Critical Essays* (2009), edited by Dana A. Williams, Eleanor Traylor states: "These decades would reveal the rise of interdisciplinary Black Studies, African American Studies, the introduction of the heretical text, as James Baldwin had put it, into the congregation (canon) of the always-already chosen righteous. . . ."[2] This observation centers the anchor essay that crowns content with context to conclude Williams's collection. Traylor is eloquent in her style of literary litany and summoning to stage a reading of Toni Morrison's *Paradise* to assert the power of storytelling in spite of shifts in the academy and losses due to increasing globalization.

Contemporary African American Literature: The Living Canon (2013), edited by Lovalerie King and Shirley Moody-Turner, is a more recent volume whose contributors introduce dynamic contemporary discourses related to what Mat Johnson in the volume's foreword describes as "an historic moment in African American literary dialogue" in which there is an even greater need for quality literary criticism.[3] He reiterates the robust moment, noting again—"This is an historical moment in African American literature, when new social realities demand new questions be asked."[4] Johnson is a novelist and professor of creative writing, but his observations parallel Africana Studies sensibilities, reminding us of the need for both specificity and dialogue about our diverse approaches to the canon. The editors provide great clarity about the myriad questions that confront the African American literary tradition, and within their primarily English-based and highly relevant concerns for their practice, they are also aware of how African American literature is practiced from multiple sites. Their summative description of the ongoing literary tradition notes: "Such a tradition is distinguishable by a history of shared formal, thematic and other concerns that have been adapted to late twentieth-century and early twenty-first-century contexts."[5] They also embrace one of the contributors' perspectives as a best practices viewpoint amid the competing debates about key questions of African American literature and the canon. They paraphrase Evie Shockley and suggest, "we should consider how the African American literary tradition is characterized by multiple aesthetics accompanied by varied and diverse, rather than monolithic, strategies for grappling with questions of race, gender, identity and tradition."[6]

The final essay of *Contemporary African American Literature: The Living Canon* is the most compatible with transcendent Africana Studies literary discourses and reveals how traditional African American literary practices within English departments are indeed attentive to the commonalities between the two disciplinary crafts. Greg Carr and Dana A. Williams celebrate that "Africana Studies seeks to theorize out of long-view genealogies of African intellectual work."[7] The authors also bespeak the contest between the two disciplines:

> The attempt to use these [Africana] conceptual categories to read a contemporary African American text is not without its challenges—the impetus to offer an Africana Studies reading (using the conceptual categories as the incubator for such a pursuit) of African American literary texts without consideration of an engagement with the full range of Africana Studies methodologies is a seductive (and potentially reductive) one. Yet, the dormant possibilities potentially made manifest by situating the two distinct disciplines (literary study as the discipline in the case of African American literature) beside each other are perhaps among African American literature's few sources of meaningful liberation.[8]

This point of view is a rare gem in contemporary African American literary criticism, and is a result of cross-departmental collaboration that stands as a beacon of possibility, all in the name of cultivating the broadest effect of the African American literary tradition. The authors also warn of "superficial" practices of *carelessly* replacing requisite literary critiques with Africana conceptual expectations.[9] Africana Studies is also plagued by outsider assumptions that the discipline is a comfy academic site where they can use texts to teach culture, thus abandoning their commitment to credential their students with layers of requisite formal skills related to literary and textual analysis, devices, and conventions.

Building upon these broad understandings of the canon this book is a study of the innovation and distinction of engaging with the African American literary canon within the discipline of Africana Studies. The thesis of this study is that the approach to structuring knowledge and inquiry in the Africana literary enterprise is a commitment to *transcendence*, which is balancing literary analysis with social science applications as a critical and pedagogical process representing the paradigmatic core of Africana Studies as a layered, multidimensional academic and practical pursuit. This is not a new argument, per se; engaging the sociology of literature or literature as sociology has a long tradition in the academy and has been a core argument of Africana disciplinary theorists since the 1960s. However, in the contemporary process of institutionalizing the subject areas of the discipline of Africana Studies—in this case writing as a manifestation of creative production, aesthetics, culture, and communication—the critical process benefits from being itemized as *transcendence* and from being modeled in a series of literary criticism applications that serve as case studies. Such an effort toward an Africana Studies orientation to pedagogy and literary criticism is stabilizing and clarifying.

This book signifies the differential between Africana literary logic and routine African American literary criticism viewpoints, including the scope of bibliographic expectations related to the canon. The chapters are in dialogue with key anthologies and sources that comprehensively define the African American literary canon, namely, *The Norton Anthology of African American Literature* (2004), *Call and Response: The Riverside Anthology of the African American Literary Tradition* (1998), Maryemma Graham's *The Cambridge Companion to the African American Novel* (2004), Bernard Bell's *The Afro-American Novel and Its Tradition* (1987) and *The Contemporary African American Novel: Its Folk Roots and Modern Literary Branches* (2004), and Gene Andrew Jarrett's *A Companion to African American Literature* (2010). Jarrett's edited volume of criticism is of particular value because it demonstrates a level of compatibility with Africana disciplinary interests in anteriority and demarcations between African-derived and European-derived literary worldviews.

The discipline's literary pursuit is indebted to the traditional and chronological framing of the African American literary canon that most university English department curricula manage in a formal and linear way. The nation's Africana Studies departments also include such traditional training in their curricula—a requisite that scholars also meet by teaching the tradition through canon summary—which is appropriate for topic-driven courses.

The chapters proceed chronologically, building a narrative about transcendence and modeling the specificity of Africana Studies–based modes of inquiry for traditional, canonical, and innovative readings of Frances Ellen Watkins Harper's *Iola Leroy* (1893), W. E. B. Du Bois's *The Souls of Black Folk* (1903), Claude McKay's *Banjo* (1929), Ann Petry's *The Street* (1946), Dorothy West's *The Living is Easy* (1948), Paul Robeson's *Here I Stand* (1958), Lorraine Hansberry's *A Raisin in the Sun* (1959), Malcolm X's *Autobiography* (1964), August Wilson's *Ma Rainey's Black Bottom* (1985), and Octavia Butler's *Parable of the Sower* (1993). Several final chapters tackle orientations beyond the canon. Daniel Black's alarming tale *Perfect Peace* presents a contemporary use of allegory that re-orients gender identity frameworks in a community-based discourse as a legacy of Toni Morrison's literary interventions. Black's novel is sure to become part of the contemporary canon.

The book ends with chapters on gendered hip-hop, Broadway as text, and transatlantic performances of cultural memory. The discipline-based pairings of literature with other subject areas, the articulation of what constitutes the discipline's atmosphere of freedom, an interest in a disciplinary application of dutiful survey, and attention to expectations of Africana reader-response theory are woven through the analysis in order to model transcendence as Africana literary phenomenology. Each chapter in the book further advances the discussion of canon alignment and innovation.

Within the African American literary tradition, Black internationalism, Pan-Africanism, migration, and cultural mythology have occasionally extended the geographical borders of the canon, and this book has several examples of such overlap wherein comparative literary and cultural analyses are natural expansions and inclusions. Chronologically, it addresses subjects of masculinity, Pan-Africanism, humor, bibliographic worldview, cultural mythology, the documentary form, demographics versus dramaturgy, liberation theology, eulogy, psychology, womanism, and hero dynamics through an Africana Studies–based view. The most popular and most utilized anthologies and literary companions to African American literature are extraordinary sources for the vital linear chronicling of the literary tradition. However, the literary enterprise in the discipline of Africana Studies often has a transcended approach that enables alternative categorizations based on the discipline's theories, logic, methodologies, and conceptual frameworks. These frameworks yield new readings and feature different variables and applications. This book is the first of its kind to sustain an argument for the Africana literary enterprise through an interplay with the canon.

Africana Studies disciplinary practitioners have been carving out academic space through the reorganization and redefinition of knowledge pertaining to people of African descent and through the creation and implementation of new epistemologies that reflect African-centered and Afrocentric approaches to knowledge. This collective activity has resulted in the emergence of Africana Studies as an academic discipline built on the foundations of the survivalist behaviors of Africans in the Americas, as well as in Africa and the diaspora. The conceptual possibilities of Africana Studies as a contemporary specialized discipline are in full bloom as new readings and discipline-specific orientations reveal dynamic and original visions of the meaning of Black life and behavior—a meaning based on unflinching attention to cultural agency and emancipated formulations of African-centered logic.

In essence, the discipline of Africana Studies gives scholars the freedom to think creatively and historically in order to organically describe phenomena and efficiently manage the challenges that characterize and affect the lives and experiences of people of African descent. The discipline as well as its literary enterprise are attentive to heritage experiences, knowledge recovery, classical African philosophy and ethics, contemporary problem-solving, cultural self-determination, global African unity and cooperation, and stabilizing cultural identity through narrative forms that intersect with the practical in a multidimensional layering of knowledge.

Scholars tend to describe work that relies on cross-sectional and layered analyses that either draw from multiple traditional disciplines or meander between the spaces and topics omitted in these disciplines as *interdisciplinary* or *multidisciplinary*; however, *multidimensional* is the optimum description that prevents Africana Studies from being overly invested in the priorities of other academic disciplines. Moving beyond these terms, *multidimensional* captures the discipline's unique method and logic for layering ideas, concepts, theories, history, and data into usable narratives and tools to advance Africana experience as a model for the human capacity for renewal and regeneration.

Another objective of this book is to provide examples of Africana literary methodology and critical modes of thinking. Readers will recognize morsels of the familiar whether through an author, text, event, or theory, but this book draws attention to the innovative critical approaches to the familiar in distinct formation of Africana Studies logic. The book's chapters demonstrate the ways in which Africana Studies reconfigures the boundaries and categories of knowledge, argument, and evidence. In *content* it offers an instructive model for audiences getting acquainted with the discipline through the lens of diverse non-fiction genres (e.g. essay, speech, eulogy, autobiography/ documentary, and historical essay) as well as fiction or more imaginative and performative genres (e.g. novel, rap/hip-hop performance and video, theatre,) that collectively comprise the *literary enterprise* in the most contemporary sense. In *structure,* it is a more advanced model to challenge advanced students to begin to formulate their own conceptual directions for interpreting the range of Africana ideas and experience represented in narrative. As a contribution to inspiring the next generation of historically informed genius and creativity, the contemporary Africana Studies enterprise demands a standard of mastering historical content *plus* theorizing the Africana experience with originality and vision. This imperative to develop communicative tools and patterns of itemizing and developing elements of African-centered historical, cultural, linguistic, political, and *literary* models into informative tools that enable practitioners of Africana Studies to speak authoritatively to advance and defend Black life is essential to the discipline's progress.

This book frames the growth and expansion of knowledge on the subject of Africana life and experience, with a lens toward the literary enterprise whose analyses rely on additional competencies in the discipline's subject areas. Its literary enterprise also reflects a layering of subject areas and critical approaches drawn from the key subject areas of the discipline: [*Black*] History, Economics, Religion, Politics, Sociology, Psychology, Creative Production, Culture, Aesthetics, Communication, Community Development, Philosophy, Pan-Africanism, Education, Gender, Linguistics, Geography, and Health/Science/Technology. The discipline trains its practitioners, even in the literary enterprise, to be conversant with many data sources across the discipline's subject areas. Literary methods filter useable data from a variety of sources. The ensuing innovation or *transcendence* is the creation of theories, approaches, concepts, and terminologies that model the nature of engaging literature in its practical and disciplinary possibilities.

There are many sites in the academy that generate Africana, African, and diaspora literary knowledge, but this book reveals the specificity of disciplinary pursuits in transcendence. The goal of professionally trained Africologists is to generate texts and scholarship that are theoretically compatible with Afrocentric and African-centered frames of reference in the matured discipline of Africana Studies. The discipline of Africana Studies encourages scholars to embrace the challenge to be well-read in African, African-derived, African-centered, Diaspora, and Western/European history, traditional culture, popular culture, and current events as a skill set to delineate extraordinary and practical relationships between world history, ancient-to-present global African heritage, diaspora evolution and adaptation, and the future stability of global African heritage identity and well-being.

Approaching the feature of transcendence chronologically and in conversation with the canon—as a traditional organization of content and excellence and coordinated with key Africana Studies subject area sources—enables various interpretations of and applications of traditional texts. This is a practice of *framing* inquiry, meandering as guide, as suggestion, and as model, with varying degrees of depth depending on topic and objective. Some chapters achieve comprehensive textual analysis; others invoke perspective, innovation, or methodological bravery. The explicative depth varies from one chapter to the next by design to demonstrate the versatility of isolating, pausing, meta-focusing, or providing old fashioned full-text explication in the processes of balancing literary and Africana idea formation and cultural analysis. The coverage is selective yet aims to inspire scholars to pursue inquiry that may fill the gaps or address complementary analyses.

Chapter 1 introduces attributes of literary Africology. As Africana Studies is further grounding its disciplinary specificity with shifts in naming the enterprise from Africana to Africology, this chapter is attentive to how the institutionalization of the literary enterprise is part of the emerging specificity. This chapter introduces the emergent language and functional contexts of Africana disciplinary literary criticism and borrows from education studies on reader-response theory to reinforce effect.

Chapters 2 through 4 represent critical analyses of the canon's more traditional texts from the turn of the nineteenth century to the mid-twentieth century, including mostly comparative studies of works from Harper, Du Bois, McKay, West, and Petry. The discourses in these chapters negotiate idea formation beyond the critical contexts maintained by canon presentation and in the collective critical bibliographies on the texts. Chapter 2 tackles topics of male mortality in readings of Du Bois and West, updated and humanized by comparisons to Black Lives Matter and Black Male Studies platforms that redirect traditional readings, especially of West's novel, which had been explored widely for its feminist and womanist value. Chapter 3 proposes a dissection of the variable of humor away from folkloric interpretations of McKay's tricksterism in favor of aligning his jocular trope of observation with a functional Pan-African negotiation of cross-cultural relationship-building. Chapter 4 is an exploratory critical redirection of bibliographic trends in existing thematic and critical choices for criticism on the scholarship on Harper's *Iola Leroy* and Petry's *The Street* that shifts attention to the understudied prominence of African cultural retentions in the texts.

Chapters 5 through 7 prompt Africana-based readings of form and genre beyond the essay and the novel genres featured in earlier chapters and align them with three different Africana literary methodologies. Paul Robeson's autobiography and documentary are the subjects of Chapter 5 which ambitiously introduces the effect of applying attributes of the theory of Black cultural mythology to comparative pairings in adaptation studies. Chapter 6 extends readings of Lorraine Hansberry's *Raisin in the Sun* through the lens of literary Pan-Africanism and relies on the Worldview Analysis Scale (WAS) to propose a Black psychology quantification of Africanity in the play. Chapter 7 deconstructs implications of characterization in August Wilson's *Ma Rainey's Black Bottom* using the demographic literary standard (DLS) to discover pre-disciplinary routes of transmitting knowledge on ancient African history and global African achievement embodied in the consciousness of Wilson's character Toledo.

Chapters 8 through 10 approach the subjects of religion, spirituality, and ethics from foundational subject area grounding in Africana Studies. Chapter 8 interrogates the new religion, Earthseed, from Octavia Butler's *Parable of the Sower*, to evaluate its proximity to Black liberation theology. Chapter 9 interprets Africana models of self-eulogy as prophetic spiritual possibilities related to contemporary theorizations of Afrofuturism. This chapter's studies respond to the archived Christian funeral program of Black Studies ancestor John Henrik Clarke in comparison to the historical record of Malcolm X's Islamic example of passing into ancestorship. Chapter 10 merges assumptions of moral ethics and communal justice drawing not only from the ancient Kemetic principle of *Maat* but also from Black psychology. This chapter anticipates an addition to the canon for Daniel Black's novel *Perfect Peace* which is a metanarrative signification on 1992 Nobel Laureate Toni Morrison's novel *The Bluest Eye* that challenges the African American community to think critically about human agency and about its reactions to fluid gender identities.

The final three chapters reflect border crossing and extend the meaning of text into areas of oratory, lyricism, performance, music, and media. Chapter 11 is a study of how African American woman speakers/performers manage form and content with the privilege of having an audience within the public sphere. The approach excavates and theorizes the achievement of abolitionist speaker Maria W. Stewart in order to measure the extent to which women in rap and hip-hop can be said to participate within a continuum. Chapter 12 examines Africana-related Broadway experiences as social and communal encounters with what are, in essence, still *texts*. Questions of audience, authenticity, assumptions, and historicity emerge as unexpected critical topics based on viewings of *Aida*, specifically, and *Hamilton*, in contemporary comparison. Chapter 13 pushes the envelope to consider canonical African American images and heroic references and utterances in diaspora rap and hip-hop as performance texts aligned with the literary and with creative production. The conclusion reinforces the relationship between transcendence and the ensuing atmosphere of freedom fostered in the Africana literary enterprise.

In reading this book's examples of literary transcendence beyond the traditional canon, I encourage readers to rediscover the diversity of the literary enterprise in its non-fiction and fiction engagements as well as in its academic intersectionality with methodologies and traditions that pioneered the topics, the African-centered points of reference, and inevitably insist that literary studies also advance Africana Studies as a discipline. It is my hope that this book inspires readers to more consciously and deliberately advance Africana Studies–based interests inspired by creative and structured writing.

The Africana Studies scholar is positioned to be a steward and agent of a very exciting moment in the history of knowledge creation. The discipline has created, stabilized, and claimed academic space in the university, and scholars have the opportunity to ask the right questions and to explore the phenomena that characterize Black life with an unprecedented academic freedom and authority enabled by the times and its technology. Literature, as a dynamic prospect for this extraordinary process, continues to be a source of inspiration and innovation.

NOTES

1. This is the publisher's summary on the back cover of the volume from 1992. It is important because it reflects how publisher and editor chose to market its innovation and value just a few years—less than five years, and subtracting the time the book was in press—after the introduction of Afrocentricity in 1987.

2. Eleanor W. Traylor, "Re-Imagining the Academy: Story and Pedagogy in Contemporary African American Fiction," in *Contemporary African American Fiction: New Critical Essay*, edited by Dana A. Williams (Columbus: The Ohio State University Press, 2009). 165 (160–171)

3. Mat Johnson. Foreword, in *Contemporary African American Literature: The Living Canon*, edited by Lovalerie King and Shirley Moody-Turner (Bloomington: Indiana University Press, 2013): xi (ixxii)

4. Ibid.

5. Lovalerie King and Shirley Moody-Turner. Introduction, in *Contemporary African American Literature: The Living Canon*, edited by Lovalerie King and Shirley Moody-Turner (Bloomington: Indiana University Press, 2013): 5 (1–13)

6. Ibid., 3.

7. Greg Carr and Dana A. Williams, "Toward the Theoretical Practice of Conceptual Liberation: Using an Africana Studies Approach to Reading African American Literary Texts," in *Contemporary African American Literature: The Living Canon*, edited by Lovalerie King and Shirley Moody-Turner (Bloomington: Indiana University Press, 2013): 302 (302–327).

8. Ibid., 312.

9. Ibid., 314.

Chapter 1

Literary Africology

Literary Africology describes the need to theorize what takes place in an Africana Studies literary world as a component of advancing the discipline and institutionalizing *literary* studies from a disciplinary point of view. Literary Africology suggests that we increase consciousness by stylizing an interpretive and applied methodology to the corpus of Black texts and creative oratory/writing by fashioning a better understanding of Africana cognitive reading. We use our stories and storytelling as catalysts for perfecting our human critical skills of analysis, deduction, research, inquiry, and to be globally and cosmologically engaged as an ongoing human enterprise of understanding each other and the world. These processes are supported by an Africana cognitive orientation that intuitively and practically engages perception, sensation, discernment, understanding, comprehension, insight, experience, and the acquiring of knowledge from an informed cultural worldview.

Strengthening and institutionalizing the literary enterprise of Africana Studies involves the circulation and expanded use of a set of features culled and arranged specifically for this purpose. These tools of literary Africology are Africana reader-response, bibliographic shift, pairing, isolation, canon summary, idea formation modeling, disciplinary competency, applied functionality, Africana phenomenology, multidimensionality, and dutiful survey. The practice relies on analyses of traditional literary features such as adaptation studies and metanarrative as well as on specific Africana-based literary criticism such as the demographic literary standard (DLS), Black cultural mythology, and literary Pan-Africanism. Collectively, the features and critical paradigms are not exhaustive, but they verify the volume's immersion in an Africana-derived literary enterprise.

Disciplinary competency is verification that, pedagogically speaking, a scholar's or a critic's theoretical and paradigmatic understanding of the discipline of Africana Studies is established and sound. The discipline organizes subject area knowledge as multi-epistemologies in a researcher's or an analyst's critical repertoire to record and respond to the culture's various phenomena in the agency of its creation and critique, particularly of forms of domination that the culture must resist for its well-being. This approach credentials practitioners as master communicators in matters of culture, race, history, and transnationalism, and as social agents able to operate with a high cultural competency. The observations and critical logic of the discipline's practitioners are naturally responsible for the creation of new knowledge and distinct idea formation based on structured training in the discipline, also primarily for the benefit of stabilizing and reinforcing the specificity of the discipline. Collectively, disciplinary competency in Africana Studies is articulated in scholars' creative confidence in their ability to offer original perspectives and readings of phenomena aligned with the discipline's priorities. A final objective is to generate ideas and tools to improve the lot of African heritage groups and humanity through an openness to activism, programming, education, community development, and policy initiatives generated from a synthesized Africana curricular expertise.

Applied functionality is a charge to readers to not only critique and historicize the text but also strive to find ways to understand the conflicts illuminated by the text within a context of social science problem-solving. It is an imperative to find ways to use the literature as a cultural tool beyond the walls of the academy. One of the most compelling anecdotes is, how critics were so enamored of Suzan-Lori Parks's play *In the Blood*'s uses of Euripedes' *Medea*, of Greek tragedy structure (chorus, confessions), influences from Nathaniel Hawthorne's *The Scarlet Letter* (1850), and references to the *Oedipus* tragedy, that they construed these as the central value of Parks's creation. They are *significations*, and do not constitute the sole function and importance of Parks's work. However, in an Africana-aligned reading, her lasting artistic contribution is challenging the audience to self-examine their race, class, and sexuality prejudices when her play proves to the audience that they, too, are guilty of having prejudicial thoughts against a homeless, unemployed, frustrated, Afro-Latina protagonist. Such a reading implores social justice and behaviors reinforcing change.

Among professionally trained Africologists, the discipline's literary pursuits are described as creative production, aesthetics, and memory-making and contemporary scholars are finding the label of "literature" to be less accurate in describing their work. What transpires in the discipline's classrooms is a dynamic response to the discipline's foundations and frames of reference; thus there are strategies and orientations to Africana literature that are discipline-specific. Chapter 4's comparison of traditional and African-centered criticism on Frances Ellen Watkins Harper's *Iola Leroy* (1893) and Ann

Petry's *The Street* (1946) is an example of this. The comparisons are not to discredit the work managed by scholars in other literary disciplines. Instead, they reiterate the atmosphere of freedom that the literary enterprise of the discipline of Africana Studies brings to Africana literary practice. We tend to do different things in the study and application of literature, and in order to advance the discipline and to institutionalize its orientation to its subject areas, Africana literary scholars are beginning to publish literary criticism and analysis with an Africana disciplinary label that actually reflects *grounding*. Differential comparisons hint at possibilities of what readers informed by various African-centered orientations and Afrocentric consciousness bring to the analysis of literature. This is a shift that expands the need to explore reading methods and reader-response theory additionally from Africology-based vision and praxis.

Africological reader-response merges with audience theory and addresses what discipline-trained readers and critical thinkers cognitively bring to the process of analyzing the culture's literatures. In the academy, this concern falls under topics such as reading methods, the sociolinguistics of reading, the cultural theory of reading, cognitive literary studies, and psycholinguistics. Additionally, much of the research is considered relevant more for K-12 pedagogies for teaching reading and reading comprehension, particularly the debate over phonics versus whole language techniques as well as cultural bias in standardized testing. Africana reader-response theory suggests that as readers and as a community informed by the discipline's paradigms, the reading and engagement of a text are distinguished by culturally specific objectives, thought-processes, intuitions, and anticipation of functionality. The unique orientations relate to the African worldview, an emphasis on increasing consciousness, a search for the African continuum, the anticipation of agency, and the ability to reconcile narratives related to oppression with a healthy sense of the tension between resistance and capitulation. At the core, readers wish to be entertained and to be intrigued. However, cultural readers desire other nuances and benefits from the experience.

Wanda Brooks and Susan Browne make strides in exploring "how culture enables literary interpretations of texts," with their theory suggesting that, "because a range of cultural positions factors into students' meaning making, we should mine texts more carefully for cultural milieu as well as find acceptance with a broader range of literary interpretations."[1] Their study confirms that reader responses to literature "are powerful personal evocations influenced by both readers and stories" that "are often mediated by the space one occupies in the world," that include "derived cultural positions" and the regular act of reader positioning "in relationship to texts with strong cultural fabric."[2] This tendency increases as readers become more acutely aware of sophisticated cultural paradigms such as those featured as premises of

Africology. The Africana Studies–trained reader approaches literature from a position of disciplinary specificity and advances practical, life-enhancing objectives for audiences of all age groups. This goal is in dialogue with children's literature experts who expose "the lack of knowledge many educators have of African American literature; they focus on familiar historical figures, rather than take the time to familiarize themselves with the contemporary literature their students find more relatable."[3] The interventions implemented for school-age readers get updated for adult readers.

The Africana literary enterprise merges interest with the subject area of Black education in order to institutionalize the discipline's paradigms, orientations, and resources not only at the collegiate and lay levels but also in primary and secondary settings of literature engagement. Katie Sciurba's school-age intervention is vital to the intergenerational vision of Africana literature. She differentiates between "empathetic" (based on a familiar or literal personal connection) and "sympathetic" (based on an unfamiliar, yet relatable, connection).[4] This ordering helps educators discern how "students either 'see themselves' in the material because they have lived through similar experiences, or they did not 'see themselves' in the text but could *imagine* having experiences similar to those depicted in the text."[5] Africana reader-response approaches for scholar, student, and adult audiences, in general, benefit from examining educational child-development research which is more attentive to and more aware of the cognitive processes at work in a literary environment. The adult encounters society has with African American literature are sometimes inhibited by such delayed exposure to cultural literary traditions, and this tragedy introduces additional research questions about the latent effects of impeding cultural awareness in school curricula that scholars have masterfully introduced in research on visibility and teacher selection of African American texts in a grade school setting.[6]

From an Africana perspective, we desire and demand certain things of our literatures, and the literary criticism and contextualization should respond well to these desires and demands. The expectations include a desire for narratives with cultural-based cleverness that additionally differentiate cleverness from humor. This includes experiencing entertainment based on intellectual and cultural satisfaction accomplished through intrigue, humor, and effect. Readers seek a balance in narratives that permit Africana cultural values to be the noblest of motives, even though society is mature enough to process stories about Africana villains or cultural undesirables. The readership expects to discover Africa as a source, however briefly referenced or sustained, in the continuum or in the text's timeline. There should be evidence of the processes of using African-derived culture as a tool for survival and as a premise for intellectual tools, many of which would likely signify the culture's actual intellectual history and genealogy. Readers are delighted to experience texts that document the culture's use of linguistic codes and code-switching for maximum communicative effect. We want to discover narratives that reveal intergenerational communication and fully developed relationships, understanding how bizarre it is to read a text or view a filmic source that shows an African individual willfully alienated from kin as he or she seeks to resolve the text's central dilemma in unexplained cultural isolation. The readership anticipates commentary—whether affirming, favorable, or ambivalent—on spirituality, the supernatural, or life forces beyond mortality. We expect that the literature will not needlessly offend or carelessly use cultural non-negotiables and that the literature will minimally offer an insulting, shallow use of stereotypes and a-cultural stock characters. This is a fair summary of the expectations and ideals of an Africana readership. From an anthropological point of view, these elements are commensurate with descriptions of African oral communicative traditions as traditional education with structural and societal functions that sustain the identity, values, customs, and worldview of the culture.

In an Africana consciousness, critics rely on an additional lens to interpret the effect and function of a text. This critical process is what reveals a text's possibilities for applied functionality—how we can increase the life chances and life experiences of people of African descent, in particular, and of humanity, in general, by transmitting, sharing, or operationalizing a compelling aspect or variable of the text as fulfillment of the discipline's necessary practical enterprise. When readers fulfill this process, we have literary transcendence. Literary transcendence is the desired outcome of Africological reader-response. Usual and customary literary analysis relies on devices, conventions, criticism, aesthetics, and attention to form plus explication based on engaging the text as an informed disciplinary reader. This means that we are equipped to complete the final step of the Africological literary engagement process. Fulfilling the practical enterprise requires finding ways to incorporate the text's genius and effect into a process of empowerment.. The intervention of a discipline-based literary criticism enables readers to decipher, discover, and appropriately respond to textual nuances, outcomes, and phenomena whether symbolically favorable or tragic.

It is also helpful to contemplate the culture's literary traditions as a sort of literary Ebonics, wherein we read from an African worldview just as our ancestors inserted English words into their African linguistic structure. Cultivating the practice of reading and analyzing our texts from a place of high cultural competency and Africana consciousness will enable us to engage literature for optimum effect and to transmit "reading from an African worldview" as an effective cultural tool.

The discipline is not and was never intended to be a random unit that relies on a practice of disciplinary border-crossing for viability, in spite of university administrations' imposition of hierarchies of intellectual value. The contemporary practices in Africana Studies permit total commitment to the discipline with an invigorating production of new paradigms, methodologies, and approaches to interpretation. Growth in doctoral programs in Africana Studies demonstrates the need for such literary praxis that models how the literary enterprise contributes to training expanding cohorts of master communicators with a high cultural competency as analysts of worldview, race, ethnicity, heritage, power, and artifact.

Another specificity is considering the meaning of Africana reader-response theory with respect to worldview, rhetoric, and discourse in *dutiful survey*. This relates to the role of rhetoric and seminal works in the canon's instruction. Non-fiction genres in the canon demonstrate the effect of rhetorical devices and link literature to sociopolitical awareness and even to movements that have complementary literary wings. Aligning canonical non-fiction with Africana Studies–based approaches to the rhetorical traditions of Black consciousness and philosophy fosters the critical reading methodology of *dutiful survey*. This describes the intellectual commitment to cyclically reading and analyzing core sources or texts of the non-fiction Africana intellectual tradition in an active search for ideas and expressions that should enhance the discourse of literary criticism as a tool to advance the liberation of African people globally. It sustains ideas about literary function and contributes to theoretical approaches to cognition, memory, and action related to Black consciousness and idea formation found in historical documents and in the traditions of speeches, sociopolitical philosophy, and manifestos. It reinforces the intersections of Literature and History. In general, it is a reiteration of the Africana cognitive practice of reading Black texts with a lens toward epistemological refinements on behalf of the discipline's literary methodologies and priorities. In dutiful survey, literary critics in the discipline engage in a process of regularly re-/familiarizing themselves with the disciplinary foundations, its cross–subject area multidimensionality, and with key primary and philosophical sources that sustain an Africana worldview. This includes maintaining an acute relationship with iconic knowledge and concepts from the broad African and diaspora traditions of non-fiction and critical writing. It is a practice of reading, interpreting, and relying on a tradition of inspired Africana philosophers and agents for foundational knowledge that is in constant intergenerational interplay with contemporary idea formation, even in literature, namely how literature intersects with historical and cultural ideas in the context of Africana multidimensionality. The volume is familiar to readers because it engages stylized and creative writing from many of the same voices that are central to the canon. The subject treatment of philosophies and intellectual traditions adjacent to literature in forms of rhetoric, stylized activism, historical narrative prowess, documentary film, and popular culture demonstrates the literary enterprise's disciplinary specificity. Layered with this is the literary enterprise's intersectionality with the discipline's micro and macro subject areas including topics of gender, psychology, ethics and moral order, social science and statistics, liberation theology, intellectual history, Pan-Africanism, masculinity, womanism, aesthetics, cultural mythology, cultural memory, and spirituality.

Transcendence compels and celebrates the intellectual freedom offered by the discipline of Africana Studies. It inspires readers to think beyond the boundaries of traditional academic categories and methodologies and to consider the depth of critical immersion in Africana Studies approaches to analyzing literary traditions in analyses that are well contextualized for arguments regarding canon, disciplinary prerogative, articulating transcendence, and reviewing trends in African American literary criticism. Pairing is a routine means of aligning one or more literary texts with a featured non-literary but core Africana knowledge source(s) naturally selected from the discipline's critical subject areas. There is room for these types of enhancements in the Africana literary setting, not as digressions or substitutes, but as ambitious comprehensive attention to form as well as function. These techniques of literary Africology offer a balance of research, contextualization, textual analysis, and Africana conceptual modeling for literature, guided by attention to Africana reader-response.

The use of Africological methodologies in literature analysis often redirects literary criticism, as readers have the opportunity to pursue and develop analyses *beyond* issues of literary form, textual close reading, periodization, categorizations such as humanism and realism, symbolism and metaphor, historical-biographical survey, politics, setting and environment, and expansions of interdisciplinary approaches and applications from fields of study such as feminism, identity studies, cultural studies, comparative literature, postcolonialism, and counter-modernity. These expansions do creative things with the literature, but literary study directly within the discipline of Africana Studies is forging its own context. The methodological interventions even for the definition of and assumptions of the word literature indicate the level of distinction.

In Africana Studies, literary activity falls under aesthetics, creative production, and "movement and memory" and "cultural meaning-making."[7] These critical interventions on the discipline's categorizations of narrative and writing are early disciplinary steps toward framing the distinct literary enterprise in Africana Studies. Framing literature different from the academy's norms reiterates the distinct vision the discipline has for literary study, and this vision is not equivalent to a periodization-restricted approach. For example, critical contexts for literary narratives such as cultural mythology and cultural memory show promise as more useful worldview-based orientations to exploring African American literature because they account for many more culturally based implications of texts.

Literary Africology also implies shifts in what constitutes acceptable narrative response and writing. Stylized critical writing in essay form naturally remains the norm, but the Africana literary enterprise welcomes the diversity of research presentation and reportage wherein the narrative forms of essay communication are not always prioritized over reportage, or even over bullet-point presentation. This leaves room for effective structural diversity for *applied* criticism, in particular, emerging from Africana reader-response choices about the most effective way to configure and respond to a text. This is especially true for critical exercises that engage in *measuring* variables of literature and literary context as well as exercises of applied functionality wherein the text serves as a catalyst to instigate a more social science or problem-solving reader-response. Ayi Kwei Armah predicts this, in a sense, when he writes of literature as a "dynamic activity" that shifts its "forms and techniques as technological possibilities expand."[8] In the Africana literary worldview, sometimes the content is a priority: not for humanistic philosophical wonderment but as a charge to expand the meaning of reader-response stewardship. In essence, the reading of a text implies participation in a process of author-instigated civic awareness of a phenomenon or problematic that the reader is compelled and dutifully bound to pursue beyond the enjoyment of a text and the celebration of the author's successful craft. This Africana literary assumption manifests itself in a critical product that is not always required to be a narrative essay. For example, in teaching literatures that advance health-related content, scholars have the option to critically respond to the text by structuring a document that relies on graphing, charting, and measuring variables and behaviors from the text, all within a format that takes advantage of the digital publishing tools available through this era's household technology. It is not only a postmodern reflection of the possibilities of what is text, but it is also an indicator that the Africana disciplinary enterprise initiates new responses to literature, including creative and visual and artistic representations of textual analysis and applied functionality.

This Africana engagement of literature embraces the flexibility for Africana literary scholars to prepare evaluations and analyses of literature that merge qualitative, quantitative, symbolic, and artistic representations of textual value and meaning. This methodology merges assessment and function in a product/artifact outcome of reader-response that can be visual, non-narrative, or limited narrative masterpieces. The product or artifact has a different appeal than a twenty-page essay of literary criticism that relies on traditional narrative explication, and it is material enough (digital, mini-poster, chart, art rendering, etc.) to be given to schools or to community centers as means of fulfilling the practical enterprise of Africana Studies which is to find ways to share the knowledge generated in the academy. Thus, Africana literary

criticism regains an aesthetic and visual attribute and participates in the negotiation of memory-making through cross–subject area documentation and
research that are *visually* or *materially* stimulating and not bound by lengthy,
prose-paragraph products. Such a potentially artistic outcome is stimulating
and philosophically communicative in forms that are reflective of traditional
African modes of icon and symbol communication such as the Adinkra system of Ghana.

Being aware of such Africana literary flexibility, which is a fulfillment
of the discipline's foundational imperative to advance both the academic
and practical/applied enterprises, becomes strategically important to communicate at all social, community, and educational levels. At the K-12 level,
instruction that adds a non-narrative component to documenting or assessing
proof of literary comprehension responds to child development benchmarks
during which youth conceptualize with either symbolic or abstract non-
narrative written tendencies. The assumptions of art therapy also highlight
the value of such an approach. At the university level, it becomes imperative
for Africana Studies practitioners and leadership to be aware of a level of
Africana Studies methodological exceptionalism, for pursuits directly in the
discipline, that emerges from the acceleration in twenty-first-century graduate training in Africana Studies. Disciplinary practitioners are invigorating
the field with such dynamic, discipline-specific orientations to traditional
bodies of knowledge, and they have the responsibility to clarify and cement
the norms of the discipline of Africana Studies in curricular practices. It is a
distinct twenty-first-century innovation in the Africana literary enterprise that
methods of graphing, mapping, charting, and quantifying a literary text, often
using digital techniques, are effective practices to create a final or artistic
product to fulfill the discipline's practical enterprise.

In a framework of transcendence, literary Africology announces a defini-
tive literary orientation with its own organic disciplinary rubrics, philosophies, and possibilities. It helps move the literary enterprise away from the
natural, early self-conscious phases of non-formalized and ambiguous
enactments of bona fide Africana literary practice. This study samples, interrogates, models, and prompts collectivity of vision for the Africana literary
enterprise and is by no means exhaustive. However, from here, institutionalization of the discipline-based Africana literary enterprise is no longer open
for deconstructionist or adverse debate.

NOTES

1. Wanda Brooks and Susan Browne, "Towards a Culturally Situated Reader
Response Theory," *Children's Literature in Education* 43 (2012): 74–75.
2. Ibid., 83.

3. See Katie Sciurba, "'The Wrong Things About Literature' Invisibility and African American Texts," *Curriculum Inquiry* 41.1 (2011): 127. It is a review of E. S. Gray, "The Importance of Visibility: Students' and Teachers' Criteria for Selecting African American Literature," *The Reading Teacher* 62.6 (2009): 472–481.

4. Ibid., 131.

5. Ibid.

6. See E. S. Gray, "The Importance of Visibility: Students' and Teachers' Criteria for Selecting African American Literature," *The Reading Teacher* 62.6 (2009): 472–481.

7. See Molefi Kete Asante's subject areas from *Kemet, Afrocentricity, and Knowledge*, Maulana Karenga's subject areas from *Introduction to Black Studies*, and Greg Carr's description of the literary arts from the Philadelphia School Board's criteria for the district's curriculum on African American Studies.

8. Ayi Kwei Armah, *Osiris Rising: A Novel of Africa Past, Present and Future* (Pompenguine, West Africa: Per Ankh, 1995), 221.

Chapter 2

Twentieth Century Black
Lives Mattered

Reading Male Mortality in The Souls
of Black Folk *and* The Living Is Easy

It is a breakthrough to find ways to link traditional literature with contemporary phenomena, and this reading of two central canonical texts—*The Souls of Black Folk* (1903) and *The Living Is Easy* (1948)—prioritizes early twentieth-century examples of Black masculinity, namely the subject of male mortality. The topic is imbedded in the canon through many testaments of the Black male predicament and is an even more emergent contemporary topic based on what scholars like Tommy Curry describe as "Black male vulnerability" and "the need for new theories beyond the generic language of intersectionality to speak to the death that disproportionately affects Black males."[1] Curry's essay begins with a critique of the 2014 questionable police shooting of eighteen-year-old Michael Brown in Ferguson, Missouri, and his book *The Man-Not: Race, Class, Genre, and the Dilemmas of Black Manhood* (2017) extends the topic into radically innovative interventions toward the creation of Black Male Studies. The broad topic of Black male mortality finds a voice and advocacy in the Black Lives Matter Movement, spurred by the 2012 killing of seventeen-year-old Trayvon Martin in Sanford, Florida, and the subsequent acquittal of his offender. The Black Lives Matter Movement lends activism to "the validity of Black life" and acts to "resist our dehumanization."[2] The Movement emphasizes "resilience" and "is working for a world where Black lives are no longer systematically and intentionally targeted for demise."[3] Black male mortality is one of many gendered and sociopolitical platforms of the Black Lives Matter Movement against forms of state violence, and this chapter isolates for explication related philosophical and structural concerns of one among many possible Africana literary pairings. The Black Lives Matter Movement is not a sustained structural comparison to the Du Bois and West texts, but it is a link that helps to frame how Africana literature is in continuous discourse with social justice and gender.

11

This analysis approaches Du Bois's essay "Of the Passing of the First-Born" as a cultural artifact that informs theoretical directions for Black masculinity studies, particularly its potential to convey a sincere paradigm of mourning. This links with a similar reading of Dorothy West's *The Living is Easy* which transcends the novel's canonical representation in Black feminist and Africana womanist criticism, this time, in favor of a featured Black masculinity analysis—that of survivalist masculinity. The chapter adds a dimension of masculinist emotionality to tropes of reading gender in the extended New Negro/Harlem Renaissance period. Definitions of masculinity have a wide range. Ron L. Jackson II's and Celnisha I. Dangerfield's "identity negotiation paradigm" presents a circular model of the variables of "community," "achievement," "recognition," and "independence" with intersectional variables of "self-efficacy" and "historical symbiosis."[4] Danté L. Pelzer's description of the "historical, societal, and internal convergence of the Black male's struggle" builds on the agency to view Black men as aspiring to be "pillars of their communities" instead of on objectified and negative nuances of Black maleness. These accurately frame Du Bois's and West's orientations toward Black male experience.[5]

The Souls of Black Folk is standard reading for courses in many academic disciplines. It is excerpted in *The Norton Anthology of African American Literature* and includes the "First-Born" essay. The *Norton* biographical entry on Du Bois notes his evolution toward using literary forms to advance the progress of the race and his gift of "introspective, impressionistic prose when impelled by the need to express his most deeply felt emotions."[6] *The Riverside Anthology of the African American Literary Tradition* also excerpts *Souls*, though it excludes "Of the Passing of the First-Born." In this chapter's featured Du Bois essay, the primary questions inspired by his writing are: "What is the critical meaning of death for Black men and boys?" and "How should the death of a Black male register in our consciousness?" While this chapter does not cite data on the challenges that Black men and boys face, it is a critical response to the familiar challenges that appear in the daily news and statistics about Black men and boys. This chapter utilizes Afrocentric measures of cultural character as the comparative norm from which to compare Du Bois's 1903 expectation of Black male character.

The Africological study of Africa and the diaspora holds great promise for reinforcing African cultural identity because it encourages the interrogation of historical construction, the interpretation of African culture based on adaptation to new environments, and the development of perspectives rooted in activism toward cultural and social restoration. Art, particularly written literature, defined as "cultural production informed by standards of creativity and beauty and inspired by and reflective of a people's life-experiences and life aspirations,"[7] contributes to this endeavor. The Africological study of these texts enables a conversation about the recovery of the cultural character of African American men, including contemporary challenges of the topic of *masculinity*.

The late 1960s ushered in not only Black Studies departments but also, by 1970, women's studies departments. California was a pioneering state with San Francisco State University offering Black Studies, with San Diego State pioneering a women's studies department, and with California State University, Long Beach offering courses that, in 1970, became formalized as a women's studies curriculum. Women's studies departments evolved to characterize themselves as *gender* studies programs in order to also accommodate LGBTQ and masculinity studies. By the early 1990s, there were enough masculinity courses offered at universities to informally identify masculinity studies as a sub-discipline. Masculinity was featured as a gender issue; however, a consistent point of contention has been the balance between heterosexual and gay male studies.[8]

Black masculinity studies does not always find its way into the curriculum of Africana Studies, yet the comparison of Du Bois's essay and West's novel transcends this omission, giving an opportunity to explore masculinity studies and traditional literary texts, and to link them with contemporary social justice approaches. The contemporary defining canon of research on Black masculinity includes Don Belton's edited collection *Speak My Name: Black Men on Masculinity and the American Dream* (1996), Christopher B. Booker's *"I Will Wear No Chain!": A Social History of African-American Males* (2000), Richard G. Majors's and Jacob U. Gordon's *The American Black Male: His Present Status and His Future* (1994) and Philip Brian Harper's *Are We Not Men?: Masculine Anxiety and the Problem of African-American Identity* (1998). Stephanie Brown's and Keith Clark's approach to masculinity as "scholarly topos" is most relevant to the direction of this chapter.[9] It offers a literary approach to masculinity studies in its prioritization of the meaning of "fictive testaments to black male social and corporeal annihilation" but with significant historical-biographical context for Black male writers, namely Ralph Ellison, Richard Wright, Charles Johnson, and Ishmael Reed.[10] The authors address "African-American literature about men [because it] has chronicled blackness in the white American imaginary, where metaphorical and occasional physical 'lynchings' . . . are part and parcel of black men's social, discursive, and physical reality."[11]

While interpreting literature's role in articulating Black male experience, Brown and Clark highlight the factors that continue to oppress Black men. They contest the era of the1990s to the twenty-first century's unfortunate "prominent cultural interpretation," per Charles Johnson, of "blackness as pathology," whereby the dominant ethos of Black men is "blackness as threatening, feral, sexual bestial."[12] They draw from an unfortunate set of contemporary examples of Black male stories including Amadou Diallo, James Byrd, and even O. J. Simpson and Jayson Blair to show White America and society's "chronic cultural construction" where "black malehood and pathology are forever sutured despite the noblest attempts to civilize. Because of the symbiosis of blackness and whiteness in the dyadic American racial mythology, the African-American male body has and will remain the repository of all that America fears, hates, and loves."[13] These myths are "concocted by a virulently racist culture to justify castration, imprisonment, experimentation (re: Tuskegee), surveillance."[14]

Brown and Clark interrogate Black masculinity studies through their critique of Clyde Franklin's 1994 essay on men's studies published in *The American Black Male*.[15] Problematic is Franklin's "line of social scrutiny [that] reductively casts African-American masculinity as a kind of melodrama of beset black manhood, with black men misguidedly embracing a singular atavistic notion of patriarchal and phallocentric masculinity that, at its core, is odious and detrimental to personhood."[16] Franklin views Black men as victims who have been denied the usual and customary male privilege of domination. In response to Franklin, Brown and Clark call for "sustained critical interventions and interrogations that gainsay the belief that African-American men aspire to a corrosive, severely flawed notion of masculinity."[17] Brown and Clark's essay continues to reflect key variables of the contemporary state of affairs for African American men and a sociopolitical context from which to explore the cultural character of Black men embodied in Du Bois's and West's creative visions of the meaning of Black male masculinity through visions of mortality.

In Africana Studies, literature is part of the cultural/aesthetic classification of subject areas and means "the creative, artistic, and inventive aspect of human phenomena which demonstrates the expression of values, art, and the good."[18] In this area, Afrocentrists seek to explore "significant elements . . . that give meaning to cultural character. By cultural character is meant the essence of a people's history and icons in harmonious tension."[19] Literature offers examples of this Black male character from an Africana reader-response orientation. Molefi Kete Asante's synthesis of African-centered epistemologies of culture, drawn from the work of Cheikh Anta Diop, considers three frameworks—the "psychic, historic, and linguistic"[20]—that facilitate this chapter's masculinist interpretation of Du Bois's essay "Of the Passing of the First-Born." For clarification, "the psychic factor is a mental factor; the historic factor deals with phenomena; and the linguistic is concerned with languages."[21] These aspects of cultural character enable dynamic interpretations of the literary record and of sources that introduce issues of Black male mortality.

Concerning Du Bois's grief and the spiritual articulation of Black masculinity, the variables of cultural character—the psychic, the historic, and the linguistic—take on special meaning in the case of Du Bois's treatment of Black male mortality in "Of the Passing of the First-Born." The psychic dimension of cultural character pertains to the human mind or psyche, the extraordinary, extra-sensory, and non-physical mental processes, including telepathy. The historic aspect is self-explanatory in its feature of phenomena, which are notable publicly documented events and occurrences of both past and present. The linguistic sphere includes applications of human speech, such as the act of expressing or describing thoughts, feelings, or perceptions through the articulation of words. The linguistic sphere also has implications for oral communication, sounds, and vocal physiology. Both Du Bois's essay and West's characterizations are optimally deciphered based on these general approaches to Diop's core concepts of cultural character.

Du Bois dedicates *The Souls of Black Folk* "To Burghardt and Yolande: The Lost and the Found," a testament to the influence of his children's lives on his work that he expands in the brief, six-and-a-half-page essay "Of the Passing of the First-Born." The essay is pure literature, making use of musical poetic language, elements of structured plot, storytelling, repetition, symbolism, metaphor, humor, understatement, pathos, and climax.

Toward a grounding for the psychic perspective, it is important that Du Bois permits readers to celebrate the birth of his son, Burghardt, and he acknowledges the interrelatedness of cycles of birth, life, and death. Spirituality is central to the psychic component of Black male cultural character as Du Bois infuses his narrative with descriptions of his child's birth in ancestral cosmology. Du Bois responded to the sacredness of the birth process, lyrically acknowledging "the sanctuary on whose altar a life at my bidding had offered itself to win a life, and won."[22] The child gave a "wail from an unknown world," which infers a belief in the processes of the ancestral world, where new life comes from a place of transcended life. Du Bois elaborates on the ancestral affiliation of his child's life when he notes Burghardt's "life but eighteen months distant from the All-life,—we were not far from worshipping this revelation of the divine."[23]

Du Bois introduces the theme of prophecy when he imagines the son inheriting the father's vision and gifts. Dreams are elements of the psychic, and Du Bois writes, "I saw the dream of my black fathers stagger a step onward in the wild phantasm of the world."[24] He offers a considerable amount of deep thought and intuitive intellectual reflection on what it means to bring a Black male life into the world.

Du Bois also introduces a notion of gender complementarity that relates to the primacy of the bond between mothers and sons. He demonstrates a vibrant respect for women's reproductive ability, or *power*. The power is biological, physical, and intuitive, or psychic. The way he honors his wife is an ancient embodiment of celebrating motherhood, symbolized in figures such as Isis or the Black Madonna/Virgin Mary. He confesses: "And I thought in awe of her—she who had slept with Death to tear a manchild from underneath her heart, while I was unconsciously wandering."[25] Like the Biblical assumption of Joseph's initial skepticism about Mary and his subsequent surrogate fathering of Jesus, Du Bois admits, "I did not love it [the baby] then; . . . but her I loved, my girl-mother, she whom now I saw unfolding like the glory of the morning—the transfigured woman. Through her I came to love the wee thing, as it grew strong."[26] Thus the cultural character of Black male life is that birth is a celebration, an event not to be aborted or lamented. The birthing experience is a fragile, life-or-death process, and male mortality is intricately related to mother-mortality, which constitutes a bond initially between mother and child and then between father and family. But Du Bois explains that it was the mother's love that initiated him into loving the child, and thus we see a balance and order of Black family life whereby a father respects the sacredness of motherhood, but he participates psychically after the mother's initial role in childbirth. Du Bois relies on his wife to initiate him into fatherhood, and fatherly love, and he presents it as a natural process. We see him, however, consistently involved in his son's earliest life experience.

The historic component merges with Du Bois's treatment of his son's birth as a transgenerational prophecy. The essay opens with a Biblical passage, "Unto you a child is born," which compares little Burghardt's arrival with the predestined and prophesied birth of Christ from the Bible's Old and New Testaments. These elements of prophecy and celebration document both psychic and historical factors. Du Bois acknowledges his son's African heritage, and quickly assesses the problems his child might face in life. In Du Bois's scholarly method, he surveys history in order to construct solutions to problems of the color line. Regarding Burghardt's place in the racist world fashioned by a history of enslavement, he writes:

> How beautiful he was, with his olive-tinted flesh and dark gold ringlets, his eyes of mingled blue and brown, his perfect little limbs, and the soft-voluptuous roll which the blood of Africa had moulded into his features! I held him in my arms, after we had sped away from our Southern home,—held him and glanced at the red hot soil of Georgia and the breathless city of a hundred hills, and felt a vague unrest. Why was his hair tinted with gold? An evil omen was golden hair in my life. Why had not the brown of his eyes crushed out and killed the blue? —for brown were his father's eyes, and his father's father's. And thus in the Land of the Color-line I saw, as it fell across my baby, the shadow of the Veil.[27]

Du Bois practices Africana survivalist parenting, and upon the birth of his male child, he is in a self-defense mode and aware of the need to protect the life of his child by examining what perils lie ahead. This is a form of what

Carolyn Bennett Murray and Jelani Mandara describe as racial socialization, "the process by which the family shapes attitudes and beliefs about race and explains how the child fits within this context."[28] Du Bois anticipates and foreshadows the possibility of his child's death in a world whose history is replete with extreme racism and violence. He contextualizes the historical time and space of his child's birth, clarifying: "Within the Veil was he born."[29] Du Bois anticipates that the son will make history in the father's footsteps. He writes, I "saw the strength of my own arm stretched onward through the ages through the newer strength of his."[30] Du Bois envisions how his commitment to intergenerational communication—to his son's social education—will be functional for his offspring for generations to come. From this testimony of his reflections on Burghardt, Du Bois's fathering is attentive to navigating a racialized life terrain.

Linguistically, Du Bois practices nommo. He speaks a legacy into existence. He writes, "I fled to my wife and child, repeating the while to myself half wonderingly, 'Wife and child? Wife and child?'"[31] He spoke his fatherhood into existence. Watching a young life develop, Du Bois is also keenly aware of the nonverbal development of his male child, as Burghardt was "so tremulous with . . . unspoken wisdom."[32] Du Bois defines the communication between mother and child as a language when he observes, "she and he together spoke some soft and unknown tongue and in it held communion."[33] He reinforces the attention required for parenting. Du Bois envisions the power of his son's words when he writes that he "heard in his baby voice the voice of the Prophet that was to rise within the Veil."[34] This statement of birthright is in direct contrast to the stereotypes and defeatism that mar Black male children's purpose in life. The perils that face Black male children today are fourth-grade failure syndrome, juvenile delinquency, school-to-prison trajectories, police brutality, poverty, food insecurity, and social stereotype. However, Burghardt was eighteen months old, and his father expressed a complete vision for his life.

The mere act of writing this eloquent narrative as confession and lamentation is an element of the linguistic facets of cultural character. The act of writing is a step toward immortalization, but in an Africana literary critique, the primacy of the oral tradition demands that the written stories be told, as elements of heritage practices and cultural storytelling. Du Bois's narrative can also be considered a type of fatherly dirge to his first-born—as he memorializes his child in the process of ancestor-acknowledgment.

Inevitably, in a world where Black male life is devalued and strategically snuffed out with too little grief, too little lamentation, and within a setting of powerlessness that stupefies rather than empowers, Du Bois's elegant survey of the meaning of Black male life and mortality is a cognitive model worthy of emulation. It captures the critical narrative and intellectualism of African

American parenting. The narrative is certainly sad and tragic, and Du Bois philosophically evaluates the meanings of Black male mortality in meandering directions that offer perspectives of healing in spite of loss, and empowerment in moments of the soul's deepest despair. Du Bois's gift is a version of Black masculinity that values young life as the elder male eagerly awaits the young male child's coming of age. Du Bois writes of "wisdom wait[ing] to speak," and of the possibility that Black man-children might bear their "burden more bravely than we."[35] Du Bois's narrative is a counter-argument to American racial stereotype bent on defining Black maleness as deviance, as pathological, and as an identity to be feared and annihilated from the moment a Black parent conceives a child, particularly a male child.

This approach of exploring the cultural character of Black males through an analysis of psychic, historic, and linguistic elements is a discipline-based Afrocentric critical methodology. This paradigm compels scholars to regard the nuances of intuition and deep thought related to Africana men and boys, along with history for self-knowledge and self-identification. This approach demonstrates the agency of men and boys in historical consciousness and reflection, reinforcing a genealogy of inspiration, achievement, and sacred testament of cultural expectations for the survival and flourishing of men and boys. In the tradition of Du Bois, language becomes a positive reinforcement of the Black male life journey, rather than a tool for the negative stereotyping that inevitably kills too many boys and men.

In the Norton Critical Edition of *The Souls of Black Folk* (1995) Susan Mizruchi identifies similar elements of the psychic, historical, and linguistic that enhance the dialogue between an Africana vision of texts and other canonical engagements.[36] She measures the essay "Of the Passing of the First-Born" in terms of the fluidity of DuBois's expressions in response to his grief and to the racism of White passersby who defy the human expectations of cross-racial sympathy and mutter "Niggers" during Burghardt's funeral procession. She writes, "Du Bois's reproof here is muted and indirect: the abrupt cropping of the paragraph expresses typographically what cannot be conveyed in ordinary language."[37] Mizruchi's critical interest is in presentations of sympathy in Du Bois's writings. She examines his choice to "locate his insights about sympathy in the funeral of his own son" and notes Du Bois's "ability to make personal tragedy resonate with collective and, in this case, political meaning."[38] Her analysis considers the possibility that Southern racist Whites regarded Blacks with a desire for their extinction and removal from society, and therefore, Whites were not troubled by the levels of Black infant mortality.[39] In her comprehensive treatment of the variables associated with death and sympathy in cross-racial encounters she defines *Souls* as "a book that crosses disciplinary boundaries while helping to define them."[40] This includes sociology and literature, with natural applications to political science and history, and an Africana literary reading updates the sub-disciplines that uniquely respond to Du Bois's legacy. In this instance, it is a deeper concern for Black masculinity.

THE LIVING IS EASY

In an Africana reader-response theory engagement of *The Living Is Easy* the contemporary Africana-informed reader is drawn to facets of this early-twentieth-century novel that also signify present-day Black masculinist realities, which extends the inclusion of gendered readings of legacy texts, like *The Living is Easy*, to the literary historiography of Black masculinity. Even though Dorothy West published the novel in 1948 it is classified as a product from the end of the New Negro Movement/Harlem Renaissance era. Additionally, the novel's setting is the turn of the century, which supports the parallels I draw between Du Bois's lamentation of male mortality and West's male characters' preoccupations. In documenting a symbolic narrative of masculine consciousness in the early twentieth century, West gives readers the opportunity to engage, to compare, and to contrast historical predicaments with accumulated and contemporary versions of reality.

Published criticism on West's novel is preoccupied with the feminine and its intersections with race and class. The novel's protagonist—the beautiful, smart, young matriarch Cleo Jericho Judson—is strikingly cunning and cynical and worthy of critical attention due to West's daring to invent an obsessive and flawed characterization, though Cleo is semi-autobiographically representative of West's Boston mother. Yet, there are multiple plots in the novel that reveal the passions, objectives, and character of African-American men. In the novel, the theme of Black male mortality relates to how the domestic sphere of Black life is influenced by the possibilities of the male provider's death. The novel presents traditional scenarios of male, female, and community perceptions of and responses to Black male mortality, and West inevitably reveals a masculine-centered emotionality. The protagonist is a selfish, manipulative Black woman, and this analysis aims to de-center her within the narrative in order to realize West's vision of and for Black men. In interviews with West and in following the point-of-view of Cleo's daughter, Judy Judson, the novel documents the father-daughter relationship. The creative nuances of personal experience that West weaves through the nuclear part of the Judson family—mother, father, daughter— reveal Judy's love, admiration, and sympathy for her father, Bart Judson. Perhaps *The Living is Easy* is a subtle tribute to Black manhood fulfilling the author's personal admiration for a father sometimes challenged by a dominant wife.

There are over a dozen critical sources and articles available on Dorothy West. Several address women's studies issues such as sister bonds, mothers, mother-daughter relationships, and feminisms; several are interviews. There is a dissertation comparing the literary careers of Black women writers. Others are general surveys of the Harlem Renaissance, social criticism, and West's career as a short story writer. None of the articles features the Black male experience, but Africana womanist and other similar theorizations emphasized in the discipline of Africana Studies reinforce a standard of pursuing balanced gender analyses that address womanism as well as masculinity.

The 1970s witnessed the rise of Black women's studies, and this movement was a response to conditions in which the Black women's experience was overlooked and subjugated in favor of white male, white female, and Black male privilege. However, the privilege that Black men received from institutionalized gender bias has been a mere and partial privilege of inclusion, but not of power. Michael Awkward writes, "It might even be argued that, before the African-American women's literary renaissance and the emergence of black feminist criticism in the 1970s and 1980s, manhood was the [literary] tradition's dominant subject."[41] After a review of how "manhood" has been defined in the African American literary tradition beginning with Frederick Douglass's *Narrative of the Life of Frederick Douglass* (1845), Awkward concludes that the period of the 1990s represents, perhaps, "the moment when African American womanhood and manhood will not compete for representational space and attention but will be seen as equally important to our understanding of art, literature, and subjectivity."[42] His point is well-taken, and corroborates the need to explore *The Living Is Easy* for the early-twentieth-century vision it also provides of Black *male* experience.

Black men in America have always lived in anticipation of death. Ida B. Wells described it as a *Southern Horror* in 1892 in the context of lynching.[43] Popular and religious scholars describe how in the distant past, when the man of the house went out to secure food for his family, there was no guarantee that he would return. Instead, "he might be fatally wounded by an animal or die of exposure."[44] Why, in the modern age, is this still a predicament for African American men? Jawanza Kunjufu insists that society must pay more attention to processes leading toward both psychic and physical Black male mortality.[45] *The Living Is Easy* has one instance of a male lynching threat, but West constructs the other episodes and inferences of a discourse on male mortality from within domestic and familial spheres that are chivalrous and sacrificial. Mortality is the quality or condition of being liable or subject to death or the death rate of a group within a certain population. In response to the Black male's sociohistorical predicament of targeting by racist Whites as a threat or as prey, this chapter operationalizes mortality as processes and enactments of literal as well as virtual death, which can be spiritual, psychological, social, or economic.

In *The Living Is Easy* a Southern Black woman, Cleo, moves to Boston, marries Bart Judson, a successful Black businessman, and works to simultaneously establish herself and her family as part of Boston's "colored" elite while obsessively working to recreate the family structure of her Southern childhood. She manipulates her three sisters into leaving their husbands and moving into her Boston home. She inevitably runs her own husband out of the home, and compensates for this loss with a resolution, at the end of the novel, to groom her six-year-old nephew to "cling" to her and grow to "be the man of the house."[46] Seymour Krim observes: "The important thing about the book is its abundance and special woman's energy and beat. The beat is a deep one, and it often makes a man's seem puny."[47] The manipulation in the novel is fascinating, and perhaps the need to explore the Black masculinist vision emerges because the reader is unaccustomed to seeing virtuous and well-meaning Black men persecuted by Black women, in addition to society's assault on their integrity, self-determination, and self-esteem.

The text's characters exhibit Black male mortality through the responsible consciousness and willingness of men who will die in order to provide for their families or through the predicaments of men whose deaths present severe social consequences for the families they leave behind. In fact, not only do Black men die for their families, but also they risk their lives for each other. In *The Living Is Easy*, the victimization of Black men is pervasive.

Several Black male characters actually die within the narrative, beginning with Cleo's father, lovingly referred to as Pa, and others exist in various well-defined predicaments of foreshadowed death. West constructs Pa's persona within a context of struggle and impending death. His struggle as a man and as a provider is evident in Cleo's childhood memories. West relies on physical descriptions of his labor-intensive work at the stable, emphasizing his "toil" and "perspiration."[48] She juxtaposes his commitment to being a provider with the novel's central conflict—that one of his daughters, Cleo, fancies money more than expressions of love. Cleo's motives and manipulations are the dominant critical subject of much of the criticism, but the scene in which Pa succumbs to Cleo's pennies-not-kisses demands is heartbreaking in its indication of Pa's dual hardship. Not only is he a toiling provider, but he also self-sacrifices for his wife and four daughters. The text tabulates the cost of this in terms of "four coopers a day, six days a week, was half a day's pay gone up in smoke for candy."[49] In spite of this type of sacrifice, Cleo abandons Pa in his old age, leaving him to fend for himself and to eventually die alone. The novel champions the rugged and responsible plight of Black men while advancing a creative, literary voice of anti-essentialist Black womanhood. In this fiction, it is entertaining that Cleo is a relentless taker, but the more sentimental subtext of West's novel is its capacity to humanize and pay homage to industrious and striving, yet dying, Black men. In situating Cleo's villainy, the text suggests that Cleo was jealous of her father's role in her mother's world; his love and companionship evokes "silver laughter."[50] Pa escapes death in Cleo's youth when a winter flood threatens his life and arrival home for Christmas. Ironically, it is on Christmas day, years later, that a party guest to Cleo's Boston home informs her that her father drowned earlier that year. Pa's barely noticed and incidental death contrasts with the other central Black male death, which can be read in both their interpretive proximity and distance to shared gender-based meanings with Cleo. In fact, the novel has great potential for psychological critique, particularly in a symptom–behavior driven analysis of mental health, narcissism, and personality disorders. In a sense of applied functionality, the novel initiates healthy critique with its timeless reading of exploitative gender relationships even in the Black community.

Mr. Binney, a cofounder of Boston's light-skinned Black elite, also dies within the narrative, with both symbolic and narrative realism implications. His tailoring business was upstaged by the growth of urban department stores, and the text presents a concomitant disorder that merges economic bankruptcy and depression. He "bolstered his delusions with his [white] gentleman's drink of decay" and he took pride in the fact that his white neighbors described his family as behaving "as if they were white."[51] With male mortality comes expectations of inheritance. Mr. Binney's death left an imaginary bourgeois legacy to his children, and the dysfunction of relying on skin color and proximity to whiteness as measures of Black elite success, damages his children. In addition, Mr. Binney's death allows a long-owed debt to be paid to a woman whom Mr. Binney wronged long ago. This is a spiritual debt, and it ends up costing the Binney family its soul. The implications of legacy get skewed in the unexpected inheritance the African American businessman, Mr. Binney, leaves his children. In cliché, this appears as a tale of the sins of the father often becoming consequences for the son. But the text's litany of social mortalities is more complicated. For example, Mr. Hartnett, another patriarch of Boston's Black elite families and a business colleague of Mr. Binney's, lost his business and "blew his brains out just like a white man. Everybody was a little proud of his suicide."[52] Yet, this imitation of a version of white manhood is an affront to a functional sense of Black male mortality. These examples demonstrate desperation among the Black bourgeois segment of Boston, and the atrophy of body and mind are proportionately related to their dysfunctional alliance with capitalistic whiteness. In addition to the businessmen's literal deaths, these episodes also represent memorial losses in which remembrance is tied to white or Eurocentric valuation of their legacy. This is also a symptom of mortality.

Mr. Binney's son, Simeon, does not die a physical death, but the contradictions within his soul lead him into a spiritual death. He is transformed from being a radical Black newspaper owner into a self-absorbed, bitter product of his father's bourgeois legacy. His spiritual death is marked by what can be considered mental incest whereby he is more attentive to his sister's needs than to his own wife's needs, as he assumes his deceased father's role as provider for the family (his sister and her son). Simeon consented to an arranged marriage for profit. This marriage fulfilled his father's debt and preserved some of his father's fortune. Simeon's transition from being a race man modeled after the legacy of William Monroe Trotter reflected a dynamic but degenerating characterization caused by illusions and confusions of Black masculinity. From his father he inherited a dysfunctional sense of being a capitalist provider that competed with the emerging Black nationalist consciousness of his youth. His sister Thea inevitably exploits his inherited, orphaned providership through her assimilationist expectations modeled on Eurocentric damsel-in-distress expectations of deference and privilege supported by colorism and classism.

The novel helps readers discern the era's version of childhood Black masculinity. When the novel first introduces Simeon, he is a thoughtful child, confused by the contradictions between his father's love of the white world and his youthful isolation. He resents the pride his parents felt that "he and Thea were always the only colored children in school, church, in their block. Didn't they know that made him feel lonely?"[53] Simeon's confusion grows with the betrayed response his father gives when children tease him for being "colored." His father instructs, "You're the color of an Indian, Simeon, and the Indians are the oldest Americans. If any boy ever asks you again why you're brown, you just say that it's because your grandfather was a full-blooded Indian."[54] This rejection of identity, framed as a denial of African heritage, is the opposite of what a father like Du Bois planned to impart to his son. Episodes like this form the root of Simeon's eventual spiritual death, which African-centered scholar Asa Hilliard explains as a type of negative socialization:

> The African American parent like any other parent is a constant teacher, more by what they model than by what they say. To model cultural surrender, self-rejection, self-negation and shame, while exalting and honoring others is to teach children to be schizophrenic, or worse still, is to produce the double consciousness that Du Bois warned about, seeing ourselves and measuring ourselves through the eyes of others.[55]

The types of dysfunction that West chronicles in *The Living Is Easy*, based on her semi-autobiographical observations of Boston society, still challenge the Black community. In the novel, Simeon expresses his childlike confusion over his father's response to the racism he encountered. Simeon is further scarred by his father's reaction to a childhood fight with a poor Black child. While Simeon feels elated that a schoolmate finally fights him "man to man," Mr. Binney is angry at the "spectacle of young Binney so demeaning himself as to fight with a boy beneath his station. It put them both in the same class."[56] The novel's many wordplays on manhood (e.g. man-to-man, gentleman) affirm a Black masculinity reading. Simeon revolts against a life full of such episodes with his father by starting a Black newspaper that highlights injustice and by hoping for his father's death. In fact, when Mr. Binney finally dies, Simeon is unmoved by his father's mortality. He says, "I suppose I've been wanting father to die for years. I wanted him to die because he was rich. I didn't know how I would spend his money. But knew I would spend it differently."[57] This is antithetical to expectations of the ancestral cycle, and frame the male Binney legacy as a tragedy of Black male mortality.

Simeon and his sister eventually live out their lives in their father's house, together and raising her son, also named Simeon, not as a Hartnett (her husband's family name) but as a Binney. Simeon realizes his dysfunction and even anticipates his own death. He observes, "Thea and I and our kind are phenomena who have bloomed and will die in one generation. Our fathers built a social class for us out of tailor shops and barber shops and stables and caterers' coats. We cannot afford its upkeep because they have taught us to think above their profitable occupations."[58] His reflection describes the complicated racial-cultural dimension of the American dream, and reflects a bidirectional economic death suggesting that the sacrifices African Americans make for wealth are damaging in literal and symbolic ways.

Robert Jones, Cleo's sister Serena's husband, is the epitome of Black male mortality because his conception, birth, upbringing, poverty, and unemployment contribute to his lifelong challenges with what appears to be a spiraling depression. He was "an orphan man, son of some straw-haired cracker too poor, too uncaring, too conscienceless to feed and clothe his bastard," so having an absent, white father predetermines, at least for storytelling, his future.[59] He was raised in the streets, and he "was like a man holding his breath waiting for something to happen."[60] Raised in poverty and shame, Robert "didn't know very much about right and wrong," and "there was in him a weakness from the years of slow hunger that would never let him be a strong-bodied man."[61] Robert is an early-twentieth-century example of what poverty is still doing to Black children. In the introduction to Kunjufu's *Countering the Conspiracy to Destroy Black Boys*, Useni Eugene Perkins, then publisher and editor of *Black Child Journal* observes:

African American boys are systematically programmed for failure so that when they become adults they pose little danger to the status quo. By their control of key social institutions, European-Americans have denied the African-American boy the fruits of his heritage, culture and "rights of passage." As a result, the African-American boy becomes the bearer of social maladies which he carries with him into adulthood. This "early seasoning" is described . . . as the "science of dehumanization" which signals the first stage of the conspiracy.[62]

By the end of the novel Robert is permanently traumatized and institution-alized. However, for a moment, he is symbolically heroic and redeems the light-skinned elite of the novel because he utilizes "passing for white" as a means of resistance. In order to earn money to finish building a house for his wife, he joins a white Southern police force, called together to keep order after a white driver runs over a black child. Robert performs his duty in peace until he encounters a Ku Klux Klan police officer among his ranks. When the Klan member fires into a crowd of peaceful Black marcher-protestors, Robert shoots and kills him. Robert flees, and in the process of helping him cross a river to safety, Cleo's father, Pa, drowns. This is an example of fraternity among Black men in the novel, whereby one man is willing to give his life for another.

Ironically, Cleo retains a Boston lawyer to go South to save Robert from indictment and hanging. Although she despises her sisters' husbands, she helps Robert in order to save the self-esteem of his son, Tim, who is Cleo's nephew, or surrogate son. Tim is described as "the man-child, who must bear his father's shame forever," and to save the child from the sins of the father, Cleo's husband agrees to pay for the attorney. [63]

There is another example of virtual Black male mortality involved in Robert's saga. In order to have Robert acquitted, Cleo concocts a story for the attorney to use to persuade the jury to release him. Cleo's attorney finds an unknown Black man to testify that Robert did not shoot the white police officer, and that it was an anonymous Black man who did. The story that Cleo creates not only demoralizes Robert, whose original defensive act was heroic, but it also supports the criminalization of the Black male. Inevitably, the story that Cleo concocts to save her brother-in-law is fuel for Southern whites to use to convict or lynch the next Black man and the next.

The most pervasive representation of Black masculinity and male mortality in *The Living Is Easy* is Cleo's husband Bart Judson. His life is dedicated to earning a good living and leaving an inheritance for his wife, Cleo, and his child, Judy. He says, "all my planning is to see to it that you'll never know want when I'm gone. No one on earth will ever say that I wasn't a good pro-vider."[64] Later in the novel when Cleo asks him for a large sum of money, he says, "It's the child's money . . . Everything I do is to secure the future. No one of mine will ever want when I'm not here to take care of them."[65]

Emancipation freed Bart when he was one year old. He developed a keen business sense at an early age, and he worked with his industrious, business-minded, formerly enslaved mother until his own business ventures led him North to Boston. Although he was twenty-four years older than Cleo, he met and married her quickly because he fell in love. Additionally, he noticed that Cleo was in danger of being molested by her employer's nephew. His courtship was brief but ardent because "She needed a good man's protection. She needed a husband."[66] It was five years before Cleo permitted the marriage's consummation, and her daughter Judy was conceived. Cleo's refusal to meet her husband's physical needs is described as another factor that contributed to his inability to resist aging. When Bart officially loses his fortune and leaves Cleo at the end of the novel, his mortality is confirmed. Cleo was aware of it, too—"For in that momentary glimpse of his haggard face, she was shocked by the showing of age. That fear of his dying oppressed her heart."[67]

Bart questions his own mortality, and the text often frames him as a dying provider. He reflected, "She was his wife. He wanted to die with her beside him. He did not know now if he would."[68] In the rare instance when Cleo showed concern for the man that she, herself, had aged, she realized, "If he ever took sick, the earth would tremble."[69] Bart's departure and the failure of his business by the end of the novel are surprising because Bart seemed invincible. His goals for his family were considerable, and he always equated his death, or passing, with his family's *success*. In one debate with Cleo about money, Bart explains his plan: "I got to leave her money. . . .I wanted to leave the child fifty-thousand dollars, anyway, when it came my time to die."[70] Eleven years after West published *The Living Is Easy* Lorraine Hansberry revisited the theme of an African American family benefiting from a cash inheritance. Thus, there are the makings of a tradition of literary texts that consider the relationship between male mortality and economics.

The novel's conclusion is open-ended enough that the reader can logically hope that Bart will find a new business venture and return to his family. However, Bart is an aged man. West's descriptions foreshadow his demise. Inevitably, in the most well developed characterization of Black male mortality in the novel, it is not only American capitalism, but also Cleo, Bart's African American wife, that are the culprits that hasten the death of the Black man. This critical angle is a shift from the current paradigms used to explore the meaning of *The Living Is Easy*.

At the end of the novel, Cleo, who struggles with a jealousy of, yet a dependence on, Black men, shifts her attention to her sister's six-year-old son, Tim. It is unclear whether or not Cleo's renewed affinity for the male child is a positive shift. Cleo appears to be the same selfish, life-consuming threat to male life. Hypothetically, Tim has the potential to emerge as either a candidate for the type of innate achievement Amos N. Wilson describes in *Awakening the Natural Genius of Black Children* (2003) or a person who can be manipulated and inevitably victimized by his selfish aunt. It is an empowering ending for countering male mortality if West is suggesting the future lies in a compassionate six-year-old boy. He is described as a mature and sympathetic child who had decided to become a doctor in order to make his father, Robert, well again.[71] In addition to mental illness, Robert had tuberculosis, which made the possibility of his death even more imminent. Tim is the primary male character who exudes life instead of mortality. He was a surrogate son for Bart, who proved to be an excellent husband and provider. Perhaps West's message is that, in the next generation, the Black male will rise above the impending doom of his mortality, and she predicts success for both Black boys and girls.

Both Du Bois's essay lamenting the loss of his first-born as well as West's *The Living Is Easy* extend the gender lens beyond expected attention to feminism and womanism, to expand the range of Black masculinity discourses in the canon and in Africana literary practices. When Du Bois wondered about the life of a Black son, he wrote, "Within the Veil was he born, said I: and there within shall he live,—a Negro and a Negro's son" and his love for the child invoked "the unvoiced terror of my life. . . . I . . . saw the strength of my own arm stretched onward through the ages through the newer strength of his; saw the dream of my black fathers stagger a step onward in the wild phantasm of the world; heard in his baby voice the voice of the Prophet that was to rise within the veil."[72] The intergenerational beauty of his words and the brief articulations of the value of Black male life get lost in traditional readings of *Souls of Black Folk*. This chapter's transcendent goal is to renew the force of both Du Bois's and West's visions of masculinity from a holistic intellectual lens of Africana Studies. The study benefits from a natural disciplinary pairing with sources such as African-centered psychologist Na'im Akbar's seminal work, *Visions for Black Men* (1992), in which he writes, "Our resilience and apparently stubborn determination to survive and thrive are nothing short of a miracle."[73] This is no less true in the culture's nonfiction and fiction depictions.

NOTES

1. Tommy Curry, "Michael Brown and the Need for a Genre Study of Black Death and Dying," *Theory and Event* 17.3 (2014): 4.

2. "About the Black Lives Matter Network," http://blacklivesmatter.com/about/ (Accessed June 12, 2017).

3. Ibid.

4. Ron L. Jackson, II and Celnisha I. Dangerfield, "Defining Black Masculinity as Cultural Property: Toward an Identity Negotiation Paradigm," in *Co-Cultures: Living in Two Cultures*, edited by Larry A. Samovar, Richard E. Porter, and Edwin R. McDaniel. (Boston: Wadsworth, 2012) 126.

5. Danté L. Pelzer, "Creating a New Narrative: Reframing Black Masculinity for College Men," *Journal of Negro Education* 85.1 (2016): 16–27, 18.

6. Gates and McKay, "W. E. B. Du Bois," *Norton* 686.

7. Maulana Karenga, *Introduction to Black Studies* (Los Angeles: Sankore Press, 1993), 393.

8. Bryce Traister, "Academic Viagra: The Rise of American Masculinity Studies," *American Quarterly* 52.2 (2000): 274.

9. Stephanie Brown and Keith Clark, "Melodrama of Beset Black Manhood?: Meditations on African-American Masculinity as Scholarly Topos and Social Menace," *Callaloo* 26.3 (2003): 732–37.

10. Ibid., 733.

11. Ibid.

12. Ibid.

13. Ibid.

14. Ibid., 733–34.

15. Clyde Franklin, "Ain't I a Man?: The Efficacy of Black Masculinities for Men's Studies in the 1990s," in *The American Black Male: His Status and His Future*, edited by Richard G. Majors and Jacob U. Gordon (Chicago: Nelson Hall, 1994), 271–83.

16. Brown and Clark, "Melodrama," 733.

17. Ibid., 735.

18. Molefi Kete Asante, *Kemet, Afrocentricity, and Knowledge* (Trenton: Africa World Press, 1992), 19.

19. Ibid.

20. Ibid. Here, Asante theorizes Diop's 1976 work.

21. Ibid.

22. Du Bois, "First Born," 227.

23. Ibid., 238.

24. Ibid.

25. Ibid., 226.

26. Ibid., 227.

27. Ibid.

28. Carolyn Bennett Murray and Jelani Mandara, "Racial Identity Development in African American Children: Cognitive and Experiential Antecedents," in *Black Children: Social, Educational, and Parental Environments*, edited by Harriette Pipes-McAdoo (Thousand Oaks, CA: SAGE Publications, 2001), 83.

29. Ibid.

30. Ibid., 228.

31. Ibid., 226.

32. Ibid., 228.

33. Ibid., 238.

34. Ibid., 228.

35. Ibid., 232, 231.

36. Susan Mizruchi, "Neighbors, Strangers, Corpses: Death and Sympathy in the Early Writings of W. E. B. Du Bois," in *The Souls of Black Folk: Authoritative Texts, Contexts, Criticism*, edited by Henry Louis Gates, Jr. and Terri Hume Oliver (New York: W. W. Norton & Company, 1999).

37. Ibid., 273.

38. Ibid., 274.

39. Ibid., 274–75.

40. Ibid., 275.

41. Michael Awkward, "Manhood," in *The Oxford Companion to African American Literature*, edited by William L. Andrews, Frances Smith Foster, and Trudier Harris (New York: Oxford UP, 1997), 475.

42. Ibid., 477.

43. Ida B. Wells, *Southern Horrors and Other Writings: The Anti-Lynching Campaign of Ida B. Wells, 1892–1900*, edited by Jacqueline Jones Royster (New York: Bedford Books, 1997).

44. Myles Munroe, *Understanding the Purpose and Power of Men: A Book for Men and the Women Who Love Them* (New Kensington, PA: Whitaker House, 2001), 21.

45. Jawanza Kunjufu, *State of Emergency: We Must Save African American Males* (Chicago: African American Images, 2003).

46. Dorothy West, *The Living Is Easy* (New York: The Feminist Press, 1948), 347.

47. See the jacket cover of the 1982 edition published by The Feminist Press.

48. West, *The Living Is Easy*, 18.

49. Ibid.

50. Ibid., 17.

51. Ibid., 328, 120.

52. Ibid., 112.

53. Ibid., 121.

54. Ibid., 123.

55. Asa Hilliard, "The Maroon Within Us: The Lessons of Africa for the Parenting and Education of African American Children," *The Maroon Within Us: Selected Essays on African American Community Socialization* (Baltimore: Black Classic Press, 1995), 68.

56. West, *The Living Is Easy*, 127, 126.

57. Ibid., 138.

58. Ibid., 139.

59. Ibid., 161.

60. Ibid.

61. Ibid., 162.

62. Useni Eugene Perkins, Introduction, in *Countering the Conspiracy to Destroy Black Boys*, edited by Jawanza Kunjufu (Chicago: African American Images, 1985), viii.

63. West, *The Living Is Easy*, 277.

64. Ibid., 9.

65. Ibid., 81.

66. Ibid., 35.

67. Ibid., 343.

68. Ibid., 346.

69. Ibid., 344.

70. Ibid., 275.

71. Ibid.

72. Du Bois, "First-Born," 227–28.

73. Na'im Akbar, *Visions for Black Men* (Tallahassee: Mind Productions and Associates, Inc., 1992), viii.

Chapter 3

"Can't the Race Stand a Joke?"

Humor and Pan-African Folk Negotiation in Banjo

Claude McKay's Harlem Renaissance era work is due for a re-reading in the discipline of Africana Studies. He was cheeky, playful, politically curious, and eclectic in his transnationalism and Marxist political survey. The playfulness in the writer's craft is due for revisiting, and the transcendence of this inquiry is featuring the broad function of humor beyond its culturally expressive role in folk culture. In an Africological reading, humor can relate to revolutionary nationalism. Humor is customarily the domain of folk studies and media studies, and an Africana-based inquiry has more to offer in exploring the role, effect, and processes of humor. Pairing a humor analysis with Pan-Africanist possibilities gives a *Banjo: A Novel Without a Plot* (1929) a critical reading beyond McKay's playfulness and often offensive, racial descriptions. The novel's cleverness, wit, debate, signifying, and wordplay, in addition to its display of Pan-African group encounters and processes, make it a rhetorical gem. McKay's novel is visionary in this respect, as it becomes a primer for Pan-African encounter and negotiation, and though not the focus of this chapter, it is also ideal for comparative analysis with Chimamanda Ngozi Adichie's *Americanah* (2013), which updates, structurally at least in the novel's U.S.-related settings, what McKay achieves in the Marseilles setting in intercultural observation, humor, wit, and levels of Pan-Africanism and transnationalism.

Mainstream points of view limit the inclusion of Pan-Africanism—as ideology, as historical marker, and as theory or methodology—as a critical priority of the canon, but in the Africana literary enterprise it is central. Pan-Africanist orientations stabilize contexts of past and present issues of migration, globalism, history, resistance, and power. In the criticism, scholars have explored Pan-Africanism in the writings of Paule Marshall, Toni Morrison, Maryse Condé, Wole Soyinka, Ama Ata Aidoo, Caryl Phillips,

and even Nella Larsen with respect to psychic and physical returns to African consciousness. Adding the study of humor to the broad dimension of
Pan-Africanism becomes a prototype study of the types of personal, or in
this case *character*, relationships that are the first and early encounters upon
which future commonality and transnational organization-building are based.
Being attentive to the negotiations and encounters between individuals of
African descent who, also in reality, managed to move beyond difference to
forge formal twentieth-century congresses and conferences and both formal
and informal grassroots and intellectual organizations, the imaginative text
prefigures the types of transnational person-to-person negotiations that occur
and must be overcome as barriers to fellowship and alliance.

Black internationalism characterized early-twentieth-century African
American writing and operates at times as a type of Pan-Africanism. McK-
ay's *Banjo* offers subtext on the challenges of Pan-African discourse based
on how the author frames comedic dialogue. African American literature
scholar Gene Andrew Jarrett points to McKay's emergent "cultural definition
of racial politics" honed in London at "a club for colored soldiers where he
could discuss the issues of race and culture."[1] Though not Marseilles, one
can imagine the race humor and jesting modeled in this environment. McKay
imaginatively initiates the challenges of rhetoric and folk sensibility among
a group of transnational characters, post–World War I. Though not the scope
of this chapter, it is also an informative comparison to consider the Diaspora
Studies iteration of the discipline of Africana Studies by layering a reading of
Banjo with its post–World War II counterparts, *The Lonely Londoners* (1956)
by Sam Selvon as well as George Lamming's novel *The Emigrants* (1954).[2]
All three writers proceed with a cultural sensibility that captures the isolation
and yearning of diaspora migrants who find themselves in European cities.
The group dynamics in the texts demand a contemporary reading that takes
advantage of advances in critical humor studies from an Africana critical lens
that highlights the folkloric and rhetorical elements of Pan-Africanism and
diaspora community building.

Most of the critical sources on humor in the African American literary
tradition frame it as a feature of folklore. The definitions of this approach
are helpful, even though this chapter demarcates humor with an interest not
in what is funny or comedic but in what is clever and rhetorically tactical
in the processes and negotiations of Pan-African community building. Literary scholar Constance Bailey offers useful context for humor when she
writes: "Not only does humor affect the way people engage with the world,
it also affects the way they interpret the world. In short, one who possesses a
humorous outlook on life has seemingly internalized the belief that in order
to make reality more palatable, one must believe that the joke is on someone
other than one self."[3] Bailey emphasizes Langston Hughes's interpretation

of humor which makes her description even more relevant to this chapter's interpretation of his contemporary's novel. Glenda R. Carpio's "Humor in African American Literature" (2010) gives a comprehensive canon-based survey of humor that evaluates the range of humor as a genre as well as its devices—from "comedy, tragicomedy, and burlesque" to "irony, satire, and parody."[4] Carpio notes how Harlem Renaissance critics "wrote about the power of humor in African American culture," but she omits McKay's work in her assessment; she credits "George Schuyler, Zora Neale Hurston, and Langston Hughes who advanced its use in African American letters."[5] The omission of McKay's writing is not surprising. He is guilty of participating in the tradition of buffoonery, but this chapter's transcendence encourages a reading of McKay's humor in a more serious context.

As a contributor to Jarrett's critical volume, *A Companion to African American Literature*, Carpio's historical survey of humor is an important intervention to Africana literary humor studies. She acknowledges that "the use of humor in African American letters has not always been encouraged or recognized" because African American writers deflected racist stereotypes by using "more sophisticated vehicles for humor."[6] She addresses how writers use literature to address political inequality and how some topics such as "the violence of Jim Crow segregation" are "too morally important and earnest to be treated through humor."[7] My Africana reader-response interest in McKay's synthesis of humor and Pan-Africanism may be an exception that meets one of Carpio's emphases regarding humor. She indicates that "a more assertive and acerbic humor that often targeted racial injustice . . . was generally reserved for in-group interactions," and this is certainly a feature of the community of vagabonds in *Banjo*. Carpio's analysis of humor features "the superiority theory, which posits that we laugh at other people's misfortunes" and that it "savors verbal wit over mean-spirited competition or insult," as in the tradition of the dozens.[8] Carpio considers the African American humor tradition and historical context in the interest of exploring the ways contemporary writers use humor, but her framing also leaves room for viewing *Banjo* from the distinct critical approach of its early modeling of the challenges of Pan-African negotiation.

As laughter is a universal ice-breaker among the unfamiliar, McKay's novel, aptly suggesting the interplays of humor in its subtitle, frames much of its conflict and resolution among its potential Pan-Africanists as a contest between negotiating what is and what is not funny. McKay describes this in the novel as an African-derived "composite voice" that includes "speech, song, and laughter" and as "sugary laughter."[9] The interplay of cultural rhetoric and colonialist instigation of sociopolitical and geographical experiences culminate with negotiations among a group of African-world men converging in post–World War I Marseilles, France. While all of the text's treatments of

Pan-Africanism are not funny and also can reflect levels of tragedy and seri-ousness, McKay's novel offers many definitions of the phenomenon, includ-ing ones that include a more expansive representation of brown brotherhood. The text's introduction of the description "Nationally Doubtful" citizenship papers is one iteration to describe seamen who do not possess official citizen-ship paperwork.[10] It seems, "West Africans, East Africans, South Africans, West Indians, Arabs, and Indians—they were all mixed up together," and the novel frames this as an "eloquent exhibition" of a "universal attitude."[11]

Definitions of humor from the lens of critical theorists allow a compre-hensive itemization of humor's constituent parts and cultural frameworks. The robust engagement of comparative humor and comedy studies through the twenty-first-century growth of media studies programs presents new configurations from which to analyze traditional literary works and their documentation of sociopolitical and cultural phenomena, such as McKay's novel *Banjo*, but it is not comprehensively based on negotiations between humor *and* Pan-Africanism. McKay's novel is part of both the canon of New Negro Movement or Harlem Renaissance literature and the transnational corpus of Black diaspora literature. One of the novel's key presentations of Pan-Africanism interrogates intercultural Africana difference and world-view wherein the group of African world vagabonds experiences a type of dialectically structured conflict-play that is a formula for many of the text's plot episodes. McKay's trope is humor; his protagonist Banjo (aka Lincoln Agrippa Daily) is the world-traveling, blues-defying protagonist from *Home to Harlem* (1928), who in the sequel *Banjo* demonstrates his international survival prowess based on wit.

Banjo is of value additionally because while McKay fashions Banjo as the protagonist, he also includes the character Ray as a semi-autobiographical (representing McKay, himself) foil, ally, and sensible sidekick who serves as a type of alter-ego for Banjo, if he were to have a more rational versus indi-vidualist identity. In the final chapter, Ray admits, "I like this rolling along, stopping anywhere I'm put off or thrown off. Like Banjo."[12] In fact, even the character Jake from Harlem is a literary type who is a thinly veiled represen-tation of Langston Hughes. The novel's exchanges are not completely humor-ous. Many of the characters share unfortunate tales, including Banjo, and his more sobering moments further reveal the psychological dimensions of acts of humor and fast-talking. For example, in the final chapter, Banjo proves his concern for race when he confesses that he saw his little brother get lynched. Yet, McKay presents this revelation without giving narrative space for the shock of a memory of violence to have any opportunity for emotional follow-through. Instead, Banjo continues his litany of proving to Goosey that he has a rational sensibility of the perils of race in America, noting that to his credit he enlisted to fight in World War I via Canada. He suggests that he was not always so jesting and that he made a choice to be "crazy for a change" along with the rest of the world.[13] However, he demarcates that he and the world "ain't gone a-mourning forevah" and that they are "jazzing to fohgit."[14] These subtle elements of Banjo's storytelling invoke the emotional and psychological processes of how humor and associated elements are responses to things such as trauma, undesired memory, and devices for self-preservation. Banjo even prioritizes skills of "self-makings" and says, "I ain't one accidental-made nigger like you, Goosey" suggesting that his persona is one that has evolved to favor his survival.[15] Ray reflectively revisits Banjo's confession, noting, "Never had Ray guessed from Banjo's general manner that he had known any deep sorrow. Yet when he heard him tell Goosey that he had seen his only brother lynched, he was not surprised, he understood, because right there he had revealed the depths of his soul and the soul of his race."[16]

These autobiographical contexts of the character Banjo, whose persona throughout the novel is based more on his identity as a musician and as a folk comic, are part of the inquiry into the model of survival that Banjo shares and even mentors among the group. Many of the seamen and vagabonds lie to customs officials in order to inhabit multiple transnational African/Black identities depending on environment and motive. The group believes Goosey to be West Indian, but he turns out to be African American. Banjo fights in World War I for Canada, but is African American. Malty tells Dengel, "Though youse French . . . you masticate that Englishman's langwitch" better than a lot of Blacks back home.[17] In the text's finale, Malty is responsible for securing a Caribbean crew for a boat headed back to the West Indies, but "Malty also took West African boys, a 'colored': South African, a reed-like Somali lad, and another Aframerican besides Banjo," an act that was successful trickery of the union bosses.[18] Even these scenarios of survival using trickery and manipulation of European unfamiliarity or disinterest in the national origins of people of African descent are comedic and humorous as contributions to a discourse on Pan-Africanist humor. They signify the external versus the internal group negotiations in the text.

McKay's insertion of himself as a literary archetype into the narrative requires us to engage his history of experience in Marseilles or symbolically abroad, in general, in a comparative autobiographical context that balances the literary (*text*), the sociopolitical and applied (*Pan-Africanism*), and the methodological (*humor*) elements of McKay's novelistic vision of the interplay between Black characters in a mid-colonialist European site. The topics of both humor and Pan-Africanism have intellectual trails in the African American and diaspora literary canon. The two variables have not been merged significantly into a single discourse. There are nearly three dozen scholarly articles on *Banjo* that lightly reference humor, but not as a primary variable. Few address Pan-Africanism as a primary variable, and several others engage associated topics of cross-cultural dialogue, transnationalism, cosmopolitanism, and internationalism.

Broader literary studies layer the history of Pan-Africanism with humor-adjacent topics in literature which scholars such as Boubacar M'Baye in *Trickster Comes West: Pan-African Influence in Early Black Diaspora Narratives* (2009) suggest is a discourse considering Pan-African folk narratives aligned with resistance practices in the writing of enslaved Africans.[19] Merging the topics of Pan-Africanism could also benefit from a long view of humor in traditional African contexts, such as what Youssoupha Mane frames in his study on humorous proverbs that appear in African fiction writing.[20] Dexter B. Gordon delineates the difference between classical European and African American approaches to humor. From a cultural standpoint he observes that "humor arises from passion and has always provided a serviceable channel for expressing human feelings, when the range of the oppressed is spoken, humorous discourse may provide a vital rather than merely convenient channel."[21] He credits New Negro Movement writers, including McKay, with using "multiple facets of humor in an effort to recover a distinctly Black folk past with its acknowledgment of basic human instincts," and he credits the movement for a collective "acidic" use of "satire, irony, and the comic imagination."[22] In *Banjo*, the writer Ray values the African-centered cultural mix from this New Negro Movement vantage point and sets the stage for the humor and Pan-Africanism that emerge there. He notes the "piquant variety of things on the dock" and the "colorful human interest."[23]

McKay's *Banjo* has a chapter specifically titled "Telling Jokes" (Chapter 14). He places it just past the novel's midway point, and it serves as a focal point in the novel to alert the reader formally that the novel requires us to pay attention to the interplay of humor and the possibilities of Pan-Africanism. McKay communicates to the reader that if we have not already noticed the value of humor, then he is giving us a gratis clue as assistance. The chapter is the culmination of defining the novel for its inroads into humor. This is in addition to the novel's reliance on storytelling for its inferences and negotiations of the different African-derived identities, philosophies, and points of view that have evolved through various African encounters with the West. It is almost as if the author is aware of the universalism of tall tales, even their value for being types of stock stories that may have versions in multiple cultures and can, therefore, serve as a common logic or reflection of worldview. The content vagabonds, or African world *tourists*, emerge with relative ease as a corps of storytellers, but the logics and expectations of humor, often as *race-based* forays into the comedic, reveal many things. The chapter "Telling Jokes" is the pinnacle of McKay's broad model of the nature of humor among the Pan-African group.

Several things happen in "Telling Jokes." The first is the reappearance of the forlorn Black American Southerner, Lonesome Blue, who prefers the company of the Corsicans over the Pan-African group. His downtrodden-ness is the catalyst for a folkloric creation story about how God accidentally gave Blacks froth for brains. Banjo's observation—"A nigger is a bohn mistake"—is the philosophical transition that temporarily shifts the observations about and conversations with the forlorn Lonesome Blue to the folk narrative creation story.[24] Lonesome Blue is the negative object of the tale proving why the world is as it is wherein "the nigger always full a froth or just dumb like this heah Lonesome Blue," and the crew has a collective "rollicking laugh" at Lonesome Blue's expense without any conflict in philosophy.[25] The justification of the group identity versus Lonesome Blue's in this episode is that Lonesome Blue's general rejection of the group in favor of a European crew (the Corsicans) framed him as unworthy of critical racial protection. The group could laugh at the joke, even with its emphasis on a derogatory hierarchy that shows God favoring whites. In fact, not only did the group laugh, but, led by Ginger, they also speculated that Black would be even more grand if it were not for the mistake.[26]

There is a subtle shift in the group dynamic just as Banjo finishes his creation story. A white vagabonding seaman, Kid Irish, and a Jew join the group. The group's shift from being an all-Black audience to now being a racially mixed one troubles Goosey who complains of Banjo's "raw nigger-ism" as he tells him "you ought to be ashamed to tell that on the race before a white person."[27] This becomes Malty's cue to inquire, "Can't the race stand a joke?" The Jew interprets this as license to participate and asks permission to tell a race joke. The joke ends up capitalizing on stereotypes of Black women as promiscuous, and it angers the only two Black men in the group who actually understand the punchline. Ray criticizes Jews for being the originators of most of the "stock" jokes about Blacks, but Goosey condemns Black women who date white men as "wenches."[28] Both Ray's and Goosey's critical discomfort with a Jew telling race jokes results in condemnations—of Jews and of Black women, the latter of which can be a jab at the Jew and not necessarily at Black women. In fact, the text introduces the Jew by his trade of selling "sex post cards to tourists."[29] Goosey says, "I think we've had enough of colored jokes" and notes that "white people don't make jokes like that about themselves."[30]

From this, now interracial, exchange of jokes, the dialogue reiterates the racial and cultural philosophies of the men. The reader learns that racially derogatory jest is best shared when there is an all-Black audience. The reader learns that Whites, like the Jew, take advantage of capitalizing on racial stereotypes when allowed. The reader learns that humor also has a political subtext, and this comes as a post-humor diatribe from Goosey naming white jokes as one of the things that impedes the race movement. He says, "You don't know why the white man put all his dirty jokes on to the race. It's because the white man is dirty in his heart and got to have dirt. But he covers it up in race to show himself superior and put it on us."[31] He adds his philosophy that "the weak and comic side of race life can't further race advancement."[32] The conversation shifts from storytelling and humor to sociopolitical ideas. This includes Ray's discourse on the linguistic difference between "nigger" and "nigguh" and an additional observation that the Black press is a comic joke.[33] The exchange of jokes strikes an emotional chord and leads to an argument between Goosey (US) and Ray (Haiti) that reveals nothing less than their collective angst associated with a dissatisfaction with the prospect that neither Haiti, Africa, life among the Senegalese in Marseilles, time among a despising Europe, nor existence in the United States feels like *home*.

In the finale of the jesting episode there are resolutions and correctives related to the interplay of humor and Pan-Africanism. In one conversation, Goosey catches himself and impressively uses the word "man" in place of "nig—," which is self-conscious growth to enable stronger ties of brotherhood with the offended Ray.[34] Kid Irish, who was also allowed to eventually tell a race joke that was successful because it chided the Irish instead of Blacks, corrected his use of the word properly to "Negroes."[35] As the chapter began with jest at the expense of Lonesome Blue, it also ends with a resolution to help him in spite of his tendency to dissociate with the group of Pan-African vagabonds. Ray insists on helping Lonesome Blue as an act of solidarity in a notable ancestral honor of an old, disabled Black British seaman in Joliette who died alone "like a dog."[36]

Joel Nickels's study on the novel's dissident internationalism itemizes the negotiations that take place in the text, and these are no less related to the interplay of humor and Pan-Africanism than they are to Nickels's interest in political formations.[37] He argues that "the group dynamics in *Banjo* evoke the rudimentary structures of local negotiation that would constitute the building blocks of any decentralized, global democracy along dissident international lines."[38] Some may even view Pan-Africanism as a dissident, non-mainstream aspect of African-based global democracy. His description of McKay's creative power to envision "sites of transnational democratic agency, while at the same time remaining embedded within community networks and ethnic solidarities" is a version of the text's Pan-Africanism.[39]

Just as chapter 14 ("Telling Jokes") is the height of the novel's emphasis on humor's cultural role, chapter 6 ("Meeting Up") and chapter 25 ("Banjo's Ace of Spades," the novel's final chapter) as a unit cement the novel's contribution specifically to Pan-African discourse. They are the first and final word, respectively, on Pan-Africanism and intersect with the novel's steady interwoven buildup of other occasional Pan-African descriptions, ideas, and contexts, which include the contests of intellect, geographical worldview, and jest between the groups. Both the African American and Caribbean (by way of the U.S.) *philosophers*—Banjo and Ray (McKay's semi-autobiographical character)—are central to these chapters' exchanges. In fact, these two chapters narrate Banjo's and Ray's first and then final meetings. Ray provides the novel's early African-centered cultural context: "It was as if every country of the world where Negroes lived had sent representatives drifting in to Marseilles."[40] The Senegalese shopkeeper added another nuance to the locale, that "White people, no matter of what nation, did not want to see colored people prosper."[41] The central Pan-African discourse began with discussions and global African familiarity with Marcus Garvey's newspaper *Negro World*. It shifted toward conflict between Senegalese views of the United States as a land of prosperity and opportunity and a critique that African Americans fail to take advantage of these privileges. Banjo's defense of his culture and his negative critique of Garvey's role in his own deportation is not the humor in this episode of interrupted Pan-Africanism, but it is the catalyst for an African cross-cultural episode of "monkey" name-calling that ends in negotiation. Notable is the Senegalese barkeeper's cultural-equating description that "Garvey was good for all Negroes . . . in America and in Europe and in Africa" and Ray's and Bugsy's (Senegalese with affinity for Afro-British identification who reveals here that he is actually just West Indian and has been engaging in Pan-African passing) correction to Banjo's reckless insults of both African and Caribbean Blacks.[42] When Banjo critically jokes of the Senegalese bartender as an "African nigger" and "a really and truly down-there Bungo-Congo," Ray intervenes to stabilize the solidarity and calls Banjo a "mean hater" and clarifies that "he's just like other Negroes from the States and West Indies."[43]

Banjo rejects this description with the caveat that the bartender could be like the "monkeys" in the West Indies, and Bugsy's angry response takes the form of the dozens—"Monkey you' grandmother's blue yaller outa the red a you' charcoal-black spit coon of a baboon moon! . . . I'll fight off any nigger foh monkeying me."[44] Both men—Banjo and Bugsy—possess an impulse to use blurred humor and comic racialized jokes as self-defense, which is an episode that falls under the purview of the novel's negotiation of humor and Pan-Africanism. However, Banjo is sensitive to his fault in deconstructing the vagabond brotherhood. His apology is profuse and healing, and inherent in the remedy is a type of confession that some American Blacks have a tendency to share these types of derogatory jungle-monkey jokes among themselves. Banjo appeases, "Scuse me, buddy, I thought you said you was American. I didn't know you come from then Wesht [sic] Indies country. . . .You and me and Ginger and Malty am just like we come from the same home town. We ain't nevah agwine to fight against one another."[45] The resolution was successful as "the little wiry belligerent Bugsy was cooling down as quickly as he had warmed up."[46] In an Africana literary context, this episode requires further analysis. First, there is a need to understand the derogatory impulse to use self-effacing and culture-effacing insults. Second, there is the matter of deciphering what constitutes healing in a Pan-African negotiation. These secondary, African-centered, community-developing and non-literary questions instigated by the text are the applied act of fulfilling the practical enterprise of the discipline of Africana Studies. Thus *Banjo*, written in 1929, is a catalyst for the successful negotiations of global African and diaspora alliances. The text also models the inevitable cross-cultural practices and assumptions that we expect to appear and then to be resolved in discursive interactions among Pan-African communities.

The final chapter, "Banjo's Ace of Spades," begins with Ray's disgust over the "lugubriously comic-procession" of a police funeral, reminding us that a more elaborate analysis of humor and comedy would reveal McKay's critique of the West's excesses in cultural performance and ideology. An early reso-lution in this chapter is Goosey calling Banjo African when he says, "Good God, man, get some American pep in you and don't act so *African*."[47] This is a clichéd description of relaxed traditional African behaviors toward time, but the characters' comfort with such straightforward heritage identity in jest has evolved over the course of the narrative. The chapter includes minor humor elements such as the wordplay in conversations between Banjo and Goosey in which they call the United States the "United Snakes" and "You-whited Snakes," reflecting a collective Afrocentric description of Black distrust of the United States which will "snake-bite wisdom into you."[48]

In the chapter reflecting the novel's resolution, McKay summarizes and enhances many central themes, including humor as an African-derived cul-tural feature, a trickster-based method for survival, and the joys of vagabond-ing among men of African descent who "assembled for the great transport lines" but saved enough energy to "laugh and love and jazz and fight."[49] In fact, McKay's conclusion takes this analysis further into a discourse on the value of folk wisdom as a tool of instruction for Black children whose sur-vival depends on learning what the African world vagabonds know. McKay's reference instigates an inquiry into precisely what is folk wisdom. In this final chapter, the character Ray reflectively itemizes the cultural gifts and features of different African groups and then synthesizes their collaborative, or Pan-African, effect in the geographical experiences in Marseilles. He is inspired and affirmed by African groups speaking their own languages and offering the diaspora a vision of its "cultural roots."[50] He understands his cultural birthright among classes of Aframericans who had "tricks of lan-guage," "unconscious artistic capacity," and "natural gusto for living down the past."[51] Inevitably, he ends this litany with a celebration of the African world's "instinctive gifts."[52] Ray's observations include a distinction between "black gifts of laughter" and the European view of African people as "minstrel niggers, coons, funny monkeys" for the West that reduces the African to being a "public performer."[53]

The novel engages the diverse Pan-African group of men as a collective, exhibiting "rude anarchy" and "legendary vitality," both elements of their particular brand of humor that balances the potential tragedies of Black life and unapologetically reflects the nuances and beliefs of their cultural worldview.[54]

NOTES

1. Gene Andrew Jarrett, *Representing the Race: A New Political History of African American Literature* (New York: New York University Press, 2011), 109.

2. See Anne Adams, "Literary Pan-Africanism," *Thamyris: Intersecting Place, Sex, and Race* 11 (2003): 137–50, which pairs McKay's *Banjo* and George Lamming's *The Emigrants* as companion texts advancing comparable aspects of Pan-Africanism on European soil.

3. Constance Bailey, "Fight the Power: African American humor as a Discourse of Resistance," *Western Journal of Black Studies* 36.4 (2012): 257.

4. Glenda R. Carpio, "Humor in African American Literature," in *A Companion to African American Literature*, edited by Gene Andrew Jarrett (Malden, MA: Blackwell Publishing, 2010), 315.

5. Ibid., 319.

6. Ibid., 315.

7. Ibid.

8. Ibid., 316.

9. Claude McKay, *Banjo: A Novel Without a Plot* (Philadelphia: Harvest Books, 1970), 314, 316.

10. Ibid., 312.

11. Ibid., 312, 313.

12. Ibid., 306.

13. Ibid., 304.

14. Ibid., 304.

15. Ibid., 303, 305.

16. Ibid., 322.

17. Ibid., 317.

18. Ibid.

19. Boubacar M'Baye, *Trickster Comes West: Pan-African Influence in Early Black Diaspora Narratives* (Jackson: UP of Mississippi, 2009).

20. Youssoupha Mane. "Visiting Humorous Proverbs in African Literary Fiction" in *Journal of Pan African Studies* (2015) 7.8: 110–20. Online journal.

21. Dexter B. Gordon, "Humor in African American Discourse: Speaking of Oppression," *Journal of Black Studies* 29.2 (1998): 255.

22. Ibid., 258.

23. McKay, *Banjo*, 68.
24. Ibid., 180.
25. Ibid.
26. Ibid., 180–81.
27. Ibid., 181.
28. Ibid., 182.
29. Ibid., 180.
30. Ibid., 182.
31. Ibid.
32. Ibid., 183.
33. Ibid.
34. Ibid.
35. Ibid., 184.
36. Ibid., 186.
37. Joel Nickels, "Claude McKay and Dissident Internationalism," *Cultural Critique* 87 (2014): 1–37.
38. Ibid., 5.
39. Ibid., 6.
40. McKay, *Banjo*, 68.
41. Ibid., 74.
42. Ibid., 77.
43. Ibid., 77–78.
44. Ibid., 78.
45. Ibid.
46. Ibid.
47. Ibid., 302.
48. Ibid., 305–3.
49. Ibid., 319.
50. Ibid., 320.
51. Ibid., 320–21, 321, 321–22.
52. Ibid., 323.
53. Ibid.
54. Ibid., 324.

Chapter 4

Africana Literary Methods and the Bibliographic Shift in *Iola Leroy* and *The Street*

Locating and identifying the subject place of Africans is a central inquiry in Africology, and an Africana critical reading of Frances Ellen Watkins Harper's and Ann Petry's novels reveals missed opportunities to feature the topic of African sensibility as a central theme of the texts. Describing this as the bibliographic shift is a way to inspire an additional re-reading of canonical texts already initially rescued from obscurity by gendered literary activism. This resuscitative literary activism is responsible for the re-emergence of many African American women's literary texts (e.g., Zora Neale Hurston, Sarah Wright, Hannah Crafts, Julia C. Collins). Such rescue and resurgence activism can be duplicated as we frame the activism around the texts' Africana disciplinary and paradigmatic readings which permit and encourage interpretations, analyses, and research into the narrative to excavate topics more central to and aligned with the discipline's conceptual priorities. As transcendence, this approach generates readings and literary contextualizations of both novels within, in this example, an Africana sensibility. There are many critical options, but this chapter models an analysis of the subject place of Africa in *Iola Leroy* and *The Street*. It is similar to Casey Howard Clabough's literary application of Afrocentricity to various works that confirms how "the experiences of Africa-descended people remain at the center of each book, making Afrocentric theory among the most useful avenues for establishing their respective and collective implications."[1] The distance between this priority and the trends of published research on the novels is the basis of this chapter's introduction of the bibliographic shift, which is subjecting existing culturally-based literary criticism to analysis to discover gaps and opportunities that can be addressed to offer a more Africana disciplinary analysis to apply the discipline's literary specificity. Carr and Williams also reiterate the significance of this when they emphasize the importance—in

African American literary analysis—of the "continuing process of tracing and re-tracing the African experience from its origins in Africa to the present."[2]

In this study of the corpus of literary criticism on two central novels of the African American literary canon—Frances Ellen Watkins Harper's *Iola Leroy, Or, Shadows Uplifted* (1893) and Ann Petry's *The Street: A Novel* (1946), the published criticism is juxtaposed with an African-centered literary criticism that reveals different analytical outcomes and interpretive priorities. This survey models new critical potential for scholarship on traditional literary texts. Contemporary Africana Studies orientations give the texts meaning that is directly proportionate to the discipline's subject areas and are advanced in ways that permit literature to inspire readers toward liberation discourses and behaviors. This is a model that reveals what elements a disciplinary reading adds to the literary enterprise. In transcendence, the Africana lens yields literary readings *plus* an additional exploration aligned with disciplinary function. In the case of delineating trends in critical approaches to *Iola Leroy* and *The Street*, the Africana enterprise suggests the possibility of shifting away from bibliographic trends to emphasize an Africana reading.

Location theory assumes new meaning in such an intervention into the role of bibliography, the bibliographic essay (including annotation), and literature reviews. The discipline's training in matters of agency and worldview is so acute that the discipline's literary research methodologies require a different assumption to determine the relevance of usable sources. The survey technique of listing general thematic trends is more useful than annotation of sources that are precursory yet not critically aligned with an Africana-centered research question. Location theory encourages readers to swiftly discern the worldview, discipline, critical orientation, centeredness, and topic of a source in order to assess whether or not the source is compatible with or antagonistic toward an African-centered agency interest. For advanced scholars, this is a swift discernment. The rationale is that citing sources that are antithetical to or so far removed from the norms of an Africana disciplinary worldview and interests is counterproductive to advancing a disciplinary or cultural-based argument. The problematic resides in the assumption that a literature review and similar forms demonstrate a scholar's immersion in the literary discipline. The literary discipline is assumed to be universal, but the epistemology of the Africana literary enterprise has a specificity of function that sometimes cannot rely on the existing bibliography, which is not so unusual when a subfield is defining its authenticity.

Western literature's disciplinary concern has been to prevent a "wandering too far from the Eurocentric core of the curriculum."[3] However, if critics cannot wander, then the opportunities for new disciplinary analyses will suffer. Proceeding in its own disciplinary direction, Africana literature criticism may opt to have little to do with the reader-response assumptions from other centered locations. This is not to suggest that Africana literary research should ignore relevant existing scholarship on literary texts. However, the discipline's literary process inevitably interrogates the notion of *relevant* and defines relevance on its own paradigmatic terms, which is part of the discipline's process of locating a text. Collectively, these bibliographic shifts are clarifications that support the institutionalizing of the literary domain of Africana Studies.

The discipline's multidimensional training in over a dozen itemized subject areas (*Black* history, politics, economics, sociology, psychology, religion, creative production, aesthetics, culture, philosophy, Pan-Africanism, gender, geography, communication, community development, linguistics, education, and health/science/technology) that are emphasized to different degrees in the majority of the discipline's introductory textbooks grounds Africana thinkers into a cognitive disciplinary approach that is attentive to the categorization and layering of interpretive epistemological lenses. This approach equips scholars to locate a text based on multiple contextual markers. This also determines how much word count should be required for narrating bibliographic sources that may be largely irrelevant to the discipline's concerns. This chapter tests applications of the bibliographic shift to interpretations of *Iola Leroy* and *The Street.*

IOLA LEROY

For nearly a century, critics believed Harper's novel *Iola Leroy* to be the first published African American women's novel, and it has always held a revered status in the canon. We now know it was the third African American women's novel to be published, following Harriet Wilson's *Our Nig* (1859) and Julia C. Collins's *The Slave Bride* (1865). *Iola Leroy* is over 120 years old, but it has powerful features that speak directly to the contemporary concerns of the intersections of history and literature and of the discipline-based and subject-area-adjacent issues of the Africana literature enterprise. The novel is the story of a young woman's choice to be African in spite of the social benefits of her light skin color. The assumption is that the novel's late-nineteenth-century romantic and genteel narrative style upstages African-centered contexts of Harper's fiction. Bernard Bell describes it as "a melodramatic study of the color line" that layers "the sentimentality and rhetoric of romance with the psychological and sociological truth of mimesis."[4] Yet, from a perspective of Africana reader-response theory, the comparative and social science engagements are dynamic. The diversity of its themes is vast, but Africana-centered readings are few. The summaries in anthologies and reference works are balanced. The *Norton Anthology* well-anthologizes Harper's

writings, especially her poetry, prose, and essays, and even though it does not
excerpt *Iola Leroy* it offers comprehensive context, noting:

> Although Iola is superficially similar to the figure of the tragic mulatta, she is
> not a suffering victim. In addition, Harper pairs her mulatto characters with
> "pure African" counterparts who are generally superior to their noble and
> accomplished lighter-skinned friends. Further extending the conventions of
> earlier African American fiction, Harper includes several characters whose
> intelligence, dedication, and resourcefulness are models for the emerging black
> middle class.[5]

This summary implies Africanity is a trope, albeit one that makes a powerful
statement about valuation, but it predicts and confirms why topics about the
middle class and biracial identity dominate the literary criticism. *The Riverside Anthology* excerpts *Iola Leroy*, several poems, and an essay by Harper
in a section on "Major Abolitionist Voices," and emphasizes the novel's
identity as part of the sentimental novel genre and Harper's feminist intervention on the stereotypes of the tragic mulatto.[6] The introduction to *Iola Leroy*
in *The Cambridge Companion to the African American Novel*[7] is particularly
well aligned with Africana literary interests in the novel. In *Cambridge* M.
Giulia Fabi credits writers like Harper for empowering representations of
Black characters in "passing" novels by avoiding stereotype and exploita-
tions of their color for "comic relief."[8] Fabi credits Harper and her peers for
characterizations that represent a "reevaluation of the distinctiveness of African-American culture" and introduce "spokespersons of those historic and
cultural values of black America."[9] Fabi also notes in *Iola Leroy* specifically,
"African Americanness as the consciousness of a distinctive historical, social,
and cultural heritage, rather than as an intrinsic condition of dispossession."[10]

The topics addressed in the published criticism reflect the sentimental
genre, feminist concerns, passing and race matters, and class concerns of the
text: (Table 4.1)

In comparison, an Africological reading of Harper's novel *Iola Leroy*
prioritizes many discipline-specific interests (which overlap with a few on
the list), and as the institutionalization of the discipline's literary enterprise
increases, scholars will produce more Africana Studies adjacent readings of
Harper's novel. As a primary early text representing the continuum of African
American women's writing, *Iola Leroy* is an influential work. As a literary
influence, it inspires and anticipates the African American literary genealogy
that is conversant with the works of many writers. It relates to Toni Morrison's *Beloved* (1987) as Harper references the Margaret Garner story of
a woman killing a child to prevent its enslavement. It overlaps with August
Wilson's play *Piano Lesson* (1987) with its references to a life traded for a
piano. Harper even plants the seeds that Nella Larsen might have used, as *Iola*

Table 4.1   **Bibliographic Themes for *Iola Leroy***

Narrative patterns of resistance	Trickster, passing/marriage
Ambivalent citizenship	Mother's milk, circulation of blood
Mulattoes as mediators	Poverty relief missions
Identity and social knowledge	Language and dilemmas
Schoolteachers	Racial discovery
Romances, mulatta heroines, passing	Reconstructing literary genealogies
Voice-paradigms	Utopian fiction
Race hysteria and politics, pathology	Invisible/invalid woman
The veil, gender, class, and labor	Pathology, secrets, racial/sexual identity
Cultural pedagogy	Black female desire
Warring fictions, color of gender	Generational connections
Class and anxiety	Black feminist orality
Reading beyond the conventions	Romancing the vote
Prisms of passing	Interracial sex
Women's era	Racial ambiguity, American gothic
Sentimental novel, true womanhood	Passing/marriage
Race, work, and desire	

Leroy introduces passages on the metaphor of "quicksand" and the topic of "passing," both of which are titles of Larsen's two novellas.

Harper's storytelling features stable community progress and activist legacies of the period's male and female citizens, with a consistent and committed emphasis on themes of lynching, immigration, and the emerging Reconstruction prison-industrialization complex. The novel's dialogue models the nation's debates about African life and mobility, favoring African characters' explanations of their own agency in matters of freedom, suffrage, identity, education, and mobility. Harper extends these themes well beyond the novel's central interest in mothering, and her approach to the sacredness of African mothering is profound. The conscious rejection of the option to "pass" reflects explicit worldviews of love for and loyalty to African mothers and African blood. As a literary model of Africana womanism, *Iola Leroy* models gender complementarity including settings of men and women interacting freely at a conference where there is space and consideration for all parties' ideas in spite of sex. In the narrative Harper also models equitable communication between African American couples as they contemplate decisions and courses of action for their families.

Harper's literary craft models priorities of contemporary Africana Studies frameworks, including Black psychology and aesthetics. The novel is scathing in its commentary on the complicity of the white plantation mistress and white northern women of all age levels in oppression, racism, prejudice, and discrimination. It differentiates Black psychology descriptions of the pathology of oppression, that it takes a greater pathology to oppress than it does to be a victim of racism. It presents African-centered aesthetics through a sustained view of enslaved African characters as intelligent, clever, and beautiful without romanticizing. The race is presented neither as phenotypi-cally ugly or based on stereotypes, nor are the characterizations ranked aes-thetically and intellectually according to hue or coloration. *Iola Leroy* also advances Africana cultural memory with a differentiation between cultural memory and cultural brooding, or victimization. A cardinal crime recalled in the novel is the cultural memory that men and women retain of the emo-tional scars of ripping mothers away from their children. The novel affirms this tragic memory as a memorialization "to never forget" this particular inhumanity of the enslavers. Finally, the novel frames the religion and forms of spirituality that Africans practiced as a higher, more authentic form of communing with the ancestor. Harper uses the novel to criticize American/ European Christianity.

The comparison does not claim a deficiency in non-Africana Studies–based criticism on *Iola Leroy*. Instead, this chapter engages the bibliography on the novel to reiterate differences in critical priorities based on the unique dis-ciplinary lenses. Africana literary scholars have an opportunity to grow the discipline's literary criticism by engaging the above topics, as it is a challenge to find the word "Africa" in the existing criticism. The demarcations aim to encourage Africology scholars to publish literary criticism with a disciplinary context and categorization, which will naturally advance a revisionist read-ing. This list of potential Africana-aligned topics reveals the content priori-ties of Africana-trained critics in comparison to an emergent content analysis of the existing bibliography. The following approach to Petry's *The Street* advances additional methods and concerns for Africological reader-response for a traditional novel.

THE STREET

Assessing Africana experiences and behaviors in literature also requires finding an author's or character's "psychological location" which is "deter-mined by symbols, motifs, rituals, and signs" as well as "the subject-place of Africans in any social, political, economic, or religious phenomenon."[11] These characteristics also apply to literature, and this section's transcendence is providing an Africological reading of *The Street* with a lens toward item-izing "African cultural elements as historically valid."[12] These are some of the priorities in the Africana-based analysis of literature, and they converge with other customary and even non-traditional approaches for the collective benefit of exploring the value of African American creative production in lit-erature. Similar discipline-based methods include exploring African-centered adaptations to treatments of characterization, historical setting, plot devices, narrative structure and strategy, and forms of conflict, as well as to myriad other devices and conventions. Society should anticipate that different disciplines advance distinct prerogatives in approaching knowledge construction, and this is no less true for contemporary institutionalized Africana Studies, which has its own benchmarks and standards.

Though considerate of cultural specificity based on regional identity, the most progressive, historically determined identity freedom in Africana epistemology is the right and privilege to acknowledge diaspora writers as African and African-derived, with an inherent understanding of the extent to which they are *once removed*, or more (and involuntarily at that), from the African heritage. This acknowledgment also supports diaspora and heritage contextualizations of agency. With these disciplinary imperatives in mind, an Africana disciplinary reading of Petry's novel *The Street* highlights distinct possibilities of the novel's function as a creative cultural product. It is not necessary to characterize the novel as an Afrocentric text, but the novel has several orientations that suggest it would benefit from the perspective of Africological reader-response. The content of *The Street* compels this reading more than attention to formalist textual elements, though it does include observations about Petry's choices for characterization, motive, conflict, and cultural logic. Africana-trained scholars will perceive additional critical and teachable phenomena based on their disciplinary expertise.

Much of the literary criticism on *The Street* emerges from the fields of Literature and Gender Studies, and as a collective the scholarship covers comprehensive dimensions of the novel's plot. In particular, available scholarship addresses: (Table 4.2)

In these studies scholars most frequently compare *The Street* to Petry's other novels and short stories as well as to other Black women's texts. They are explications of the novel's plot, major themes, and constructions of

Table 4.2   Bibliographic Themes for *The Street*

Class consciousness	Mothering
The "street" as theme	Black women's identity
Domestic service	Rape/sexual violence
Harlem's urban landscape	Resistance
Counter-modernity	Survival strategies
Intersectionality	Separate spheres
Demythologizing America	Social terror
Surveillance	Racial privacy
Spectatorship	Feminism
American Dream	Masculinity
Naturalism	The blues
Realism	Scarring/disfigurement
Social terror	

conflict, but the most significant difference is the limited Africana disciplinary cultural framing of analyses. I offer this not as a negative criticism but as an indication of the opportunities for revisionist disciplinary readings of traditional texts. Literature is a cultural artifact as well as a repository of Black experience, storytelling genius, and critical thought that requires an additional cultural–historical and social science interpretation and application. This chapter's example of an Africana topical intervention to the reading of *The Street* highlights textual examples that indicate Petry's sustained contribution to defining the value and role of African heritage in the novel. She does this through thoughtful character reflections on cultural point-of-reference and in passages reflecting identity construction in Harlem's realistic fictionalized populations.

The *Norton Anthology* excerpts the first chapter of *The Street* with a critical biography on Petry. She shares that the novel was "inspired by a newspaper story of an apartment house superintendent who taught a young boy to steal letters from mailboxes."[13] Petry's objective was to "show how simply and easily the environment can change the course of a person's life."[14] Of her literary craft, Petry said, "Over and over again, I have said: These are people. . . . Look at them and remember them. Remember for what a long, long time black people have been in this country, have been part of America; a sturdy, indestructible, wonderful part of America, woven into its heart and into its soul."[15] Petry's motivation to write, her cultural interests, her reference to a much larger heritage and background of African Americans, and the active role of memory in her characters' daily struggles are cues for readers to pursue in Africana criticism. The novel reveals heightened African-centered cultural awareness beyond its primary focus on gendered racial exploitation of Black urban-dwellers in the 1940s.

The Street is a straightforward, brutally honest, and at times, witty and sarcastic, narrative of Lutie Johnson's saga of survival in 1940s Harlem. This separated, single mother, lives hour-by-hour and day-to-day in an attempt to master the many lessons from childhood, employment as a live-in domestic, a failed marriage, and life's sordid predicaments in order to gain financial mobility to move her son Bub away from the threatening streets of Harlem. Readers admire the brilliant skills of observation with which Petry endows her protagonist yet are baffled by the heroine's non-characteristic defeat at the conclusion of the novel.

The character Granny is the most prevalent African presence in the novel. An early reference to Lutie's collective cultural consciousness is the memory of her Granny that appears in the protagonist's reflections during the course of her problem solving and analysis of her struggles. Petry's use of a reliable, third person limited narrator gives Lutie's reflections the integrity of experiential truth. She credits Granny for a stable intuitive corroborated by:

All those tales about things that people sensed before they actually happened. Tales that had been handed down and down and down until, if you tried to trace them back, you'd end up God knows where—probably Africa. And Granny had them all at the tip of her tongue.[16]

Lutie summons Granny's survivalist wisdom when she encounters and assesses the building Super, acknowledging, "there was no explaining away the instinctive, immediate fear she had felt when she first saw the Super. Granny would have said, 'Nothin' but evil, child. Some folks so full of it you can feel it comin' at you—oozin' right out of their skins.'"[17] In another encounter, "She was smelling out evil as Granny said. An old, old, habit. Old as time itself."[18] Granny is a central figure, though physically absent, to Lutie's worldview. Granny's wisdom and instructions guide her critical processes as a type of African-centered or African-derived philosophy that Lutie ponders throughout the text. She honors Granny in these ancestral memories, noting: "Of course none of them could know about your grandmother who had brought you up, she said to herself. And ever since you were big enough to remember the things that people said to you, had said over and over, just like a clock ticking." These things had "gravity" and "become a part of you, just like breathing."[19] The most powerful recollection of Granny's wisdom acknowledges the confidence, respect, and truth of Granny's experience and advice. It is a powerful cultural memory to acknowledge the discerning power of an elder, and Lutie's recollections are a type of ancestral libation and request for help. Granny's effect is not just her knowledge and instructional legacy, but how the memory lives through the aesthetic rhythm of speech layered with rocking movement. Lutie recalls, "Granny could have told her what to do if she had lived. She had never forgotten the things Granny had told her and the things she had told Pop. Mostly she had been right. She used to sit in her rocking chair. Wrinkled. Wise. Rocking back and forth, talking in the rhythm of the rocker."[20]

These types of remembrances appear early in a novel whose characters, especially Lutie, critically analyze their situations and survival strategies like sleuths and detectives, deducing facts and possibilities with acute forms of logic and intelligence. The text even suggests telepathic intelligence. The African grandmother is the core source whose influences—sayings, observations, perspectives, and repetition of instruction and values—establish Lutie's identity and inspire her agency. In essence, Granny is responsible for the intuitive part of Lutie's personhood, and Granny's influence is an African one, maintained by worldview, wisdom, oral tradition, and spirit. Even Boots, the musician who introduces Lutie to the possibility of singing for a living observes Granny's influence on her personality. He says, "Probably why you sing so well. . . . You feel things stronger that other folks."[21] As an aside, beyond Granny's influence on Lutie's intuitiveness, Super's live-in girlfriend Min brokers the novel's documentation of the ancient science of conjuring using potions, lit candles, and religious symbols.[22]

The crises Lutie faces throughout the novel suggest that Lutie desires a utopia, and her consistent anticipation of a place where Granny's values reign implies that the ideal environment or setting could be an African home. A central problem Lutie seeks to fix is her environment, and Petry's skills of characterization chart African sensibility, consciousness, and even sub-consciousness, framing Lutie's desire for an environment that fulfills her needs as a Black mother of a Black son. She observes and critiques the symbols of poverty around her and struggles to capture a vision of the ideal place. She envisions a place and a setting for her family with an intuitive feeling that there must be a place out there that fulfills the African American need for *home*. Her desire is not blatantly revolutionary, Pan-African, or aligned with a *return* awareness, yet there are many examples of this type of symbolic envisioning, such as her evaluation of what 117th Street has to offer within a context of anticipating an *ideal* place.

In her description of the food available in her neighborhood there is a sense of it as culturally substandard or as a product of a dystopia. She ponders— "Yet the people went on living and reproducing in spite of the bad food. Most of the children had straight bones, strong white teeth. But it couldn't go on like that. Even the strongest heritage would one day run out. Bub was healthy, sturdy, strong, but he couldn't remain that way living here."[23] Here Petry features a reference to "heritage" running out. Of which heritage is she speaking? If she laments the pork leftovers and rejected produce that were expected to be the mainstay of Black meals since enslavement, then the heritage she references is an ideal of the African tropical heritage of communal plenty and of comfort—of a genetic heritage that still gives Black children strong bones and teeth. It is at least a reflection of a time when Blacks had sufficient food and subsistence whose availability was not predetermined by race or street address. That would be Africa. August Wilson uses a similar example in his cultural manifesto to the theater world. He surveys the "different culinary values, different culinary histories . . . . In our culinary history, we have learned to make do with the feet and ears and intestines of the pig rather than the loin and the ham and the bacon," which is the result of enslavement practices.[24]

An Africana reading of *The Street* also challenges readers to itemize a White worldview, double standards, and challenges to Blackness. Lutie conceptualizes several solutions to the problem of survival for her small family. She evaluates versions of America's wealth and its beneficiaries and in the course of her employment as a domestic she proceeds as if race is not responsible for the discrepancies in wealth and opportunity. At times, her immersion in the reality of her White employer causes her to drift into daydreams of dislocation as she tests the norms and values of a White worldview.

Lutie's ideal home for her family is "an apartment some place where there were trees and the streets were clean and the rooms would be full of sunlight."[25] The contrast is that she seems unfamiliar with where such scale is possible—an apartment on "a street" with the benefits of the Chandlers' country home. While the image of a clean, sunny home should not be inaccessible to Lutie or to other Blacks, this image is a mixture of a geographically nondescript ideal—certainly not her neighborhood in Harlem. She imagines, "Bub growing up in some airy, sunny house and herself free from worry about money."[26] This healthy, safe, and economically stable image of what she experiences in the world of the Chandlers defies the "common sense" of which she reminds herself.[27] Lutie's vision for her son and herself is a manipulation of the "Country Living" with which she becomes acquainted with the Chandlers.[28]

What Lutie does not summon in her fantasies of sunlight, being a stay-at-home mom, and cookies and milk is the image of a complementary male figure in her household. During her two years with the Chandlers she bears witness to limited communication, therapeutic materialism, alcoholism, infidelity, suicide, and in-laws' effect on the family, but her fantasy does not account for the practical matters of transplanting her and Bub to a new environment. Earlier, Lutie describes the White world of the Chandlers as an "enchanted garden" full of rivers, gardens, and woods—a "very strange world that she had entered. With an entirely different set of values."[29] In the midst of these fantasies, Lutie recalls that the household's lifestyle is only allegedly "perfect." She recalls, "after six months of living there she was uneasily conscious that there was something wrong. She wasn't too sure that Mrs. Chandler was overfond of Little Henry; she never held him on her lap or picked him up and cuddled him the way mothers do their children. She was always pushing him away from her."[30] The discrepancy between what Lutie experiences as normal in the Chandler household and Lutie's fantasy of sunlight and cookies indicates a break in the manifestation of the American Dream. When Lutie's singing career collapses, she readjusts her consciousness back to the African American experience and away from the White American Dream. It is here that Afrocentric methodologies encourage us to speculate what are the contexts of her desire for security, freedom, and well-being for her son.

In Lutie's climactic breakdown, when she realizes that she did not protect her son from harm, she accuses herself of prioritizing borrowed European-American fantasies while she "underestimated the street."[31] With this self-condemnation, Lutie accuses herself of rejecting her son's needs and parallels it to the way Mrs. Chandler neglected Little Henry's needs. In an

Afrocentric analysis of time and place, Lutie's reminder of her blackness might be a configuration of relocating herself in time and space, which is an act of "discovering chronology and geography as keys to interpretation."[32] Perhaps the setting of sunlight and open spaces she sought was an extended community of African people in a region or cultural cradle less hostile than what Calvin Hernton described as the novel's "urban ghetto environment."[33] The Chandlers' worldview is not the prototype for Lutie's worldview and African American reality, and this realization challenges those affected by the meaning of Petry's novel to configure our possibilities for survival in other creative contexts, including Black nationalism, which in its formal meaning anticipates a land or a nation where Lutie's ideal of progress is possible.

Another topic of Africanity in *The Street* is its approach to aesthetics, namely the form and beauty of the black body. *The Street* is full of references to Black aesthetic issues. Most are affirming, even if Lutie's health and beauty are the basis for other characters' attacks against her. Some reveal dysfunction and the challenges the Black community faces that African-centered orientations help to remedy. Lutie's reflections in response to Bub's question about White racism indicate how Black self-love is normative. She affirms the value of Black skin and the Black body, yet it took her son's acuity to observe the racism.[34]

Petry embellishes the character Lutie with an organic cultural sense of identity. She does not know all the answers, yet she is thoughtful and culturally concise in the intellectual process of idea formation. In the novel, men pursue her because of her "long legs, straight back, smooth brown skin, and smiling eyes."[35] The narrative description is an affirming valuation of the body, though characters seek to exploit it. The text's description is attention to her Black physical perfection in terms of—"Soft skin and pointed breasts. Straight slim back and small waist. Mouth that curves over white, white teeth."[36] This description of her womanist beauty counters another character's insinuation that Black Pullman porters are prone to rape white women. While the novel problematizes the fact that those who desire Black women are able to successfully exploit them, the description of Lutie's desirability is intended here to reiterate Black women's desirability to Black men. The text ultimately describes Lutie as "extraordinarily good-looking."[37]

Aesthetically, the narrative is also preoccupied with Black skin and hair. Mrs. Hedges, the ever-gazing neighbor who manages prostitution from her first-floor window, lost her hair and its ability to grow back in a violent fire of which she was the only survivor. She envies Black (or African) hair, not the aesthetics of White hair, and this is a revision of the assumptions of Black desire for White hair. Mrs. Hedges is aware that wearing a long, straight-haired wig looks absurd. She laments the loss of her own hair, and calculates how this is a deficit in her desirability to Black and White men. Mrs. Hedges describes Lutie as having "thick, soft hair," and its value is not assessed based on its proximity to whiteness.[38] As she watches Lutie, "she could still . . . see the shining hair piled high on her head and the flawless dark brown of her skin."[39] Characteristic of Petry's binary and comparative narratives, these types of textual deductions affirm Black aesthetic norms, even in the face of objectification. In fact, in addition to affirming dark brown skin as flawless, Petry even frames desire in cross-racial affection between Junto and Mrs. Hedges. This makes Petry's treatment of Black aesthetics even more normative because Mrs. Hedges's girth, lack of hair, and scars from the fire are not conditions that upstage her desirability as an African phenotypical woman.

Another Africana aesthetics dimension is the novel's inclusion of music and performances as cultural indicators. Music and rhythm continue to be valued as cultural assets to the Black community struggling in *The Street*. The bar is valuable for transmitting music and African rituals of celebration—"It was the one thing that the Junto offered that she sought: the sound of laughter, the hum of the talk, the sight of people and brilliant lights, the . . . rhythmic music from the juke box."[40] Gayl Jones critiques Petry's literary craft in the context of jazz and blues music structure, and her analysis informs the possibilities of Petry's attention to African-derived creativity.[41] Jones is attentive to how Petry "reorders the ways events, characters, and motive are presented to the reader," and Petry's treatment of Black musical aesthetics in *The Street* indicates an additional level of social challenges and cultural resistance.[42] Boots's earlier observation that Lutie sings well because she feels things strongly characterizes Lutie's blues sensibility. However, what Petry does with male musicians is tragic. Racist exploitation of Black music and musicians causes Black male artists to either lose their crafts or to hate their talent. This disruption of the function of music in an Africana cultural narrative is tragedy. The character Boots also has a personal tale that serves as precursor to sharing his own love-hate trials with music.

Collectively, *The Street* documents the African-centered worldview in positing norms of African American aesthetics of the body, of hair, of music, and of elder wisdom. This chapter's itemization of the types of critical engagement of particular interest to an Africana disciplinary reader is not exhaustive. Instead, it covers many of the diverse topics addressed in the existing criticism yet with a specifically Africana Studies orientation that can be expanded in multiple directions. Comparing and contrasting critical trends with Africana critical priorities extends the life and meaning of both Harper's *Iola Leroy* and Petry's *The Street* and instigates new interest for invigorated Africana disciplinary critical study and research on both texts.

NOTES

1. Casey Howard Clabough, "Afrocentric Recolonization: Gayl Jones's 1990s Fiction," *Contemporary Literature* 46.2 (2005): 247.

2. Carr and Williams, *Toward the Theoretical Practice of Liberation*, 303–04.

3. Bernth Lindfors, "Emerging and Neglected Literatures: Their Place in the Traditional Spectrum of Comparative Literature," *Report, Council on National Literatures* 1 (1974): 4.

4. Bernard W. Bell, *The Afro-American Novel and Its Tradition* (Amherst: University of Massachusetts Press, 1987), 59.

5. Gates and McKay, *Norton*, 493.

6. Hill, *Riverside*, 347.

7. Maryemma Graham, ed., *The Cambridge Companion to the African American Novel* (New York: Cambridge UP, 2004).

8. M. Giulia Fabi, "Reconstructing the Race: The Novel After Slavery," in *The Cambridge Companion to the African American Novel*, edited by Maryemma Graham (New York: Cambridge UP, 2004), 40.

9. Ibid.

10. Ibid.

11. Asante, "Betrayals," 77.

12. Ibid., 76.

13. Gates and McKay, *Norton*, 1496.

14. Qtd. in Gates and McKay, Ibid.

15. Ibid.,1497.

16. Petry, *The Street*, 15–16.

17. Ibid., 20.

18. Ibid., 413.

19. Ibid., 45, 45–6.

20. Ibid., 76.

21. Ibid., 160.

22. Ibid., 285.

23. Ibid., 153–54.

24. August Wilson, "The Ground on Which I Stand," *Callaloo* 20.3 (1998): 498.

25. Petry, *The Street*, 151.

26. Ibid., 311.

27. Ibid., 309.

28. Ibid., 50, 49.

29. Ibid., 38, 41.

30. Ibid., 39.

31. Ibid., 389.

32. Asante, "Betrayals," 77.

33. Qtd. In Gates and Mckay, *Norton*, 1497.

34. Petry, *The Street*, 70–71.

35. Ibid., 263.

36. Ibid., 265.

37. Ibid., 276.

38. Ibid., 256.

39. Ibid., 246.

40. Ibid., 145.

41. Gayl Jones, *Liberating Voices: Oral Tradition in African American Literature* (Cambridge: Harvard UP, 1991).

42. Ibid., 98.

Chapter 5

Autobiography and Documentary Forms of *Here I Stand* as Black Cultural Mythology

Literature functions as a resource and vehicle for memory, and the Africana literary enterprise is attentive to this process in multiple manifestations. The discipline's African-centered worldview prioritizes understanding of ancestral cycles that converges with topics of ancestor acknowledgment, immortalization, heritage practices, legacy tools, and spirituality. With respect to genre, historical writing, autobiography, and biography document heroic and acclaimed lives that become a stable source for narrative remembrance. The documentary form contributes, as well. The transcendence here is expanding a critical method for adaptation studies related to an Africana-derived paradigm of Black cultural mythology.

This is a multidimensional subject area analysis of history, creative production, culture, and aesthetics attentive to how two non-fiction African American literary genres distinctively capture the legacy of the historical figure Paul Robeson—his memoir *Here I Stand* (1958), and the documentary film *Paul Robeson: Here I Stand* (1999) by St. Clair Bourne. Bourne is an African American documentarian who has also made films on other cultural figures such as Amiri Baraka, Langston Hughes, Gordon Parks, and John Henrik Clarke. Structurally, memoir is different from autobiography. Memoir is an account of one's relationships and experiences during a limited period of time or experiential encounter. Autobiography is a relatively chronological life story. Readers engage with Robeson's memoir *Here I Stand* as a chronological "autobiographical account"[1] of his life, and it is the single comprehensive life story Robeson left. The memoir tradition maintained by Marita Golden and Maya Angelou provides the prototype for contemporary understanding of the craft, in its distance from the chronological life narrative of the autobiographical form. This chapter takes license to describe Robeson's *Here I Stand* more as autobiography because it functions as such.

Layering the critical survey of these two genres is a unique approach to Black cultural mythology. It adds new variables to the customary approaches and canonical expectations of legend analysis and to achievement-based attributes of the genres of autobiography, memoir, and personal narrative. These are in addition to the need for balance and critical demarcations of hagiography, silences, bias, lapses in memory, fictions, embellishment, and one-sided interpretation of accolade. For example, one of the striking oversights of Robeson's autobiography is the invisibility of his wife and life partner, Eslanda Robeson, whose memory Barbara Ransby has properly excavated in *Eslanda: The Large and Unconventional Life of Mrs. Robeson* (2013).

This process begins with surveying documentary aesthetics, which in *Crafting Truth: Documentary Form and Meaning,* Louise Spence and Vinicius Navarro approach with differentiations between key discussions of authenticity, evidence, authority, and responsibility.[2] The authors are concerned with "actuality" and the ways the form can manifest different truths or reproduce what is real, and they describe the form's balance between aesthetics and "subject matter." Documentary is "lived reality on film," and the "recording of actual occurrences."[3] Spence and Navarro note—"we think of documentary not as simple records of reality but as complex and sophisticated pieces."[4] They add—"It has always been easier to recognize documentary than to define it," which is an opening that welcomes innovation and culturally specific studies of the form.[5] This chapter explores another complexity of African American documentary and shifts sway from such inquiries into truth and authenticity of representations in favor of using documentary in an adaptation studies pairing with autobiography that yields a reading of hero dynamics within a paradigm of cultural mythology.

Adaptation studies addresses how scholars translate a text from one genre to another such as fiction to film or autobiography to film. Of the many forays into merging one genre into the other, transposing autobiography into documentary is a lesser studied phenomenon. This chapter aims to introduce how the Africana literary enterprise is attentive to routine structural literary phenomena such as adaptation, and in this case, layered with the Africana methodology of Black cultural mythology. Paul Robeson's autobiography and the documentary on his life are key sources of this approach as a case study in form and criticism, modeling and framing the comparative analytics of the paired phenomena. In introducing this example of layering traditional and Africana critical methodology, this chapter approaches the two sources structurally, rather than as an in-depth content analysis, as a contribution to the structure of discourse for two frequently taught sources in Africana Studies. The pairing becomes an opportunity to advance new understandings related to cultural mythology, specifically through the method of layering multiple genres of literature and film for the purpose of structurally assessing the way each genre contributes separately, and then collectively, to sustaining the subject's mythology.

Black cultural mythology is a foundation of the emergent subfield of Africana cultural memory studies.[6] Africana cultural memory studies critically orders the field's generic and relatively unstructured approaches to cultural memory through the introduction of a stable set of variables that include: hero dynamics, sacrifice, ancestor acknowledgment, mythological structure, hyper-heroic impulses, epic intuitive conduct, commemoration, memorialization, cognitive survival, immortalization philosophy, inheritance, ritual and sacred remembrance, and anti-heroics. As both vocabulary and conceptual categories of the larger Africana cultural memory enterprise, these attributes take on a critical life of their own, which is too comprehensive for detailed exploration in this chapter. Many of these categories are quantifiable in Robeson's legacy inasmuch as it is maintained through his autobiography and the documentary on his life. Inevitably, these variables are tools from which scholars may select to explore meaning not only when studying Robeson but also as a standard Africana literary and cultural methodology for exploring Africana legacy and hero dynamics.

There was much consternation over the adaption of Malcolm X's *Autobiography* into Spike Lee's film *X*, and viewers' dissatisfaction with the creative license Lee used to embellish the hero's story in film is a predicament largely avoided by this methodology's reliance on the documentary genre as a more curated filmic source. Many attributes of Black cultural mythology methodology could be useful for explicating other dual genre pairings with autobiography and personal experience narratives, such as Gordon Parks's adaptation of *The Learning Tree* from semi-autobiography to film. Parks's contribution to the production introduces a unique caveat of adaptation related to iconic remembrances and experiences of his childhood and their relationship to his more subtle and artistic development and activism, but the methodology, as an Afrocentric tool for demarcating memorial heroic value, is still relevant. It is also useful for a more eclectic critical demarcation of heroics that critics and scholars need to sustain cultural agency in critically analyzing the sometimes troubling or interruptive distractions that are commonplace in sources where non-Black agents participate in narrating Black life, history, and experience. White author Rebecca Skloot's *The Immortal Life of Henrietta Lacks* (2010) is an example, though there are many. Skloot's narrative is reportage and memorialization of the contributions of an African American woman whose cancer cells were co-opted to sustain the contemporary medical research industry, yet the filmic version of Skloot's book merges the narratives of a heroic white researcher, played by Rose Byrne, with the heroism of the Black subject via Lacks's daughter, played by Oprah Winfrey.

Black cultural mythology's itemization of over a dozen attributes of cultural memory provides an innovative and Africana-derived set of critical variables and additions to the lexicon on memory and mythology. In deciphering layers of cultural mythology, this chapter's treatment of the Robeson legacy is just one model drawn from many possibilities. Robeson is an ideal persona on which to base this chapter's modeling, and his hyper-heroic conduct, epic intuitive behavior, and immortalization have predecessors, contemporaries, and inheritors whose legacies are equally suitable for a Black cultural mythology analysis. Naturally, Black cultural mythology is useful for guiding critical discourses on the legacies of figures such as Gabriel Prosser, Nat Turner, Harriet Tubman, John Henry, Frederick Douglass, and others whose hyper-heroic feats represent the culture's survivalist legacies and appear in literary transmission ranging from oral folk narratives, song, autobiography, biography, children's literature, drama, poetry, fiction, and prose, to film.

Khonsura Wilson's approach is to Paul Robeson's "importance to Africana intellectual history" based on his role as the early- to mid-twentieth-century prototype of an international renaissance man.[7] Born in Princeton, New Jersey in 1898, Robeson's accomplishments and identity emerge from immersion in the Black community his father led as pastor, to athletic and academic achievement at Rutgers University, to a brief law career after training at Columbia University, and to a vibrant life as a global performer and social justice agent. This chapter departs from Wilson's interest in Robeson's "creative ideal, that is, a set of creative values, principle framework, and ethics of beauty" but favors Wilson's contemporary description of Robeson as "an artist, an activist, world-class citizen, and dedicated cultural nationalist."[8] Mark Alan Rhodes's exploration of Robeson's placement in an Africana philosophical framework describes his legacy as one of the "greatest musicians, scholars, athletes, actors, and activists of the 20th century," but he focuses on the need for a corrective.[9] He writes, "despite a worldwide generation of commemoration, publications, albums, films, plays, poems, and documentaries, there is still little recognition or memory of him."[10] Rhodes's interest in Robeson's cultural memory status does not go unnoticed, and Black cultural mythology's theorizations and itemizations of foundational conceptual attributes of African American mythological processes should initiate and stabilize a broad revisionist project on Africana cultural memory studies.

Wilson and Rhodes published their artistic and philosophical studies on Robeson as Africana Studies topics in order to enhance how the discipline engages Robeson. Their reminders of Robeson's legacy parallel the function of Black cultural mythology, which is to serve as a methodology of Africana cultural memory studies that adds a comparative and survivalist dimension to the study of the *function* and *effect* of autobiographical and non-fiction-themed works and that is a framework for an Africana disciplinary engagement of legacy, myth, and cultural memory. Managing hero dynamics through this parallel approach within a Black cultural mythology framework is consistent with the discipline's interest in the applied functionality of texts and the canon. As a cultural-literary theory with a distinctive vision of literature's role in cyclically stabilizing Africana hero dynamics, Black cultural mythology itemizes variables such as mythological structure, ancestral acknowledgment, inheritance, memorialization, and anti-heroics for Afrocentric cultural discourse. It utilizes mythology's archival documentation of lived, *not imagined*, heritage experience, even though in the hands of literature there may be innocuous embellishment and symbolic uses of storytelling to sustain the culture's engagement of the original nonfiction mythological persona or event. A pairing with an adaptation studies approach adds an expanded critical dimension to the study of how narrative and genre function toward a legend's hero dynamic.

A category of adaptation studies is translating literature into film, and scholars approach this from many directions. Intertextual comparison is one approach by which scholars measure the differences, if any, in the order, structure, chronology, and loyalty to characterization, description, and plot. Filmmaker Julie Dash modeled the process in reverse by creating the film *Daughters of the Dust* (1991) before writing the novel. Tara Green researches the literature-to-film phenomenon in *Presenting Oprah Winfrey, Her Films, and African American Literature* (2013) to explore Winfrey's role at the turn of the century in producing filmic versions of Alice Walker's novel *The Color Purple* (1982), Toni Morrison's novel *Beloved* (1987), and Zora Neale Hurston's novel *Their Eyes Were Watching God* (1927). Winfrey's contemporary adaptations dominate society's memory of examples of literature-to-film adaptation, even though the subgenre is quite vast. The consistently expanding tradition includes classic and contemporary works of fiction, autobiography, and drama such as the book and filmic versions of Gordon Parks's novel *The Learning Tree* (1963)[11], Sam Greenlee's *The Spook Who Sat by the Door* (1969), Richard Wright's *Native Son* (1940), Lorraine Hansberry's *A Raisin in the Sun* (1959), Alex Haley's *Roots* (1976), Suzan-Lori Parks's *Topdog/Underdog* (2001), and Solomon Northup's *Twelve Years A Slave* (1853). Fewer African American autobiographies undergo genre adaptation, and Spike Lee's adaptation of Malcolm X's *Autobiography* (1964) generated much analysis.[12] An additional challenge within the public domain's consumption of these types of films is that society is so unfamiliar with the actual text of the African American literary tradition that viewers can watch, for example, Tyler Perry's adaptation of Ntozake Shange's *for colored girls who have considered suicide* (1975) and never know that it is an adaption of a play, or in this case, of a choreopoem. This list of the African American tradition of adaptation reminds us of how society's reading and consumption of African American literary texts should not only keep pace with but also prefigure the creation of film adaptations.

In a view of transcendence, Robeson's legacy grows from the historical and philosophical to an even more nuanced literary representation beyond the autobiographical text. Understanding Robeson's autobiography *Here I Stand* and its adaptation into documentary as an example of Black cultural mythology directs the interpretative lens toward narrative processes and their reliance on testimony, storytelling, memory, imagery, and confession as practices of key variables of Black cultural mythology such as hero dynamics, immortalization, epic intuitive conduct, and anti-heroics. Collectively, itemizing the appearance of these elements in creative texts reiterates the act not only of commemoration but also of the *deliberate preservation* of hero dynamics through socio-literary models of ancestor acknowledgment, immortalization theory, and iconic historical interpretation. The process of literature-to-film supports the Black cultural mythology endeavor as a functional and practical consciousness that enhances Black life by recycling a sacred legacy worldview. One of the objectives of literature is to transmit myths and legends of a culture. The evolution of literature from the spoken, or oral tradition, to writing, to film in the modern era represents a fulfillment of nommo[13] whereby the image invoked by language receives life. Film's audiovisual technology has great power to transmit culture and to influence and contextualize meaning.

The *Facets African American Video Guide* (1994) documents "those films which contain a substantial African-American theme and significant participation by African-American artists," but it does not include the "many documentaries, films and videos on African-American issues which are distributed through the educational channels and which can be rented for public or educational screenings."[14] The rationale is that "they are not readily accessible to the consumer," and compiler Patrick Ogle anticipates that "certainly, in the future, as these 'non-fiction' films gain greater acceptance within the home video marketplace, more and more of them will become available in video stores at home video prices."[15] Ogle does not offer a reminder that many titles are available at no cost from public and university libraries, but his observation does highlight an issue concerning the consumption of one form of literature that becomes film. The documentary form, which converts memoir, autobiography, and biography into film is the most important genre of film that helps to promote and stabilize the endeavor of Black cultural mythology. In fact, the paradigm of Black cultural mythology's most distinctive conceptual innovation is its premise of encouraging a reversal of the prioritization of writing above the oral tradition, as the paradigm values writing specifically for its ability to capture narrative in order that society can recycle it through subsequent oral transmission. Black cultural mythology aims to invigorate the oral tradition of storytelling and characterizes creative and literary processes of memory-making.

This relates to the documentary form through the latter's reintroduction of orality as *text*. While the script of the documentary is based on narrative culled from memoir, autobiography, biography, and other primary and secondary sources, it also preserves as visual text, unscripted accounts of testimony, storytelling, memory, and confession. While interviews may be re-ordered through editing, the authenticity of the unscripted oral narrative remains. The documentary form is a synthesis of modern audiovisual technology and the oral tradition. It is functional in preserving and transmitting cultural memory, cultural mythology, and storytelling in traditional parameters—human to human transmission—that are timeless strategies in the maintenance of human memory. This is a radical departure from society's auto-historical and noncritical consumption of documentary. Society makes assumptions about documentary, first, that it is realism, and second, that it documents fact. However, because the genre is based on primary historical and archival forms presented as a visual phenomenon, the critical analysis seems to halt with a documentary being a final installation on a topic. Society confers about point-of-view and biases, but not about structure and the cultural, and in this case an *Africana* functioning of filmic testimony, eyewitness account, and historical documentation. Black cultural mythology instigates new conversations about hero dynamics, a persona's mythological structure, cognitive survival documented in a legendary figure's feats and accomplishments, and the source of the figure's conviction toward epic intuitive conduct and hyper-heroism.

Documentary, as a living visual experience, is an even more authentic form of orality because it features extemporaneous and spontaneous content as well as formally scripted and directed performance. This attribute is an updated reading of what Kariamu Welsh and Molefi Asante suggest about Western technology, that it:

> murders the traditional myth; science is no longer merely *theoria*, it is profoundly practical in ways that destroy the traditional myth. Only in the most passionate rhetoric of African Americans do we still find the *pathos* that accompanies *muthos* into the twentieth century. Because technology introduces machines that reduce mystery, it also reduces the possibility of the transcendence of the spirit.[16]

The writers "discuss the nature of myth in African American thought as a way to discover the values of a spiritual, traditional, and even mystical, rhetoric as

it confronts a technological linear world."[17] The technology of the documentary form, however, as it invites testimony and generates orality, is empowering, rather than murdering. Black cultural mythology is an extension of an
Afrocentric contextualization of myth, and Asante's articulation of myth in
The Afrocentric Idea (1987) confirms the impact the documentary form has
on African agency. He writes that "the managing of myths in discourse could
lead to a renewed emphasis on deep style in orature."[18] Welsh and Asante
identify an even greater connection between myth and orature. They write:

> Myth is important as an organizing principle in the area of human discourse.
> What is it that we speak of if it is not life or death? Between the beginning
> of consciousness and the unknown is a great amount of philosophical discus-
> sion and activity about the prior-to-consciousness and the after-consciousness.
> Rhetoric is therefore the discussion of life and death, consciousness and uncon-
> sciousness, being and nonbeing.[19]

With this in mind, the collective narratives of the documentary form contribute to sustaining Black cultural mythology. Specifically,

> Rhetoric becomes mythological action when it considers the prior-to and the
> after-consciousness, even while occurring in consciousness. These analyti-
> cal utterances, or rather utterances with embedded messages, can be found in
> most contemporary speeches of African Americans. Baraka's "epic memory"
> exercises itself in the oratory of a Jesse Jackson, Benjamin Hooks, Maulana
> Karenga, or Louis Farrakhan, as it did in Malcolm X, Martin Luther King, and
> Elijah Muhammad.
>   Myth becomes in the language of the African American speaker an explana-
> tion for the human condition and an answer to the question of existence in a
> racist society.[20]

This explanation of myth permits a critical analysis of the documentary form
based on African agency and on African cultural meaning. Asante describes
myth as "poignantly eschatological."[21] He explains: "What we notice when we
examine African American myths is that they possess a kind of epistemological maturity . . . The idea of hope and possibility rises on the shoulders of an
African American imaginative mythology that sees the future as brighter than
the present."[22] Memoir, autobiography, biography, and personal testimony are
elements that evaluate and critique life experience and performance. Since
the documentary features individuals who represent or bore witness to great
achievements, the collective narratives, though interpretational, are critical,
reflective, and profoundly humanistic. They often end with a note of encouragement for future generations, in spite of the film's likelihood of revealing
pain or tragedy, and the documentary preserves a human record of heritage.

A comparison between Paul Robeson's memoir, *Here I Stand* and the documentary on his life, *Paul Robeson: Here I Stand* validates the interpretation of the documentary's value in sustaining Black cultural mythology. This chapter's model of transcendence suggests curricular, pedagogical, and research opportunities in the Africana literary endeavor, and the remainder of this chapter highlights structural and limited analytical features of both Robeson's memoir and the documentary.

Robeson lived from 1898 to 1976 and published *Here I Stand* in 1958, when he was about sixty years old. Robeson insists that it is not an autobiography, but even as memoir, it is Robeson's lasting, self-authored life story. He clarifies his objective many times, and his own words convey the depth of an oppression that he seeks to excoriate by sharing his own narrative. He writes:

> At the outset let me make one thing very clear: I care nothing—less than nothing—about what the lords of the land, the Big White Folks, think of me and my ideas. For more than ten years they have persecuted me in every way they could—by slander and mob violence, by denying me the right to practice my profession as an artist, by withholding my right to travel abroad. To these, the real Un-Americans, I merely say: "All right—I don't like *you* either!" [23]

It is not uncommon to hear contemporary testimony about how ordinary citizens fight and experience ridicule in school-age and adult environments for attempting to recognize Robeson's hero dynamic. Because of the McCarthyism that shadowed Robeson's career and activism, there was a period when he was shunned, removed from history, and forgotten. Robeson's legacy fits well into the study of memory/re-memory/remembering, and Black cultural mythology is an effective tool for re-centering Robeson's legacy into active consciousness. Beacon Press reissued *Here I Stand* in 1988 with an introduction by historian Sterling Stuckey, a reprint of Lloyd Brown's 1971 preface, and the author's original preface. Structurally, the memoir has a prologue, five topical chapters, and an epilogue. The prologue is a statement of ancestry, heritage, the dominance of his father in his life, and racial episodes of his early years that created a man whose major concern is "the struggle of my people for freedom."[24] It is imperative to survey Robeson's narrative structurally in order to compare its adaptation into the documentary form.

The autobiography begins with "I Take My Stand," which confirms that Robeson's audience is the youth, the younger generation that may not understand his plight because of the loss of credibility he experienced through blacklisting and the Black community's fear of embracing a leader associated with communism. The chapter introduces his performance career and

activism on behalf of Black freedom and human dignity and significantly
confirms Robeson's African identity and his attention to culture. A Pan-
African Robeson emerges. He is proud of his African heritage, and he is an
active spokesman against colonialism. African intellectuals introduce him
to the socialist experiments of the Soviet Union. In essence, we learn Robeson's geography—his interests and his travels. The text documents primary
sources that confirm his perspectives, and he liberally cites the Black Press's
treatment of his statements and of the tricky interpretive politics that helped
to defame his character. These function as anti-heroics, which are not merely
polemical reductionist perspectives but aggressive acts of domination that
seek to deconstruct Robeson's mythological structure. In this sense, the
memoir/autobiography itself is Robeson's testament of mythological structure—his nurtured and selected communal worldview and his philosophy of
intergenerational well-being. Robeson defends his ideas, and offers a well-
documented and well-researched narrative in his defense. The memoir is not
immersed in the standard bias that we anticipate when we read personal narrative. Legitimately, after his wrongful persecution one would expect Robeson to exonerate himself in his narrative, but his narrative personal agency
(paired later with the documentary) prevents anti-heroics from leveling the
final word on his legacy.

The deliberate process of using autobiography and memoir to preserve
one's integrity, or even one's hero dynamic, is a significant component of
Black cultural mythology. The early-nineteenth-century abolitionist Maria
W. Stewart significantly engaged in this process when she chronicled her life
story in the years before her death. Her life is the premise of several explorations of immortalization being a deliberate exercise of Black leaders whose
righteous passion on behalf of the race was forgotten, belittled, or miscon-
strued through character assassination or social neglect.[25]

In the next chapter, "Love Will Find Out the Way," one would expect some
mention of Robeson's wife, Eslanda Cordoza Goode Robeson, and family,
but it is, instead, a tribute to the bonds of affection that Robeson developed
for constituencies all over the world. It is a chapter about "the oneness of
humankind."[26] Robeson writes of mutual camaraderie between himself and
primarily the "common people"—Russians, the British (English, Irish, and
Welsh), those who fought against fascism in the Spanish Civil War, and the
Canadians and others who advocated for the reinstatement of his passport.
Robeson's musical performance repertoire was of the world's folk songs.
Ironically, since we are dealing with the documentary form, Robeson did
contribute to a film project sponsored by the World Federation of Trade
Unions. This is one film project that, being nonfiction, permitted Robeson
to perform as his authentic self [which we find a rarity in his film career, as
the documentary *Here I Stand* analyzes], as he recorded "a song for peace

and freedom, a song of brotherhood for working peoples of all lands."[27] The documentary was entitled "Song of the Rivers" and was completed by the Dutch moviemaker Joris Ivens.[28] In Robeson's chapter here, he is a bold and willful character who fights for cognitive survival and is sustained by mythology maintenance provided by other cultures and nations. Paul Robeson is an international hero, lauded and praised far beyond America's shores, and even respected by the world while America was persecuting him. His chapter highlights the models of reciprocity in the struggle for freedom, whereby other cultures are empowered by Black activism. Inevitably, Robeson has a global cultural mythology, which is sustained by sacred memorials and images such as Antonio Salemme's sculpture entitled "Lost in Europe Pre-WWII." In fact, Robeson is memorialized in public arts for the prowess narrated in his personal writings and documentary, such as the sculpture entitled "Here I Stand" in the Pentworth neighborhood of Washington, D. C., the Sir Jacob Epstein *Portrait Bust of Paul Robeson* housed in the York City Art Gallery in the United Kingdom, and statues or busts on college campuses such as North Carolina A&T and Central State University.

Robeson's next section, "Our Right to Travel," is about his passport case. The U.S. government revoked his passport for eight years, from 1950 to 1958. As a leader, Robeson does not view his struggle in isolation. Correctly so, he places his activism within the tradition of Black protest and honors the legacy of those who came before him and who struggled against racism as his contemporaries. This is an aspect of Black cultural mythology's attributes of ancestor acknowledgment and immortalization practice. In general, his narrative is historical, and he places himself in a continuum of Black resistance. He spends a large part of this chapter remembering Frederick Douglass, the Underground Railroad, and other freedom-seeking, formerly enslaved Africans who fled the United States and sought refuge among sympathizers abroad. As an icon of Black cultural mythology, not only does he call the names of forefathers and foremothers, but also he offers relevant historical context, noting—"The good work they did abroad lives on in our own time, for that pressure which comes today from Europe in our behalf is in part a precious heritage from those early Negro sojourners for freedom who crossed the sea to champion the rights of black men in America."[29] This is an emphasis on the attributes of inheritance and sacrifice. He clarifies that "the concept of *travel* has been inseparably linked with the concept of *freedom*."[30] The documentary *Here I Stand* does not feature this specific historical interpretation, and this selective omission is a reminder that the best formula for stabilizing Black cultural mythology is to read the memoir/autobiography *and* to view the documentary, which complements the text, particularly the collective eyewitness community's critique and assessment of the value of the hero as mythoform. In this chapter Robeson also mentions W. E. B. Du Bois as a dynamic contemporary doing significant national and international work on behalf of Black freedom.

The fourth chapter, "The Time is Now," is a particularly relevant contribution to Black cultural mythology because Robeson spends a considerable amount of time identifying the anti-hero. The anti-hero dynamic is imperative to an understanding of the positive hero dynamic. Often, a hero cannot exist without combating a villain or constant foe. In this chapter Robeson deconstructs the "myth of white supremacy" and leads readers into understanding the war for freedom.[31] He writes, "Some of our 'best friends' are really enemies," and he critiques the concept of "gradualism," defining it as nothing "but a mask for one of their double faces."[32] In this chapter Robeson addresses issues of "agency" [the resistance need for people of African descent to be subjects of our experience rather than objects], and he offers a platform for activism for Black rights in the United States. The earlier chapters feature Robeson's activism among multinational and multicultural freedom organizations, and here he re-emphasizes his attention to the Black freedom struggle in the United States.

Black cultural mythology is aimed at developing Black leadership models, and Robeson's narrative fulfills this objective. As a literature form, the documentary is the natural next phase that succeeds the personal narrative because it helps to preserve and transmit the living, visual, human character of Black leadership models such as Robeson. In this interpretation, technology through the documentary enables greater levels of ancestor recognition by preserving living image and voice as well as the community, whose memory of the legend is the act that sustains ancestorship.

The final chapter of Robeson's memoir, "The Power of Negro Action," reiterates Robeson's conclusion that the Black freedom struggle requires "coordinated action" and political mobilization. However, it is the epilogue entitled "Our Children, Our World" that is Robeson's final statement of the memoir/autobiography that reiterates the text's function as Black cultural mythology. Robeson confirms his vision for future generations by directing his summary to the youth. He offers an instructional letter to Black youth, including the "young heroes of Little Rock."[33] Here he refers to the Sputnik satellites as two new "little moons" and ends on a note relating the new heights of scientific achievement with the new heights Black children will reach once Jim Crow no longer bars "most Negro children from an equal education."[34]

The 1999 documentary *Paul Robeson: Here I Stand*, directed by St. Clair Bourne and written by Lou Potter, is 127 minutes long and features commentary and interviews from forty-one scholars, activists, friends, and family members of Paul Robeson. Singer/actor/activist Harry Belafonte, historian Sterling Stuckey, biographers Lloyd Brown and Martin Duberman,

Robeson's son Paul Robeson Jr., and theatre director Lloyd Richards are some of the most significant contributors. The documentary has a dynamic effect of Black cultural mythology because it encourages heritage practices. It documents the oral tradition surrounding Robeson, presents footage of his performances and commentary, and illuminates archival, primary, and secondary sources for further study. Collectively, the voices that speak to Robeson's legacy affirm his epic intuitive conduct and his hyper-heroism. The narratives also exhibit processes of remembrance and immortalization through storytelling to transmit and maintain mythological structure which is a model for future generations' culturally grounded sociopolitical agency and stability.

The documentary also enhances the realism of Robeson's life by critically evaluating his strengths and weaknesses. Robeson's memoir/autobiography does not directly mention his wife, Eslanda Cordoza Goode, but she is a central feature of the documentary. The documentary fills in the gap of what appears to be a gendered narrative in which men make history and women remain unrecognized. The documentary elevates Robeson's wife to her proper legendary status, and reminds viewers of the untold stories of Black women's achievement that would benefit from intellectual "search and rescue" missions.

Finally, the documentary situates Robeson as an ancestor by documenting his death and his funeral with visual footage of his casket, the pallbearers, and the international mourning to create a visual context for the grandeur and magnanimity of Robeson's life from which the documentary narrates an interrogation of society's unfamiliarity with the details of Robeson's legacy. The last voice of the documentary is Susan Robeson, and this is compatible with the final audience of Robeson's memoir—the future generation. This generation bears responsibility for finding ways to incorporate hero dynamics and cultural memory into quotidian practice—every day, in cyclical, repetitive, and regenerative libation. Many voices corroborate the tragedy of memorial neglect and the need for mythological grounding to ensure the legacies of exemplars who engraved courageous African American identity on American soil. In response, the tools of Black cultural mythology, which are configured to sustain the foundations of the discipline's formal establishment of Africana cultural memory studies, alleviate this looming conceptual cultural crisis—that heretofore African American and diaspora cultures have not had adequate structured conceptual tools to reinforce cultural memory. The discipline of Africana Studies is the fertile ground from which Black cultural mythology blooms.

Memoir and autobiography, as first-person narratives, are characterized by a level of understatement. The author reveals details about his or her life, but superlatives, which evolve from the community's collective interpretation of the individual, are generally absent. It takes a documentary, a survey of forty-one living (at the time) references, to convey to future generations that Paul Robeson was an early- to mid-twentieth-century global ambassador. He was a popular and political international figure who was the largest international recording star of his day. One journalist of the Black press wrote—"If there is a mystery about Paul Robeson it is this: By singing spirituals he can be popular and wealthy; by fighting for his race he becomes despised and doors are closed against him. For the answer as to why he made this choice you will have to search deep in the recesses of his soul."[35] The documentary visually fulfills this superlative beyond the understated memoir, and pairing the study of these two literary genres implies a method for comprehensively explicating Robeson's hero dynamic.

In summary, the documentary form permits that necessary phase of critical community analysis and debate about the value of one's legacy. This is part of the process of the traditional West African funeral dirge and has great implications for the ascendance of and the remembrance of African American and diaspora leaders as ancestors. Black cultural mythology rejects blind consumption of heroes and legendary figures based only on accolade, for the value of heroes is that they are also human. This humanity enables us to value their achievement and to learn from the experiences that challenged them. Many times these challenges emerge as models of transformation that are inspirational. The documentary *Paul Robeson: Here I Stand* ends with a challenge for society to "know him; [to] revere him." Lloyd Richards describes the lasting photographic images he has of Robeson in which Robeson is standing, surrounded by a group of young men—the next generation. He describes Robeson as a huge Christmas tree, of which "we are the ornaments." This anecdote of Robeson's legacy illustrates the process of Black cultural mythology whereby we have a responsibility to aesthetically embellish and adorn the past with deliberate contributions that sustain and recycle a confident narrative of Black survivalist prowess and achievement in a world that negates the processes of Black survival. This is an intergenerational intellectual exercise that makes liberal use of history, personal narrative, and film to maximize a centered interpretation of the past.

NOTES

1. Many legends die before they have an opportunity to write and publish a formal autobiography. Others, like W. E. B. Du Bois, wrote several autobiographies because they kept outliving their own life story. Structurally, Robeson's memoir is compatible with the autobiographical form in spite of Robeson's protests that it is a memoir. One of the biases of personal writing, in this sense, is the individual's

natural ego which does not wish to concede to death or admit that his years on this earth may be shorter than anticipated. The general public, consumes the personal narrative more as an "autobiographical account" than a memoir, as seen in Elton Weaver's www.amazon.com review "Robeson's life and legacy, July 2, 2014." In this chapter, I take license to generally describe *Here I Stand* based on how it functions, which is more as an autobiography. We are indeed indebted to Robeson for telling his own story. See https://www.amazon.com/gp/customer-reviews/R2QSI5N8LM4ZDL/ref=cm_cr_dp_d_rvw_ttl?ie=UTF8&ASIN=0807064459. (Accessed June 29, 2017).

2. Louise Spence and Vinicius Navarro, *Crafting Truth: Documentary Form and Meaning.* (New Brunswick: Rutgers UP, 2011).

3. Ibid., 2.

4. Ibid.

5. Ibid.

6. Introducing Africana cultural memory studies as a subfield of the discipline of Africana Studies has been my objective in over ten years of work on identifying Black cultural mythology as the foundation of the subfield. It began with a chapter on Black cultural mythology in *Literary Spaces: Introduction to Comparative Black Literature* (Durham: Carolina Academic Press, 2007). Expansions include "Malcolm X and Black Cultural Mythology," published in *International Journal of Africana Studies* 12.2 (2006): 213–22; "Interpreting a Brighter Past: Molefi K. Asante's Prediction of Black Cultural Mythology," pp. 191–226, in *Essays in Honor of an Intellectual Warrior*, edited by Ama Mazama (Paris: Menaibuc, 2008); and a section on immortalization theory in "The Cosmology of Afrocentric Womanism," published in *Western Journal of Black Studies* 36.1 (2012): 23–32.

7. Khonsura A. Wilson, "The Cosmopolitan Creative-Intellectual: The Creative Ideal of Paul Robeson," *Journal of Black Studies* 44.7 (2013): 725.

8. Ibid., 726.

9. Mark Alan Rhodes, "Placing Paul Robeson in History: Understanding His Philosophical Framework," *Journal of Black Studies* 47.3 (2016): 235.

10. Ibid., 236.

11. Bernard Bell, *The Afro-American Novel and Its Tradition* (Amherst: University of Massachusetts Press, 1987) describes Gordon Park's text as "literary neorealism" and as a type of "traditional realism" (p. 245) that distinguishes it from autobiography in spite of its semi-autobiographical reliance on the writer's life experience.

12. See Spike Lee's film *X* and Malcolm X and Alex Haley's *Autobiography* (New York: Ballantine Books, 1965).

13. This is based on Paul Carter Harrison's exploration in *Nommo*, which is not applied much to studies of film and cinema, even though there is a large corpus on work that traces the concept in African American writing.

14. Patrick Ogle, *Facets African American Video Guide, 1994* (Chicago: Academy Chicago Publishers, 2005), ii.

15. Ibid.

16. Kariamu Welsh and Molefi Kete Asante, "Myth: The Communication Dimension of the African American Mind," *Journal of Black Studies* 11.4 (1981): 387.

17. Ibid.

18. Molefi Kete Asante, *The Afrocentric Idea*. (Philadelphia, PA: Temple UP, 1987), 103.

19. Welsh and Asante, "Myth," 388.

20. Ibid., 388–89.

21. Asante, *Afrocentric Idea*, 101.

22. Ibid.

23. Robeson, *Here I Stand*, 4.

24. Ibid., 27.

25. See Temple, "Cosmology of Afrocentric Womanism," as well as expanded discussions of Stewart in Chapter 11.

26. Robeson, *Here I Stand*, 48.

27. Ibid., 59–60.

28. Ibid., 61.

29. Ibid., 67.

30. Ibid.

31. Ibid., 75.

32. Ibid.

33. Ibid., 109.

34. Ibid., 110, 111.

35. Ibid., 4.

Chapter 6

A Raisin In The Sun and the Tradition of Literary Pan-Africanism

This chapter is an exploration of the dimensions of Lorraine Hansberry's African-centered worldview in the play *A Raisin in the Sun* (1959) based on transcending traditional canonical approaches to the play. In *The Colored Museum*'s (1988) "Last Mama on the Couch Play," George C. Wolfe enacts an early intervention on the ways the canon and classic performances confine the effect of *Raisin*. Here, the interest is in measuring the African worldview documented in the play through the symbolism of Hansberry's African character Asagai and through the African heritage sensibility she embeds in the Younger family. Additionally, an updated look at *Raisin* is an opportunity to study one of the Africana subject area priorities—Pan-Africanism (sometimes framed as transnationalism) using the critical framework of literary Pan-Africanism. As one of many priority Africana literary interests, critical theories such as literary Pan-Africanism explore the cyclical meanings and iterations of African identity and consciousness conveyed in creative writing.

Raisin has a place of critical importance because the character Joseph Asagai is not only one of a scattered set of African characterizations in African American literature through 1959 but also "perhaps the first African intellectual on the Broadway stage."[1] The seminal theoretical objective of literary Pan-Africanism was an orientation for studying African writers' depictions of African American characters and measuring their Pan-African interest, curiosity, and creativity as trans-global post-enslavement renewal.[2] This original study anticipated expansions of literary Pan-Africanism to include creative writing that explored cross-directional geographical exchanges between people of African descent who, as Wole Soyinka assesses in his discussion on African ethnocultural debates, take advantage of the liberated rights of all African people to assume an African identity based on an "autonomous sense of being."[3] Though not an African writer, Hansberry's act of giving voice to Asagai, who resides in the United States during the play, is suitable for a literary Pan-Africanism analysis. This reading also advances a more mature conceptualization of literary Pan-Africanism that relies on more discipline-specific methodologies in its articulation of possibilities for measuring variables of African worldview, that can be applied in the future to a broader set of globally authored Africana texts.

Raisin is among the first dramas to predict the social effect of contemporary African migration to the United States. Extending the play's implied negotiations of the African and African American relationship through a method of social science speculation encourages us to question the realities of the trope of "the return," whether in its traditional, trans-global, or even contemporary heritage-DNA-testing dimensions. An innovation of this chapter is speculation on how the Younger family would score on the Worldview Analysis Scale (WAS), a tool from the field of Black Psychology to measure African cultural sensibility in United States populations. Considering the social science agency and applications of a canonical play illuminates the freedom and transcendence in the Africana literary enterprise to augment the effect and multidimensionality of *A Raisin in the Sun*.

In 2004 critics nominated *A Raisin in the Sun* for a Tony Award for Best Revival of a Play, and though it did not win in this category, the public's thirst to cyclically engage Hansberry's masterpiece through periodic revivals is not lost. The 2004 Tony Award cycle of *Raisin* boasted a unique celebrity cast, as did the 2014 cycle of performances with Denzel Washington playing the lead character of Walter Lee Younger. However, interest in the play's revival is not merely because of cycles of celebrity performances. In 2008, the 2004 Tony-nominated cast, including Phylicia Rashad, Sean Combs, Audra Mac-Donald, and Sanaa Lathan performed a television film version of the play that marked an update from the black-and-white traditional reel from 1961 starring Sidney Poitier and Ruby Dee. The life of *A Raisin in the Sun* runs from being a creative testament to twentieth-century African American ethos and experience to being a dramatic text whose recurring contemporary study within the canon of African American literature invigorates both traditional and futuristic sociocultural sensibilities. Viewing the live performances on national stages reminds us how the drama's features continue to represent an African American reality. The historiography of Hansberry's play is still active and relevant, like Ta-Nehisi Coates's itemization of similar variables in the essay "The Case for Reparations"[4] that demonstrates how the challenges of the African American past and the African American present are so compatible and aligned.

African American families are still communal and intergenerational, sharing housing and merging resources for survival. Housing still poses a crisis determined by skin color and uncertain economics. Young Black men and women continue to assess choice and regret as well as desires and dreams as they manage Black personhood amid the demands and constraints of employment, entrepreneurship, education, family life, religion/spirituality, and the pull of tradition and African-ness. Thus, considering the effect and inspiration the 1959 play has on the present, *A Raisin in the Sun* continues to evoke questions about the specificities of life for people of African descent in the United States. Including these types of considerations in an Africana literary approach instigates dynamic practical directions for the text.

These traditional approaches to the study of *Raisin* are diverse and cover masculinity, dance scenes, the U.S. metropolis, the Black body, racial discrimination, studio racism, the meaning of home, signifying, the contemporary portrayal of Walter Lee, heroines, Black womanhood, Black female space, influences on August Wilson, lynching, abortion, mothers, and human destiny. There is also a set of essays on *Raisin* with key subject interest in Africa and African-centered cultural topics.[5] These essays advance some of the strongest analyses of the African worldview, Hansberry's heritage sensibility, and the implications of the dramatist's creation of a Nigerian character in a 1959 play that emerged as the best-known African American drama of the twentieth century. The literary criticism with topical foci on Africana-adjacent topics offers important antecedent viewpoints that are a foundation for this contemporary pivot analysis toward Africana literary transcendence.

The two central anthologies on African American literature take different approaches to *Raisin* and Hansberry. *The Riverside Anthology of the African American Literary Tradition* (1998) frames the period of *Raisin*'s 1959 publication in terms of "Win the War Blues" and the "Post-Renaissance and Post-Reformation" period. [6] The anthology's authors describe this as a progressive period of African American attention to events at home and abroad. They mention Hansberry among the list of "cultural activity" that received acclaim through awards and honors from "the white literary establishment," but note that "most of the writers were not as fortunate as they were."[7] Perhaps in part because Hansberry's literary career was cut short through her untimely death in 1965, *Raisin* can be said to have remained suspended in stereotyped debates of integration and assimilation, or as "kitchen melodrama."[8] It is invisible in the *Riverside* narrative and gets lost in the valuation of "the dynamic tension between modernist integrationist poetics and African-centered poetics" that compares approaches of the 1941 publication of *The Negro Caravan* with LeRoi Jones's (Amiri Baraka) 1961 *Preface to a Twenty Volume Suicide Note*.[9] Hansberry's mention in the anthology is so minimal that neither she nor *Raisin* are indexed in the volume. In comparison, *The Norton Anthology of African American Literature* (1997, 2004) takes a more comprehensive approach to exploring Hansberry. *Norton* anthologizes *Raisin* in its entirety in the section on "Realism, Naturalism, and Modernism," phrasing that enables students in English to align the Black literary tradition with the European American tradition. Like many texts that get overshadowed by the filmic versions, the performances of Poitier and Dee, and now even Rashad and Combs, contribute to society taking the literary *texts* of the dramatic arts for granted. The legacy of the text and the legacy of the media serve distinct functions: one is for study and philosophical applications that inspire analyses of worldview, and the other becomes part of entertainment's cultural archive.

Recent studies on *Raisin* represent a shift in the critical bibliography on the drama. For instance, Lawrence P. Jackson's final chapter of *The Indignant Generation: A Narrative History of African American Writers and Critics, 1934–1960* (2011) introduces Hansberry through her interview during which she shocked Mike Wallace. As Jackson describes it, "To begin with, Hansberry had her head on straight about her African heritage, which she did not see as a source of shame and ignobility. She was not humiliated to be a descendant of Africans or slaves."[10]

In viewing the 2004 Broadway performance in which Billy Eugene Jones, the understudy, played Walter Lee Younger, one was struck by *Raisin*'s capacity to demonstrate angry Black manhood that borders on narcissism and verbal abuse of his mother, wife, and sister. Viewing the 2008 television film, the panning and cinematographic angling of Sean Combs's performance shows a cunning and seemingly unstable Walter Lee Younger whose character would benefit from *therapy* to help with his apparent advanced case of race-based traumatic stress. Jackson describes these types of incidents as Hansberry's depiction of "a series of explicit criticisms of Walter's masculine heroism."[11] Wolfe also suggests this realm of Walter Lee's characterization in his parody that merges Ntozake Shange's Vietnam veteran Beau Willie Brown (from *for colored girls who have considered suicide/ when the rainbow is enuf*) and Walter Lee Younger into the same character. The contemporary era is more nationally attentive to gendered power threats and interventions against misconduct, battery, abuse, and conflicts based on traumatic stress disorders. These nuances shift our reading of *Raisin* toward interests in mental health and racial stress in addition to the core variables of Africanity and the African worldview.

Africanity appears in *Raisin* with the Nigerian student, Asagai, who has continental African nationalist ideas, but Hansberry also parallels his African past with Walter Lee's narration of heritage. In the final confrontation with Karl Lindner, the representative from the Clybourne Park Improvement Association, Walter Lee says, "This is my son, and he makes the sixth generation [of] our family in this country."[12] Hansberry specifies that there is another country of heritage for the Younger family, and this fact of identity is not lost in Africana reader-response. In fact, not only does an Africana Studies disciplinary approach encourage readers to go a step further in pursuing a deeper analysis of African worldview documented in the play, but the limited treatment of matters of cultural depth permitted in non-Africana and other paradigmatic approaches is a primary reason why readers and students seek out an Africana approach to literature in the first place. Thus not only Black psychology but also Africana worldview are intersectional critical considerations beyond analyses of Hansberry's literary craft that find space and authority for explication in the Africana setting. An exploration of the possibilities of racial traumatic stress is a fairly straightforward analysis that has a bibliographic trail in the criticism on *Raisin*. However, as an exercise related to Hansberry's effect on creative literary characterization and realism, it is a new direction to situate the characters' African-derived personhood, which determines their motivations, expectations, and assumptions, within Black psychology measures of the WAS.

This reading of *Raisin* borrows the *Norton* anthology's reminder, from Hansberry's own words, of what the notion of "genuine realism" can mean in an Africana literary context.[13] *Norton*'s critical biography on Hansberry provides the necessary cues from which we can advance a more Africana-based analysis. First, it reminds us that radical Black critical reception was both polite and fierce, and at times dismissive of *Raisin* as "a fable of a rejected strategy of 'passive resistance.'"[14] The play's biographical note in *Norton* describes Amiri Baraka's initial view of the play as "a period piece with outdated topical concerns."[15] Later, Baraka amended his stance, now accepting *Raisin*'s "profoundly imposing stature, continuing relevance, and pointed social analysis."[16] It is here, pivoting on Baraka's description, that we pursue an Africana Studies, discipline-based literary analysis that prioritizes literary Pan-Africanism and the possibilities of a subject area intersection with Black Psychology's WAS.

A seminal essay on *Raisin* that is easily the most compelling prototype for Africana-adjacent interest in how literature advances an African worldview is acclaimed theatre scholar Harry Elam's essay on "Remembering Africa, Performing Cultural Memory" (2008). It meets the methodological expectation that a reading in search of the play's Africanity or African worldview would survey the text's lines, dialogue, and stage notes that signify the Africanity present in the Youngers' world. His critical interventions are cross-disciplinary, representing historical, sociological, literary, and anthropological knowledge toward a goal of explaining what in Africana disciplinary terms would be *epic memory*. Elam's version of epic memory is the cultural engram, which gives a scientific explanation related to "neural tissue in response to stimuli."[17] He frames the scientific core of the concept into a definition as "that trace of cultural memory that persists stimulated by . . . cultural materials."[18] Elam's analysis is a critique of how *Raisin* conjures the African past and documents cultural tradition, how the characters perform Africa, and the text's ways of "enacting an image of Africa that has meaning for the African American present."[19] Elam provides a cultural analysis distinct from a literary one when he notes, "For this African interlude in *Raisin in the Sun* does not move the action of the play forward but rather comments on and even seeks to direct the socio-political location of its subject and the political resonance of Africa within their particular cultural context."[20] He clarifies that the cultural implications are distinct from the literary implications as the performances of cultural memory "interrupt the action" and both "shed new perspective on the African and African American past" and "on the character's current social reality."[21] This thesis and its variables are consistent with Africana-based cultural-literary explications, even though the transcendence of this chapter initiates expanded Africana-specific readings of *Raisin* based on ancestral implications and on measuring the Youngers' African identity through the Black psychology WAS tool.

Elam's interest in *Raisin* is its relationship to cultural memory's embodied performance, which he writes, "functions as meta-performative, as an occurrence within the play that calls attention to itself as play, as performance."[22] "Play" refers to Walter's and his sister Beneatha's literal performances of African memory as Nigerian records play and as a drunk Walter Lee loses inhibitions enough to, as Hansberry's stage notes repeatedly instruct us, look "back to the past." Africana-trained scholars quickly relate Hansberry's words to the Akan cultural philosophy of *Sankofa* that translates as *return to the past* or *it is not taboo to go back and retrieve that which is lost*. However, most people engage with *Raisin* through either film or a dramatic performance in which they never encounter the text or its stage notes that literally reproduce an African philosophical concept. The African worldview in *Raisin* is also a form of literary Pan-Africanism, which has evolved to have multiple applications for the intersections of Africans and African worldviews in creative literatures, including nonfiction.

From an Africana reader-response theory approach, a primary question when reading the familiar socioeconomic variables of *Raisin* is how does Hansberry successfully integrate a functional and recognizable Africanity both in the play's African character and in the Younger family? This is a key fascinating element of cultural artistry in this 1959 drama. It leaves Africana readers wondering about the intellectual genealogy of African characters in African American drama and other genres up to 1959. Who are Hansberry's precursors who could do such a thing successfully? Several monologues from Alice Childress's *Like One of the Family* (1956) were examples of a peer dramatist advancing a consciousness of Africa in dramatic form, and there are multiple examples from a range of nonfiction and fiction genres.

Michelle Gordon remarks that Hansberry "turns to Asagai to confront fundamental questions of the play," particularly when he asks, "Then isn't there something wrong in a house—in a world—where all dreams, good or bad, must depend on the death of a man?"[23] What follows is arguably the longest monologue of the play, and Asagai delivers it. Beneatha interrupts Asagai's two philosophical reflections with the exclamation, *"The martyr!"* but her exclamation is not substantial enough to be an official break in his meanderings, which continue via ellipses and the repetition of "perhaps." The meanderings in the first nineteen lines of dialogue escalate with his considerations of "perhaps" mentioned four times. When Beneatha calls him a martyr, he is still in the midst of his monologue, resumed with another fourteen lines after he pauses and responds with a smile to the death sentence she predicts, and another set of ellipses and the subsequent repetition of "perhaps" appears three additional times. This monologue rivals Walter's thirty-line monologue about his hopes and dreams, shared with Travis, as it falls short of Asagai's thirty-three-line-long monologue.[24] Structurally, this feat reinforces the value of Asagai, even though in many critical analyses of the play, he is invisible, peripheral, and simply not relevant.

In the filmic versions of *Raisin*, the text comes alive visually with a neat, British-accented Nigerian whose certainty and composure contrast starkly with the collective anxiety of the Youngers. Visually and for the majority of the studied text, society tends to give Asagai a class designation. His suit, his diction, and his elaborate gift-giving of the African gown and records, represent a bit of luxury and internationalism that readers misinterpret, at least temporarily. However, the play comparatively reminds us of the realities of family-based identities—the Youngers, the Murchisons, and the Asagais. Inevitably, we learn of Joseph Asagai's familial and communal context in this monologue. Perhaps in a form of baiting and dramatic trickery, Hansberry introduces us to the international African of America's mythology and imagination—with a measure of elitism, globalism, and exceptionalism— then, she demystifies his allure to share conditions of family and community in *his* African *home*. He says, "In my village at home it is the exceptional man who can even read a newspaper . . . or whoever sees a book at all."[25] He then adds, "But I will look about my village at the illiteracy and disease and ignorance," which then certifies that his trajectory as a student in the United States is indeed exceptional and is a stark deviation from his home.[26] The comparison of the African and African American male experience between Walter Lee and Asagai shows that activist death seems more imminent for Asagai as an anticolonial than it does for the Younger family, as claimants of the residential American dream. Even though Hansberry at first gives Asagai a Négritudinist romanticism as a suiter and traducer, it is in stark contrast to the more predictable narrative that his education and anticolonial nationalism will indeed make him a martyr and make Beneatha an African American widow to a Nigerian husband.

Inevitably, *Raisin* has a significant concern with death, and in an African ontological view (and ontology is a philosophical variable of worldview), the subject matter of death is also a matter of ancestry, inheritance, and an active communal spiritualism beyond death. Advancing this discussion amid the topic of literary Pan-Africanism expands the critical framework from just a geographical and migration-based exploration of culture, heritage, or general kinship exposure/relocation/encounter to the spiritual realm instigated by several of the play's conversations about the deceased, Big Walter. Elam approaches this analysis, as well, when he writes:

> Although it does not flashback, *Raisin in the Sun* makes tangible the lessons of the past through the tangible import of the ten thousand dollar insurance check left to the family by the deceased patriarch Big Walter. The family must determine what to do with their legacy and ultimately how to honor their father's memory. As they turn "back to the past," cultural memories . . . rub against the present and become a place where history finds reinterpretations and potential new meaning.[27]

Elam may not intend it, but his observation catalogues a cognitive process through which Africana cultural readers respond to an African-centered narrative by naturally inserting reader-response memories into the text's assumed narrative. Elam notes that Hansberry's play "does not flashback," which is the usual and customary technique, even in drama, through which writers convey knowledge necessary for the fulfilled and proper interpretation of a text. This is an acute nuance of Africana reader-response theory. Elam's essay offers one more example that supports Africana audience/reader-response theory. He emphasizes the role and response of the "black members of her audience" who respond to *Raisin*'s challenge to what they know about Africa in 1959 and after.[28]

Otherwise, Elam's coding of legacy and honor imply the ancestral view, similar to what Ghanaian writer Ama Ata Aidoo captures in her play *Dilemma of a Ghost* (1965), which emphasizes what literary critic Brenda Berrian examines with the speculative question of what happens when Asagai and Beneatha get married and relocate to his African home. In *Dilemma*, a hypothesized marriage between an African favored son returned from abroad with an urban, working-class African American wife is plain chaos and is only remedied by the African husband's grandmother's acknowledgment that the African American deceased are also ancestors to whom all Africans must be respectful. In essence, the grandmother shifts her stance toward the African American Eulalie because she recalls that the orphaned Eulalie has a mother in the ancestral realm with African blood. Aidoo's play also asks central questions, seemingly in conversation with *Raisin*, and using Asagai's description; the question is, are "New World"[29] Africans (African Americans) *still* African? In both plays, the deceased African Americans have the requisite spiritual currency to influence, positively, the lives of their progeny. This introduces an additional African-centered question of characterization based on the role of ancestors. Are they active, involved, or influential in the plot, and how should scholars address this in the literary criticism? Asagai's casual, stress-free interrogation of Beneatha's anxiety over an economic death benefit is more about cultural worldview than about hopes, dreams, and social costs.

Africana literary engagement permits a level of discipline-based transcendence that enables, and even requires, written creative production to intersect with not only the discipline's multiple subject areas but also with their methodologies and critical instruments. This is an expansion of the late-twentieth-century approaches to literature as sociology with Africana-applied specificity. Elam's essay eventually engages Africa as "metaphor," noting that "its utility lies beyond its geo-political reality . . . in its symbolic significance."[30] A uniquely Africana-disciplinary reading enters here as a corrective that relies on worldview, empirically measured by the WAS, as a reliable indicator of African identity, though geographically and temporally removed. Particularly, the discipline's emphasis on worldview, measurable in the text through speculations using the WAS, aligns the literary with what Hansberry describes as "genuine realism" and what Baraka describes as "pointed social analysis." The WAS is a set of forty-five questions that respondents must answer on a six-point scale ranging from *strongly disagree* to *strongly agree*. The questions inquire into respondent beliefs on matters such as, "I enjoy participating at family reunions," "Spiritually blessed objects can protect a person from harm," "Everything in the universe is joined together by spiritual forces," and "Knowledge of my cultural history is very important to me."[31] The WAS measures the variables of materialistic universe, spiritual immortality, communalism, indigenous values, tangible realism, knowledge of self, and spiritualism, and each variable has from two to eight descriptive items associated with it.[32] As a tool applied to literary criticism, the variables of the WAS permit a uniquely ordered evaluation of characterization, plot, conflict, and resolution. While characterization and resolution can be dynamic and subject to growth and evolving, plot and conflict will be more descriptive in nature through a WAS itemization.

While there is not space enough to do a comprehensive analysis of how each of the eight African American characters (Ruth, Travis, Walter Lee, Beneatha, Lena, Murchison, and Bobo) and the one European American character (Mr. Lindner) would score on the WAS, the objective of this chapter is to introduce the measure as a transcendent Africana methodology. This approach not only has the capacity to enhance and regularize expectations or acknowledgments of artistic deviation from realism (measured by the WAS) in the creative construction of believable or reality-aligned characters, but it is also compelling from a performance point of view. In the hands of an actor, this orientation to character study has much to offer in challenging a theater artist to first, learn as much as she or he can about his character, and second, to find ways to use the verbal and nonverbal elements of performance to convey these philosophical and behavioral realities on the stage.

Many acting methods have techniques and tools for character study for performed drama, ranging from method acting to writing one-page synopses of one's character's personalities, beliefs, frames of reference, and more. According to Obasi et al. the WAS:

> was designed to operationalize measurable dimensions of worldview associated with an African and European worldview orientation, such as perceptions of the universe, spirituality, immortality, communalism, knowledge of the self, reality, and indigenous value systems. Individual perceptions of these dimensions exist in the fabric of culture and are believed to influence cognitions, decisions, and behaviors.[33]

This definition of worldview layers precisely with literary approaches to characterization. *Raisin* is an ideal prototype for a WAS literary application because the play represents African American, African, and European cultural contexts as central plot and conflict elements. The WAS itemizes "within group" and "between group" points of view and "philosophical assumptions" that are productive critical approaches for the text.[34] While the WAS is useful for its introduction of useful thematic variables, it in no way implies that the Africana literary setting requires skills of quantitative research. However, familiarizing readers with cross–subject area points of intersection prompts a more mature and well-rounded critical survey of a text's effect—its meaning, application, and value in a reader's consciousness, both immediately and over time. It is a new way to promote what literary critic Sandra Seaton describes as a "subtle probing" of "culturally specific conflicts" that help to define *Raisin* as a "cultural document."[35]

Seaton considers the irony that the matriarch Lena Younger is unfamiliar with Africa but is familiar with Mrs. Miniver, a white Englishwoman evoked by Lena's new gardening gloves. Seaton credits Hansberry with teasing her readers about the "deplorable realities" of some family members' dissociation from symbols and trivia reflecting a level of functioning Africanity. She writes: "Although some critics interpret such remarks as evidence of Hansberry's ideological confusion, I would argue that these passages display her conscious, skillful use of dramatic irony."[36] Literary critic Margaret B. Wilkerson contends that "while Mama may seem to be merely conservative, clinging to an older generation, it is she who, in fact, is the mother of revolutionaries; it is she who makes possible the change and movement of a new generation." [37] Critics have thoroughly engaged with *Raisin* with comprehensive cultural and structural acuity, and the Africana Studies literary enterprise builds on this wealth of analysis while also expanding the critical possibilities in the directions of the discipline's aligned subject areas. This expansion permits the literature to more thoroughly emphasize, for example, on Wilkerson's sense of Hansberry's "heightened realism" and on what the play's characters imply for the future.[38]

So, in the example of Walter Lee, Wilkerson suggests that he "signals the wave of the future. He is restless, hungry, angry—a victim of his circumstance but at the same time the descendant of his proud forbears, struggling to transcend his victimhood."[39] She also suggests that he "*unconsciously* embodies that proud and revolutionary spirit which is his heritage" (emphasis added) and "becomes the symbolic father of the aggressive, articulate black characters who would stride the boards in the 1960s."[40] In this sense, Walter Lee is a literary trope in African American literature who evolves to symbolize grandfather, great-grandfather, and eventually, ancestor to those who successively engage with *Raisin* throughout its literary life, which has not waned. With recent and new performances of *Raisin* that give the 1959 play a sense of contemporariness, Walter is also a model of his generation—a young man or a young father who is grappling with key questions of the Black experience. The other Black characters serve a similar function. This exercise shows a cultural process of literature that is not necessarily limited to Africana literature, even though the worldview-based approach will yield results specific to each culture of readership.

The transcendence of applying the WAS to *Raisin* is that it is a successful research instrument that does not require society to rely on African Americans' historical, cultural, trivial, learned, or cognitive knowledge and memory of Africa to authentically measure Africanity. Seaton scolds Harold Cruse that he "should know better than to require that every aspect of the Youngers be limited to what sociologists consider typical for families of their race and economic condition."[41] The sociology of the play is of interest, but the WAS as a measure of psychology—of cognition, behavior, and beliefs—is a more reliable index that informs historical and sociological predicaments.

The question then is, how to proceed? How can Africana literary criticism borrow from the WAS in order to enhance the practical experience with the text of *Raisin*. First, the categories provide a wealth of variables for offering a systematic approach to characterization. The caveat is that Asagai, as an African and not an African American, is not formally represented in the application of the WAS. It reliably measures African Americans and European Americans. Seaton suggests that Hansberry's "portrayal of the

Youngers recognizes that Afro-Americans who have lived in the United States for five generations or more have surely absorbed many aspects of the majority culture,"[42] yet the WAS is still specific enough to measure indigenous culture. Obasi et al. write: "Worldview cannot be simplified into being a nationality-bound construct. Although African Americans and European Americans live and interact together in the United States, they demonstrate significantly different worldviews that are linked to their distinct cultural pasts with which they may or may not have little to no direct contact."[43] Thus, in this comparison between the views of a literary critic, for example Seaton, and a psychological instrument for measuring cultural worldview, the literary methodology falls short of being able to most accurately reveal deeper cognitive realities of characters which Hansberry deliberately imbued with noticeable (and now quantifiable) traits of African American reality and cultural humanism. In addition, "the WAS can be used to investigate cultural factors that influence spiritual, psychological, and/or behavioral phenomena that race-based constructs cannot."[44] Applied to *Raisin*, this tool illuminates not only the Youngers' family structure, their identity constructs, the roles they play at home and in public, and their emotional responses to one another but also in the context of the play's central anticipation—the insurance check—it measures an anxiety possibly born of mourning or grieving a lost patriarch. This suggests a transference of the emotion of grief to emotions representative of greed or yearnings for financial rescue and security that are the family's coping mechanisms. Though beyond the domain of this chapter, an Africana transcendent approach could also consider the play's links to the subject area of economics in addition to the variables of the WAS, as suggested in chapter 2 that linked readings of *Raisin* with the topic of "inheritance" in Dorothy West's *The Living Is Easy*.

The Africana literary engagement enables literature to inspire speculation in a cultural context, wherein the hypothetical scenarios, conflicts, and events of the text direct us toward sources such as the actual historical, sociological, psychological, and economic records that reflect the quantifiable and demographic dimensions of Black life. Permitting creative texts to function this way benefits its readers by empowering us with empirical points of reference that become skills and training for when identical types of conflict appear in our lived experience.

Maulana Karenga's *Introduction to Black Studies*, a regularly updated core text of Africana Studies since 1982, imparts a key observation of the relationship between literature and reality that has become central to challenging the discipline's literary practitioners to get things right. Karenga introduced this as "a problematic deserving a creative solution," and this current approach is part of such an enterprise to offer practices for institutionalizing the discipline's specialized approaches to literature.[45] While the application of the

WAS is too lengthy to be included in this chapter, perhaps introducing it as an orientation toward literature can inspire thesis and dissertation projects that take advantage of any number of exciting possibilities of the discipline's multidimensionality.

NOTES

1. Harry Elam, "Remembering Africa, Performing Cultural Memory: Lorraine Hansberry, Suzan-Lori Parks, and Djanet Sears," *Signatures of the Past: Cultural Memory in Contemporary Anglophone North American Drama* (Bruxelles: Peter Lang, 2008), 34.

2. See Christel N. Temple, *Literary Pan-Africanism: History, Contexts, and Criticism* (Durham: Carolina Academic Press, 2005).

3. Wole Soyinka, "The African World and the Ethnocultural Debate," *African Culture: Rhythms of Unity* (Trenton: Africa World Press, 1985), 16.

4. Ta-Nehisi Coates, "The Case for Reparations" *The Atlantic* http://www.the-atlantic.com/magazine/archive/2014/06/the-case-for-reparations/361631/ (Accessed December 12, 2016).

5. It is of note that the majority of the essays that advance an interpretation that prioritizes Africanity are international in some way. S. Kanakaraj's "Heritage of an Old African Culture: A Study of Lorraine Hansberry's *A Raisin in the Sun*" (1998) is in an Indian source, *Indian Views on American Literature*. It is of great interest that an Indian cultural interpretation of the play delimits the play's Africanity. Edde Iji's "African Cross-Currents and American Echoes: Ego-Identity Crisis in Two Plays" (1987) is an Ibadan, Nigeria publication with Heinemann. "Remembering Africa, Performing Cultural Memory" (2008) by Harry Elam is published through a Brussels, Belgium branch of Peter Lang. And, Brenda Berrian's "The Afro-American-West African Marriage Question" (1987) is in *African Literature Today*, founded by Heinemann London, though it is out of the University of Michigan, Flint. Stateside, Sandra Seaton's "*A Raisin in the Sun*: A Study in Afro-American Culture" (1992) defends Hansberry from the Harold Cruse integrationist critique.

6. Patricia Liggins Hill, ed., *The Riverside Anthology of the African American Literary Tradition*, (Boston: Houghton Mifflin Company, 1998), 1065.

7. Ibid., 1067, 1068.

8. Qtd. In Gates and McKay, *Norton* 1769.

9. Hill, *Riverside*, PAGE.

10. Lawrence P. Jackson, *The Indignant Generation: A Narrative History of African American Writers and Critics, 1934–1960*, (Princeton: Princeton UP, 2011), 486.

11. Ibid., 489.

12. Hansberry, *Raisin*, 148.

13. Qtd. in Gates and McKay, Norton, 1769.

14. Ibid., 1769.

15. Ibid.

16. Ibid.

17. Harry Elam, "Remembering Africa, Performing Cultural Memory: Lorraine Hansberry, Suzan-Lori Parks, and Djanet Sears," in *Signatures of the Past: Cultural Memory in Contemporary Anglophone North American Drama*, edited by Marc Maufort and Caroline de Wagter (Bruxelles: Peter Lang, 2008), 33.

18. Ibid., 34.

19. Ibid., 32.

20. Ibid.

21. Ibid.

22. Ibid.

23. Michelle Gordon, "Somewhat Like War: The Aesthetics of Segregation, Black Liberation, and A Raisin in the Sun," *African American Review* 42.1 (2008): 124, 135.

24. Hansberry, *Raisin*, 108–9.

25. Ibid., 135.

26. Ibid.

27. Elam, "Remembering Africa," 33.

28. Ibid., 34.

29. Hansberry, *Raisin*, 137.

30. Elam, "Remembering Africa," 35.

31. Ezemenari M. Obasi, Lisa Y. Flores, Linda James-Myers, "Construction and Initial Validation of the Worldview Analysis Scale," *Journal of Black Studies* 39.6 (2009): 957.

32. Ibid., 944.

33. Ibid., 939.

34. Ibid., 940–41.

35. Sandra Seaton, "*A Raisin in the Sun*: A Study in Afro-American Culture," *Midwestern Miscellany* XX (1992): 48.

36. Ibid., 44.

37. Margaret B. Wilkerson, "The Sighted Eyes and Feeling Heart of Lorraine Hansberry," *Black American Literature Forum* 17.1 (1983): 10.

38. Ibid., 11.

39. Ibid., 10.

40. Ibid.

41. Seaton, "*Raisin*," 41.

42. Ibid., 43.

43. Obasi et al., "Construction," 956.

44. Ibid.

45. Maulana Karenga, *Introduction to Black Studies* (Los Angeles: University of Sankore Press, 1993), 428

Chapter 7

Ma Rainey's Black Bottom and the Demographic Literary Standard

The previous chapter introduced the relationship between quantitative possibilities and even demographics. As a methodological extension, this chapter charts qualitative history in literature by applying the demographic literary standard, an intersectional tool that layers literature and social science data analysis, to a study of characterization in one of August Wilson's most popular plays of his Century Cycle, which are all canonized to some extent.[1] The character "Toledo" is symbolic and encourages Africana Studies–trained readers to delve into the genealogy that is responsible for his education in knowledge bases reflecting radical African-centered sources on history and civilization that are the core content of his dialogue and soliloquys. The analysis is a procedural itemization of the ways the dramatic literary text maps unique Africana cognitive and investigative processes. The chapter explores the routes and possibilities through which Toledo could have acquired training or expertise as an early-twentieth-century race man, and suggests African-centered imperatives that challenge canonical assumptions about literary structure, namely that literary characterization is standardized.

With the completion of the set of ten plays representing each decade of the twentieth century for the African American experience, August Wilson's work, known as The Century Cycle, is a stable part of the canon of African American literature. Both *The Norton Anthology of African American Literature* (1994, 2007) and *Call & Response: The Riverside Anthology of the African American Literary Tradition* (1998) anthologize Wilson's *Joe Turner's Come and Gone* (1990), and certainly, other plays of Wilson's Century Cycle will be anthologized in the future. The corpus of literary criticism and scholarship on Wilson's plays is extensive; however, teaching Wilson's works within the Africana Studies curriculum benefits from a set of uniquely Afrocentric tools, matrices, and criteria. In charting Afrocentric qualitative history in literature by applying the demographic literary standard (DLS), an intersectional tool that layers literature and social science data analysis, this analysis makes use of social science observation, phrasing, and bibliographic lists as significant parts of the text. The analysis is attentive to itemizing the ways Wilson's play implores readers to map and decipher characterization in an investigative cognitive process. The chapter addresses a single character—Toledo—whom Wilson constructs as an African-centered and Afrocentric educated man. The Africana reader is struck by and curious about Toledo's trajectory and opportunities to emerge as the play's "race" man, and the DLS leads readers to consider aspects of history, worldview, and Black consciousness.

August Wilson became an ancestor on October 2, 2005, just months after the premier of the play *Radio Golf* (2005), which was the final installment of his Century Cycle. In the Century Cycle, Wilson worked for over twenty years to write a series of ten plays, each representing a decade of the twentieth-century experiences of Africans in America, most with the Black community in Pittsburgh, Pennsylvania as the prototype. With the series of plays complete, the publisher Theatre Communications Group (TCG) released the ten-volume set (although consumers are able to purchase the plays separately as well) in 2007, and the plays include introductions by artists and scholars such as Laurence Fishburne, Toni Morrison, Suzan-Lori Parks, Phylicia Rashad, and Ishmael Reed. Wilson has made literary history, and his works, which are considered epic, are and will be a significant part of both the African American and American literary canon.

Ma Rainey's Black Bottom (1985) is the third play in the Century Cycle, representing 1927 or the decade from 1920 to 1930, but is the first play that Wilson published. Wilson did not write the plays in chronological order. He relied on inspiration for each decade as it came to him. While the character Toledo is not the play's protagonist, the characterization lends itself to Afrocentric inquiry due to Toledo being the character who "constantly attempts to create historical context" and who "retrieves the historical circumstances that have brought Ma Rainey, her band and her entourage to this time and this place."[2]

The DLS is a newly conceptualized framework for Africana literary analysis that solicits social science follow-through in Black literary study. It invites qualitative and quantitative historical and social factors (including politics and psychology) into literary analysis, which is a usual and customary space for the "humanities." The objective of the humanities is often framed as a subjective exercise of exploring and understanding important intellectual issues related to human experience, while the social science objective is often framed as a more applied exercise such as providing insight into the development and implementation of programs and policies designed to improve people's lives. Historical context is essential to both enterprises, and the DLS approach merges humanities and social science skills and methods into a functional engagement of literature.

The DLS model radically amends the engagement of the "sociology of literature," wherein literature increases "social awareness and social responsiveness,"[3] from its late-nineteenth-century exploratory period and its 1990s re-articulation as cultural studies, both of which were and are philosophically concerned with relationships between literature and history as well as questions regarding the extent to which society influences the artist and vice versa.[4] The DLS is also a point of information to English disciplinary purists who suggest that culture "can no longer take literary studies where it needs to go."[5] Their arguments completely dismiss Africana cultural and Afrocentric criteria of literature, much of which is taught directly through or as cross-listings with their discipline.[6] Instead, the DLS is an African-centered and Afrocentric tool that emphasizes the function of enhancing literary analysis with qualitative and quantitative explorations of a text's collective elements and meaning.

The DLS confirms that it is possible to demarcate the line(s) between fiction and social science realism presented by and inspired by the text. It proffers an awareness of demographics, generally understood as typical group or population characteristics expressed in variables such as categories of age, sex, race, ethnicity, education, geographic residence, employment, income, marital status, religion, dwelling, language, mobility, or generation cohort. The DLS encourages the creation of an exhaustive list of all documentable and verifiable topics, themes, situations, predicaments, historical and contemporary events and figures, proper names, streets, addresses, cities, locales, social movements, eras, businesses, and economic references that are related to the various demographic conditions introduced in the text. It is also attentive to historical–biographical contexts of the work wherein knowledge of author biography, experience, influence, date/era of publication, and historical setting are even more meaningful than prescribed by conventional literary analysis. The DLS encourages an interpretation of literature as an integrated art form with aesthetic and structural conventions as well as social science implications. It is also attentive to determining the functionality of the narrative based on comparisons of the text's thematic and causal variables to quantitative and qualitative social science data sets generated through research, polls, surveys, interviews, and statistics.

The DLS reveals a critical willingness to refine or create conceptual and content categories that are not adequately represented or measured in data sets, as a means of generating ideas for new areas of quantitative and qualitative research that could better inform conditions of Africana life. With attention to the cycles of tradition and innovation[7] in Black literature, the DLS ensures that literary analysis regards advances and shifts in creativity in the context of the historical continuum of the Africana literary tradition. The DLS directs attention to the text's location in time and space[8] with respect to prioritizing an interpretation of chronology and geography, especially for literature that is structured based on measurable units of time. Its attention to the text's relationship to ethics and values[9] relates to its usefulness in inspiring solution-seeking discourse by encouraging critical thinking for the benefit of contemporary social change. Its potential to reflect literature study's need for scientific application,[10] especially concerning the use of technology in research and training of content expertise, has implications for literary classroom technology and grant funding for community center technology. Revising research directives and evidence categories in order to systematically expand literature's function beyond the humanities permits a reliance on research beyond literary bibliographical databases for criticism and analysis and enables a functional multidimensional layering of knowledge that increases the social value of literary analyses. Finally, structurally, the DLS gives critics opportunities to suspend the format of prose narrative of literary analysis in favor of listing and short description for effective highlighting of demographic and social science variables.

All attributes of the DLS may not be relevant for a particular work, and from this exhaustive list of procedures and methods of applying the DLS, those that enable a better understanding of and illuminate an effective critical directive for understanding the character Toledo of *Ma Rainey's Black Bottom* are of interest. Toledo is the band's middle-aged (likely early 50s) pianist and has been working with the other musicians for twenty-two years, or since 1905. The play presents him as the band's philosopher, and he has been and is willing to be again a farmer, which he was years earlier in Plattsville, Ohio. Levee, the band's horn player, says to Toledo, "I'd just like to be inside your head for five minutes. Just to see how you think. You done got more shit piled up and mixed up in there than the devil got sinners."[11] He accuses him of reading too many books. Levee also tells him, "Toledo, you sound like you got a mouth full of marbles. You the only cracker-talking nigger I know."[12] These types of character observations are clues to the disciplinary reader to pursue a culturally centered analysis beyond structural and other critical approaches to the text.

Regarding both pedagogy and discerning the cultural context of characterization, a primary inquiry is on how to best analyze and teach this character, his ideas, and his philosophies. The answer benefits from an emphasis on select elements of the DLS method that reveal Toledo's worldview and the historiography that informs his characterization. The key question is, "What is Toledo reading?" This is the basis of a speculative inquiry for readers, and to the literature specialist with a lens toward Afrocentric phenomenology, this is one of the key matters introduced in the literature that supports Africana discipline-based inquiry and research. First, readers must demarcate the line between fiction and social science realism to contextualize the fact that Toledo is Wilson's created literary characterization. It is productive to assess Toledo's demographic to infer the exposures that inform his consciousness. The analysis is attentive to Wilson's historical-biographical location with respect to him identifying his characters as African and his work as Afrocentric. This process helps to historically corroborate the potential sources of Toledo's broad African consciousness. The narrative as well as its characterizations suggest functionality with thematic and causal variables that could potentially benefit from analysis of early-twentieth-century data, if available. The sociopolitical setting and characterizations fall within the New Negro period, and Wilson's construction of setting and characterization reflect the Afrocentric category of "tradition and innovation" with respect to Toledo's role and function. This inquiry also benefits from a survey of African-derived ethics and values that the culture claimed and adapted in 1920s United States.

This analysis seeks to underscore the specificities of historical context, era, regional or urban landscape, migration, education, cultural literacy, and political engagement. Understanding these categories suggests the scope of the African-centered worldview and lessons that Wilson wishes to transmit through Toledo. Historically, Toledo is a representative of the New Negro Movement/Harlem Renaissance (neo-New Negro). This identification supports a comparative study of place, environment, or experiential sites encountered by real-life personas symbolized by Toledo. Delving into a study of the nature of the New Negro Movement in Chicago and the other sites of Toledo's background is an informative foray into viewing Toledo as a symbol of the era's migration. Readers wonder, "Where else has he been?" We also learn from his discourse and observation that he has been in farming communities and in the South.

Following the African-centered and Afrocentric clues of Toledo's characterization leads readers down a path of inquiry and study beyond the general scope of the play's criticism. Readers may consider what characterizes the nonfiction studies of the New Negro Movement, in general, and how Toledo's discourse on racial and social uplift, creativity based on the motifs of heritage, Africanity, and Pan-African politics filter these components of the era. Toledo's discourse leads readers to consider the nature of and the continuum of ideas from early "Negro Studies" to contemporary Africana Studies.[13] A study of the era can reveal the bibliographic sources from where Toledo learns of the ancient and traditional past. These inquiries become priorities in the disciplinary curriculum on *Ma Rainey's Black Bottom*, and the discipline's paradigms help readers to prioritize the Afrocentric and African-centered elements of the play. This engagement is commensurate with earlier conceptual, procedural, and critical orientations to African-centered literary criticism.[14]

The above considerations are also conversant with the existing scholarship on the character Toledo, but first a review of Toledo's African sensibility is in order. In the first significant passage, Toledo introduces Africa, African conceptualization, kinship, ancestral retention, and naming the gods. When he defines Slow Drag's behavior as African, a debate ensues between him and Slow Drag. Slow Drag bombards Toledo with rhetorical questions, doubtful and rejecting of Africanity to the extent that Toledo describes him as "ignorant." Slow Drag's ignorance forces Toledo to explain, and he says, "That's what you call an African conceptualization. That's when you name the gods or call on the ancestors to achieve whatever your desires are."[15] Although Slow Drag adamantly rejects being named as African, Toledo continues to describe the men's sharing as "a bond of kinship" and as an "ancestral retention."[16]

Toledo is not derailed by Slow Drag's insults such as dismissing Toledo's insights as "African nonsense." In fact, Toledo offers peaceful closure to the argument by educating his bandmates, particularly Cutler, who is interested and inquisitive about the African-centered education that Toledo attempts to impart. Toledo does this by instructing them on the value of "abstract" concepts that go on "around you and you can't even see it" and by describing an African belief in supplication to African gods who can be successful if "the gods is [sic] sympathetic with his cause for which he is calling them the right names."[17] In this passage, Toledo, though unpolished and remarking on something as basic as smoking, shares a cultural sensibility with which the other characters are unfamiliar. They initially reject the identity of African; however, Cutler does replace the word "nigger" with "African" in his follow-up inquiry, demonstrating that he has taken one small step toward increased consciousness. It is clear that Toledo is aware of some version of African cosmology and ontology. Even though the band members are all African American, this intra-cultural exchange bears a resemblance to chapter 3's fraternity among the vagabonds in Claude McKay's novel *Banjo*, set in Marseilles, France.

Toledo makes additional observations. He identifies racial pathologies, noting, "As long as the colored man look to white folks to put the crown on what he say . . . as long as he looks to white folks for approval . . . then he ain't never gonna find out who he is and what he's about. He's just gonna be about what white folks want him to be about."[18] Toledo's discourse is about agency. Sandra D. Shannon in her introduction to *The Dramatic Vision of August Wilson* (1995) suggests Wilson's intent is to use Toledo as a mouthpiece to remind readers that it is important to advance knowledge about African cultural heritage and identity as resistance to derogatory notions about

Africa. However, she later frames his role as more ambiguous. She contends that "the failures of Ma's band seem to stem from their own ignorance, their own apathy, and their own denial of their past. Thus, the play suggests that if African Americans continue to repress both their African and southern roots, they are destined to live troubled, stagnated lives."[19] This may be true of the other characters but not necessarily of Toledo. Shannon goes on, "Ma's pianist, Toledo prides himself on being the resident African griot; however, his uninvited lesson concerning an African oral tradition is taken as an insult, not as an earnest attempt to school his unenlightened brothers on some revered African ancestral customs."[20] While this analysis offers morsels of Africana intent, the DLS method demands deeper cultural analyses beyond the rhetoric of cultural nationalism. In effect, the DLS and the Afrocentric enterprise that undergirds it may be able to inform authentic cultural antecedents that Wilson is referencing through Toledo. Or, at least the attempt should consider broader bibliographic possibilities.

Shannon appropriately links Wilson's motive with Paul Carter Harrison's description of "the cultural potency of the African continuum as a psychic and spiritual repository of values and survival strategies,"[21] with the text's underlying messages concerning "cultural ancestors" and its suggestion that African Americans equate Africa and the South as "distant world[s] of painful memories and associations."[22] However, among an Africana-trained readership, the DLS may instigate additional points of view related directly to disciplinary contexts. Finally, Shannon refers to Toledo as a "pseudo-philosopher."[23] The Africana reader is interested in the themes and merits of his philosophy including the school of thought it represents, the line between real and "pseudo," and the correctives required to authenticate and amend Toledo's narrative for accuracy.

As a dramatic text and creative production, Toledo is a fictive character, yet writers like Wilson research their characters, topics, and historical periods for plausibility. The writer's ability to tell an informed story, a story that could have likely occurred based on the known narratives of history, is what empowers literature. Of course, some authors choose more abstract and symbolic routes, but Wilson is engaged in an exercise of realism. The DLS framework instigates an investigative inquiry that is a qualitative engagement of history. It is not narrative history but is a deductive practice of subjectively distinguishing the associated variables and points of reference of time, place, era, and orientation. The attention that the Afrocentric reader or teacher gives to the supporting character Toledo (he is not the protagonist of the play) verifies that an Afrocentric orientation to data—to this play as a cultural artifact—is infused with a productive and affirming sense of heritage, tradition, and legacy, and anteriority. Thus asking the question of "What has Toledo been reading?" is relevant in Africana reader-response. The approach confirms the Africana literary enterprise's functional and applied interest in the variables introduced in the text. This is what makes literature study a social science–aligned exercise.

Critic Alan Nadel refers to Toledo as a "historian,"[24] but we have the critical opportunity to be even more specific about the narratives and exposés of African cultural antecedents. Eileen Crawford describes Toledo without mentioning the description "African." Instead she features his ambition to self-educate and his "perfectibility," and characterizes him as a misunderstood autodidactic whose conflict concerns cultural identity. [25] The DLS instigates a deeper, Africana-centered study of Toledo's race consciousness and cultural influences.

For a focused historical analysis on the questions and inquiries introduced by the character Toledo, an essential source is Daryl Zizwe Poe's work on the "evolution of Black Studies as part of a continuum in the expression of the collective African voice within the Western academy."[26] Poe's discussion of the early-twentieth-century field of Negro Studies is vital to contextualizing the intellectual environment with which Toledo is familiar. There are several key points in Poe's analysis that inform the possibilities of Wilson's character Toledo. In question is the period from 1902 to 1927 (the twenty-two years that Toledo has been on the road and playing blues music), but we can also configure a relevant historical timeline in approximate years of Toledo's lifetime. He is about fifty years old, so he was likely born around 1875. This suggests that at the turn of the century he was twenty-five years old. He speaks of periods of fast living with women and periods of married domesticity ideally in the South, and from his narrative we can infer that his exposure to these "books" that the text keeps mentioning was likely after his farming years, thus between 1902 and 1927. Several exchanges address Toledo's interest in reading, and after Slow Drag and Cutler complete their banter, Toledo sentimentally redirects the conversation to the plight of Africans in America. He laments—"Ain't nobody talking about making the lot of the colored man better for him here in America"—but the bandmates chide him for being like Booker T. Washington.[27]

When Levee compares Toledo to Booker T. Washington, he notes that the men share a general awareness of Washington's self-study in the pursuit of his goals and ascension. These are cues, or Afrocentric markers that tell the reader to go back and trace the genealogy of the African American intellectual tradition. Thus the pursuits of creative literature and historical bibliography are inseparable.

From Toledo's speeches, it is apparent that he is reading nonfiction—history books and sociological studies. He believes "the colored man ought to be doing more than just trying to have a good time all the time" and he frames a discourse about solving the "colored man's problems."[28] He is also attentive to Black people around the world, or to Pan-Africanism, even though he speaks of it in vague terms in his philosophical meandering. He says, "What you think . . . I'm gonna solve the colored man's problems by myself? I said, we. You understand that? We. That is every living colored man in the world got to do his share . . . I'm talking about all us together."[29] Poe writes that "the Garvey Movement and the Pan-African Congresses organized by Du Bois deeply influenced the Negro History Movement," so the quest is to link Toledo with the actual "books," articles, and coverage in print media and the Black press that would have been likely sources for the Africana education he seems to have. Poe notes that in spite of what Africana Studies was called or named back then, "the essence was always the African voice in its role of enhancing African agency,"[30] and this is precisely what Toledo attempts to offer in his conversations with the rest of the band.

E. E. Thorpe in *Black Historians* (1971) identifies three broad periods of the evolution of Black history, and the second category, "The Middle Group, Builders of Black Studies, 1896–1930" is the group that represents the period referenced by Toledo's personal timeline. The first wave, or the "Beginning School, Justifiers of Emancipation, 1800–1896" are also important possibilities for what Toledo could have been reading.[31] Poe's essay quotes Thorpe who notes that the authors in the Beginning Group had an objective of highlighting the Black American's African "inheritance."[32] Authors in this group lived and published from 1816 to 1939 and include Robert Benjamin Lewis, James W. C. Pennington, James Theodore Holly, William Cooper Nell, William Wells Brown, William Still, Joseph T. Wilson, George Washington Williams, Benjamin Griffith Brawley, and Booker T. Washington. Poe's critique of this list is essential because he notices that Thorpe left out another important writer who should have been categorized here, Edward Wilmot Blyden, the prolific nineteenth-century Pan-Africanist.

According to Poe, Thorpe viewed the Middle Group of Black historians as the founders of what has become Africana Studies, and this group was attentive to the meaning, the role, and the plight of Africans globally. Toledo seems to have an awareness of this in his reference to "every living colored man in the world."[33] Some of the scholars who lived and published between 1866 and 1967 are Charles H. Wesley, Monroe Nathan Work, W. E. B. Du Bois, and Carter G. Woodson. Readers could also infer that if Toledo's repertoire included "books" then it certainly could also include magazines such as *The Crisis*, *Opportunity*, or Marcus Garvey and United Negro Improvement Association's *Negro World*. Also, he could have had exposure to works such as *The Papers of the American Negro Academy* (1916), *Racial Integrity: A plea for the establishment of a chair of negro history in our schools and colleges, etc.*[34], and of course Alain Locke's edited collection on *The New Negro* (1925).[35]

There are significant functional results of doing such an extended historical genealogy of Wilson's character Toledo. Readers engage with literature
not only as a symbolic artifact that presents broad cultural, sociopolitical,
historical, aesthetic, communicative, and psychological messages but also as
inspiration and a *directive* to send them back into the nonfiction sources of
the past. As we create and consume new knowledge, it gets harder to keep
the historical record alive, and the DLS demands that we revisit this process.
Students and readers who engage with *Ma Rainey's Black Bottom* using the
DLS methodology gain a sense of the discipline's multidimensionality which
requires a layering of African-centered and Afrocentric sources to make the
best practical and realistic sense of symbolic artifacts. A study of Toledo's
character directs the study toward required and recommended sources such
as the discipline's *Handbook of Black Studies*[36] and the Library of Congress's
complete holdings on "Negro History" through 1927. There is value added
in this exercise because it forces students to hunt, or to engage in a "search-
and-rescue" mission of the sources of the distant historical past. While we
follow the trail of what "books" Toledo has been reading, we also liberate
the academic space to permit literature students to pursue additional directions and research on Africana heritage using the most recent and the most
thorough texts available. This means that through a literature class, students
encounter traditions from scholars and exemplars whose academic identities are not necessarily *literary*. Literary critics do this regularly with Frantz
Fanon and Karl Marx.

In the final scene of *Ma Rainey's Black Bottom*, Levee stabs Toledo in
the back, killing him. In an interview, Wilson confirms that "[Levee] does a
tremendous disservice to blacks by killing Toledo, because he's killing the
only one who can read, he's killing the intellectual of the group."[37] This is a
cultural loss, and the ending is symbolic, suggesting the need for Toledo's
intellectual descendants to emerge as a new generation that builds on the
old. This ending leads readers to assess the role of the intellectual as cultural
mediator and cultural leader in the past as well as the present. At the end of
the play, the intellectual is dead, and there is now a need to raise up others
in his legacy. The task is more literal than symbolic—to raise up future generations to revive and incorporate into the culture's collective consciousness
and behavior the ideas and philosophies of key thinkers of the traditions of
Black consciousness. There is also the consideration that Toledo would not
have been in a position to transmit knowledge if he had not been among the
people—among those who could not read and those who had so few skills
to interpret and transmit history. Toledo's character is a reminder of the
Africana imperative to cultivate meaningful, reciprocal relationships with the
community in spaces that are not traditionally academic. These are spaces that
should be reclaimed as productive communal sites of learning and exchange.

Not only does this chapter introduce the DLS, but it also solicits possibilities for qualitative historical research that can help expand Africana-based literary character studies on intriguing cultural creations like Wilson's Toledo. The institutionalization of the literary enterprise within the discipline of Africana Studies occurs as scholars enhance evaluations of literature with disciplinary idea formation and disciplinary objectives.

NOTES

1. An earlier version of the section defining the scope of the demographic literary standard (DLS) appears in my essay, "Africana Literature as Social Science: Applying the Demographic Literary Standard (DLS) to the Works of August Wilson and Suzan-Lori Parks," in *Africana Theory, Policy, and Leadership*, edited by James L. Conyers, Jr. (New Brunswick, NJ: Transaction Publishers, 2016), 1–30.

2. Alan Nadel, *"Ma Rainey's Black Bottom*: Cutting the Historical Record, Dramatizing a Blues CD," in *The Cambridge Companion to August Wilson*, edited by Christopher Bigsby (New York: Cambridge University Press, 2007), 105.

3. See a summative review-essay by Kingsley Widmer, "The Sociology of Literature?" *Studies in the Novel* 11 (1979): 104.

4. See Jeffrey Williams, "Toward a Sociology of Literature: An Interview with John Guillory," *Minnesota Review* 61.61 (2004): 95–110, which surveys Guillory's treatment of the sociology of literature in terms of canon formation, the canon of theory, and possibilities of relating the literary to the political. They discuss Guillory's *Cultural Capital* (University of Chicago Press, 1993), but their ideas have little to do with African American literature.

5. See William B. Warner and Clifford Siskin, "Stopping Cultural Studies," in *Profession 2008*, the journal of opinion for the Modern Language Association of America, pp. 94–107.

6. See Chantal B. Dalton, "Teaching Black Literature to Undergraduates: The Problem of a Sense of Perspective," *Black American Literature Forum* 11 (1977): 102.

7. The next several concepts are aspects of Afrocentric work identified in Molefi K. Asante's "African Betrayals and African Recovery for a New Future," in *Africa in the 21st Century*, edited by Ama Mazama (New York: Routledge, 2007), which offers methodological categorizations. *Tradition and innovation* ensures that "preservation and generation are instruments of the interplay of change and continuity" (p. 77).

8. Asante offers *location in time and space* to address "discovering chronology and geography as keys to interpretation" (p. 77).

9. Asante views this as "enhancing and promoting critical thinking in the area of effective human behavior" (p. 77).

10. Asante identifies this as using "science and technology to create and enrich the community" (p. 77).

11. Wilson, *Ma Rainey*, 25.

12. Ibid., 31.

13. See Daryl Zizwe Poe, "Black Studies in the Historically Black Colleges and Universities," in *Handbook of Black Studies*, edited by Molefi Kete Asante and Maulana Karenga (Thousand Oaks, CA: Sage Press, 2006), 204.

14. See Christel N. Temple, *Literary Spaces: Introduction to Comparative Black Literature* (Durham: Carolina Academic Press 2007), particularly Chapter 2 on "Comparative Analysis and Writing," which includes a section on "Suggestions for African-centered Literary Analysis" (pp. 50–51).

15. Wilson, *Ma Rainey*, 32.

16. Ibid., 32.

17. Ibid., 33.

18. Ibid., 37.

19. Sandra D. Shannon, *The Dramatic Vision of August Wilson* (Washington, DC: Howard University Press, 1995), 79.

20. Ibid.

21. Ibid., 78. See also Paul Carter Harrison, "August Wilson's Blues Poetics" in *August Wilson: Three Plays*, edited by August Wilson (Pittsburgh: University of Pittsburgh Press, 1991), 316.

22. Ibid., 78–79.

23. Ibid., 78.

24. Nadel, "Historical Record,"108.

25. Eileen Crawford, "The Bb Burden: The Invisibility of Ma Rainey's Black Bottom," in *August Wilson: A Casebook*, edited by Marilyn Elkins (New York: Garland Publishing, 2000), 36.

26. Daryl Zizwe Poe, "Black Studies in the Historically Black Colleges and Universities," in *Handbook of Black Studies*, edited by Molefi Kete Asante and Maulana Karenga (Thousand Oaks, CA: SAGE Press, 2006), 204.

27. Wilson, *Ma Rainey*, 41.

28. Ibid., 42.

29. Ibid.

30. Poe, "Black Studies," 211.

31. Qtd. in Poe.

32. Ibid., 212. Thorpe is qtd. in Poe, 212.

33. Wilson, *Ma Rainey*, 42.

34. According to Poe, it was read before the teacher's summer class at Cheyney Institute in July 1913.

35. See Library of Congress search under "Negro History"—approximately 260 works appear.

36. Asante and Karenga, *Handbook*.

37. Qtd. in Bigsby, 105.

Chapter 8

Parable of the Sower's Earthseed as Black Liberation Theology

From Octavia Butler's novel *Parable of the Sower* (1993) there emerges a speculative fiction creation of the religion or belief system of Earthseed, and this chapter interrogates its value, and even genealogy, as a version of African American spirituality. The protagonist's new belief system of Earthseed emerges from a structured intellectual process compatible with Black liberation theology, which is an African-centered, Black nationalist paradigm for balancing African American spiritual-based resistance and liberation ideas and practices. This chapter's transcendence is how it veers away from canonical readings of *Parable of the Sower* in favor of the discipline's paradigmatic attention to cosmology and ontology. This innovation, framed in this book's interest in Africana reader-response theory, accounts for the view that Earthseed has obvious links to Black liberation theology and to Black womanist theology, even with the new religion's amended approaches to Christianity. This appraisal of the novel as a spiritual narrative aligned with historical and traditional African American responses in a survivalist crisis demonstrates transcendence based on the vitality of exploring canonical texts from the Africana literary point of view, which links literary criticism with the discipline's paradigmatic and methodological priorities.

Butler's novel *Parable of the Sower* is a canonized text in the genre of science fiction and in the African American genre of speculative fiction. Butler's literary genius is well documented through her accolades, including winning a Nebula Award, two Hugo Awards, and the MacArthur Genius grant. *Norton* anthologizes her short story "Bloodchild." *Dark Matter: A Century of Speculative Fiction from the African Diaspora* (2000) anthologizes her short story "The Evening, the Morning, and the Night." *Literary Spaces: Introduction to Comparative Black Literature* (2007) excerpts Butler's *Parable of the Talents* (1998), which is the sequel to *Parable of the Sower.*

Parable of the Sower is the futuristic tale (2024–2027) of life in Robledo, California, from the perspective of Lauren Oya Olamina, a fifteen-year-old African American girl who comes of age in a volatile dystopic society. Raised in a Christian household with a Baptist minister father in a struggling, sub-sisting, communal, interracial, gated community, Lauren's critical analysis of society and of her future compel her to focus on "arranging to survive."[1] The central feature of this survival is shifting her ontology and worldview from African American Christianity to a thoughtful, organic view of God, his attributes, and his relationship to humanity in a new belief system called Earthseed.

Traditional critical approaches to Butler's text include studies on the absent father, gifted children, gated communities, utopia, desire, citizen-ship, nature, technology, power, migration, sexual identity, enslavement, environmentalism, urban communities, pollution, and feminism/womanism. Tuire Valkearakari's study on religious idiom[2], David Morris's essay on revolution[3], and Clarence Tweedy's essay on faith[4] approach the novel from a critical perspective of spirituality. Butler describes the religious import of her work, noting, "Religion is everywhere. There are no human societies without it, whether they acknowledge it as a religion or not. So I thought religion might be an answer, as well as, in some cases, a problem."[5] There is even a hearty cyber trail that approaches Butler's fictional religion as a realistic spiritual possibility.[6]

Religion is a key subject area of the discipline of Africana Studies, and layering explication with Black liberation theology leads readers to critically consider not only the literary elements of Butler's craft but also its thematic instigation of African-centered discourses related to religion. The literary elements include aspects such as the text within a text, journalistic narrative point-of-view, dystopic and utopic sensibilities, possibilities of an African-centered bildungsroman, and contemporary innovation to the enslavement narrative genre.

Lauren's development of Earthseed is the novel's most sustained treat-ment of religion in response to her society's need for liberation. It evolves from being a rebellious polemic of teenage journaling and idea formation to becoming a thoughtful, conscientious, and survivalist experience-based writ-ten sacred text as Lauren eventually organizes her collections of wisdom and ideas into a linear and presentable theology. Bernard W. Bell characterizes the novel based on how it "follows the visions and religious philosophy" of "a black hyperempathetic prophet who creates a Californian religious commu-nity in a twenty-first century dystopian world."[7] The bibliographic entry on Butler from *Norton* describes Lauren as "the prophet of a new faith."[8] Bell's description captures readers' and the textual community of supporting char-acters' impulse to view Earthseed as a cult, and many other critical readings obscure the fact that the novel introduces at least three additional religious worldviews on which characters of African descent rely to advance freedom and equality. The original theology is the Baptist faith of Lauren's father, Rev. Olamina. A secondary theology is neighbor Richard Moss's pursuit of traditional West African beliefs and practices. The third is more subtle and is based on the clues Butler gives in the creation of Lauren's full name—Lauren *Oya* Olamina. Oya is a Yoruba and Candomblé deity or *orisha* that represents elements associated with storms, such as lightning and wind. The deity also invokes processes of death and rebirth. Significantly, Oya is a warrior. She is skilled and cannot be defeated.

African American Baptist Christianity as Black liberation theology frames the survivalist activism of the Olamina family, led by Rev. Olamina, his Latino wife Cory, his Black and biracial (Black and Latino) children, and the church flock under his leadership. As the partner in an interracial marriage and as an elder leader in a community fortress, Rev. Olamina enacts Black liberation theology on behalf of a mixed-culture family, which broadens the beneficiaries of a liberation theology traditionally practiced within the ranks of the Black community. Lauren's converts to Earthseed are also a multiracial and multicultural group that benefits from her intuitive and survivalist Black experience as a leader and liberator. The text's survivalist logic meanders between recognizable Black cultural memory responses to oppression and a contemporary skill set used to identify racial threat, which liberate humanity and not just characters and communities of African descent. Butler's vision, which is about Black culture's survivalist precision steeped in an organic belief system born out of Lauren's Black and female experience, challenges readers to respond to the ways Black nationalism, worldview, and Black liberation theology evolve. The creative text can take such liberties, but the practical Africana-based inquiry into the text's invocation of humanistic realism forces readers to respond to the speculative possibilities of reorienting traditional Black liberation theology for futuristic predicaments that are cross-cultural.

Parable of the Sower captures the evolution of an African American teenager's social, spiritual, and intellectual maturity during a believable mid-twenty-first-century setting of U.S.-based social upheaval. The novel is constructed as a series of the heroine's journal entries which offer philosophical critiques of race, oppression, and spirituality—particularly of her Christian upbringing as a preacher's daughter. She keeps a notebook of ideas that eventually becomes *Earthseed: The Books of the Living*, an alternative to the teachings of the Bible. Earthseed evolves into a spiritual philosophy based on the premise that "God is change" and that humanity's destiny is to create functional societies built in space. Butler's novel is part of the African American science fiction and speculative fiction genre that is prophetic and visionary within an African diasporic cultural context.

Considering the fact that images of the 2005 Hurricane Katrina tragedy could be be lifted directly from the pages of *Parable of the Sower*, the text introduces a powerful set of historical and future variables in its social realism. An analysis of Butler's text offers a timely critical survey of individual leadership and community organization regarding issues of spirituality, oppression, and apocalypse. Africana scholars have many options to pursue in critically studying *Parable of the Sower*. The novel's interest in change and intergalactic planetary settlement is a science fiction and speculative fiction topic as well as a historical topic possibly related to ancient Kemetic awareness of the cosmos. The novel's discourse relates to the radical Black tradition and to a broader Africana philosophy that articulates a survivalist and activist commitment to people of African descent and to humanity. The Underground Railroad parallels the Black female protagonist's leadership model, and spirituality is an influential power in the novel's episodes of Black survival and social revolt.

Inevitably, although Butler's narrative reveals versions of Black spirituality that diverge from the tradition of Christianity seen in Black literature, Lauren's new religion of Earthseed emerges from a structured intellectual process compatible with Black liberation theology. The radical reappraisals the narrative offers of African American spirituality, humanism, and organized religion remind society that Butler's science fiction legacy is a rich source from which to view, analyze, interpret, and improve our present and future life chances and life experiences.

James H. Cone, in *A Black Liberation Theology* (1970, 1990), offers the standard variables of Black liberation theology. Of interest to this chapter's treatment of the critical paradigm in a literary context is black theology's response to *failures* of one religion to address the needs of Black citizens in a racist world, and the need for *liberation* from oppression. The interpretation of scriptures is based on the experience of blackness. Specifically, Cone defines that Black liberation theology "believes that the liberation of the black community *is* God's liberation," and that the oppressed "will see the gospel as inseparable from their humiliated condition and as bestowing on them the necessary power to break the chains of oppression."[9] Cone's emphases, including that Black theology's goal is "to interpret the religious dimensions of the forces of liberation," are relatively aligned with the impulses that stir Lauren toward the evolving and creative act of consciousness that emerges as Earthseed.[10] A departure of Earthseed from Black liberation theology's assumptions is Lauren's decentering of Jesus; however, Earthseed retains features that Lauren learned from a childhood steeped in Christianity, such as a methodological and meditative focus on identifying revelations and on the pursuit of righteousness amid a society that, like Cone's modeling, includes "the weak and helpless in human society."[11] In fact, Lauren's formation of

Earthseed centers the types of interpretation that Cone insists are a feature of Black liberation theology. He notes—"The goal of black theology is to interpret God's activity as related to the oppressed black community."[12] In both Cone's traditional explanation and Lauren's practices in *Parable of the Sower* "black theology affirms the black condition as the primary datum of reality to be reckoned with."[13] Cone credits abstractions of what he calls the "Jesus-event" as a white cultural tendency, but in Lauren's hands and in the service of Earthseed, it is the abstraction and re-envisioning of God's identity that permits a more diverse or multicultural type of socially effective liberation theology. It is still *Black* because Lauren's prophetic leadership for survival is based on the skills of cultural survival transmitted through her father's Christianity, through her lineage's confident African consciousness that can even include prophetic naming, and through the legacy of her grandparents' maps that enable her to perform a northward journey that also parallels the trope of the Underground Railroad experience with contemporary Black female leadership.

Cone's version of Black liberation theology is relevant in a society where skin color and anti-black racism are still oppressions central to the Black experience, yet in the historical setting of Lauren's America in *Parable*, which covers the years 2024–2027, class, not race, is the central division. In fact, the "black community" that Cone takes for granted is, in 2024, a multiracial community that embodies the worldview of the Black experience. In spite of Lauren having a Yoruba surname, "Olamina," that her grandfather selected and had legally changed[14] in the 1960s, she has a Latino stepmother, Black-Latino siblings, and lives in a *multiracial* compound that embodies elements of the twentieth-century *Black* community, such as mutual cultural identification and an organized system of behaviors against oppressive outsiders. While the multiracial compound reflects trends of "the browning of America," by the time chaos strikes Lauren's community, she is among "a heterogeneous mass—black and white, Asian and Latin, whole families are on the move with babies on backs or perched atop loads in carts, wagons or bicycle baskets, sometimes along with an old or handicapped person."[15] It is from this interracial and diverse group that Lauren draws her Earthseed community.

The principle that makes it possible for Earthseed to be considered Black liberation theology is the principle of "adaptability" that supports Lauren's interpretation of God. Each chapter begins with an epigraph or alternative scripture from Lauren's writings, which become the belief system called Earthseed. Readers are first introduced to *Earthseed: The Books of the Living* in the prologue, where we learn that "without adaptability, what remains may be channeled into destructive fanaticism."[16] This idea of adaptability is a foundation of Lauren's interpretation of God, and her interpretation of God's shifting relationship to humanity relates directly to the chaotic, near apocalyptic world in which she lives in the 2020s. The epistolary, in journal form, gives the narrative a philosophical and confessional resonance from which Lauren explicates the idea that "God is change," a theology that concedes that, if the human status has changed in a near apocalypse or dystopia, then God's relationship to humans must also change.

Unlike Cone's interpretation, Lauren's liberation theology does not prioritize Jesus Christ and the New Testament gospel, however, Lauren synthesizes her belief that "God is change" with a human understanding of the Old Testament. She frequently quotes Old Testament scriptures in her interpretation of God. She uses the word *Change* to indicate God=Divine=Omnipotent=Change =Omnipotent: *God exists to be shaped. God is Change.*[17] Her experience with the Creator as malleable redirects the agency of prayer and of the forces that shape reality. Lauren then synthesizes her understanding of human nature, science, and the Old Testament to test her belief system. She writes, "Everyone knows that change is inevitable. From the second law of thermodynamics to Darwinian evolution, from Buddhism's insistence that nothing is permanent and suffering results from delusions of permanence to the third chapter of Ecclesiastes ('To everything there is a season . . . .'), change is part of life, of existence, of the common wisdom."[18] Early in the novel, Lauren grapples with whether her interpretation is an idea, a philosophy, or a religion, but many of her theology's descriptions, such as her verse that "Belief/Initiates and guides action—/Or it does nothing" are compatible with Cone's version of Black liberation theology.

Lauren's theology is a survivalist response in the face of a version of apocalypse. In the 2020s the United States is plagued by natural disasters such as hurricanes and tornadoes. Cholera is epidemic in Mississippi and Louisiana. The North is plagued by a measles epidemic, and blizzards are severely impacting the region. Many citizens cannot afford immunizations, and "there are too many poor people—illiterate, jobless, homeless, without decent sanitation or clean water . . . [and a] drug that makes people want to set fires."[19] At fifteen years of age, Lauren behaves as a leader or messiah, who teaches a two-fold message of physical and spiritual survival. Her maturity and vision are evident in a conversation with her peer, Joanna, when she says, "We can get ready. That's what we've got to do now. Get ready for what's going to happen, get ready to survive it, get ready to make a life afterward. Get focused on arranging to survive so that we can do more than just get batted around by crazy people, desperate people, thugs, and leaders who don't know what they're doing! . . . And if we're not ready for it, it will be like Jericho."[20] Once again, Lauren references the Old Testament, and her vision toward the future implies a rebuilding from the ground up. Lauren's vision toward survival during social upheaval turns out to be farsighted, and it saves (and liberates) a group of victims from her community as well as those the group admits along their journey to safety.

Lauren's Earthseed verses share a vision from Cone's theology, that God works for the weak and helpless in society, but Lauren equally embraces the prerequisite that people must also help themselves. Lauren's survivalist theology aims to save human life. As she collects her verses, she hopes—"Then, someday when people are able to pay more attention to what I say than to how old I am, I'll use these verses to pry them loose from the rotting past, and maybe push them into saving themselves and building a future that makes sense."[21] Lauren's attention to saving herself and her community is based on the fact that a northward migration is taking place in 2024 in the United States. However, state borders (Oregon and Washington) as well as international borders (Canada) are protected. People are getting shot at these borders when they attempt to trespass, thus the new type of U.S. national slavery based on poverty confines people to regions based on class, not race. Lauren's leadership takes her Earthseed group on a journey, and she bears similarity to a modern version of Harriet Tubman who is enabled by a new belief system that seeks a spiritual liberation as well as a physical salvation against the trend of subsistence in company towns and growing national trends of debt slavery, privatized cities, and economic colonies.

By the end of 2026, Lauren refers to herself as "preaching" Earthseed verses.[22] They comfort her, and she expects them to comfort others. Earthseed evolves into a liberation theology that frees people from fear. Earthseed embraces diversity and does not have the opportunity to develop as a racialized response to oppression because the oppression Earthseed resists is based more on class than on race. Earthseed reads—"Embrace diversity . . . / Or be divided, robbed, ruled, killed / By those who see you as prey."[23] The prophetic penalty for not embracing diversity is destruction. Lauren and her community of survivors realize that mixed-race groups, thrown together by circumstances of survival and safety in numbers, are "natural allies" of one another.[24]

Lauren's first "converts" to the Earthseed community are Black, even though her group is comprised of whites and Latinos. Zahra, her first Black woman convert says, "if you want to put together a community where people look out for each other and don't have to take being pushed around, I'm with you."[25] Zahra responds to Earthseed as Blacks have traditionally responded to the Christianity-based Black liberation theology, which prioritizes spiritual responses to Black oppression. In this sense, traditional Black liberation theology supports Lauren's Earthseed because of its identical focus on protecting its members from social oppression. When the fledgling Earthseed community (made up of two Black women, two Black men, one White man, and one Latina woman) saves two white women from attack, Bankole, the most recent Black male traveler, tells the women, "You're very fortunate. . . . People don't help each other much out here."[26] The young woman, Jill, asks, "Who are you guys anyway?" to which Harry, the white man, responds, "Earthseed."[27] This is a significant scene in the novel and in its appropriation of an adaptation of Black liberation theology. The group, by its behavior, admits that it shares ideas and intends to set up a community in the North. The Black cultural context of this is reminiscent of the Underground Railroad journey, which was a multiracial network, and the ensuing Earthseed community is not hindered by segregation or racial divisions as in the past.

Bankole's discussion of Lauren's belief system illuminates the type of adaptability that permits Earthseed to be an extension of Black liberation theology. Their conversation addresses humans, society, religion, and change, but the starting point of the discussion is Earthseed's heaven, which is the idea that humans must create communities on other planets in order to survive Earth's impending demise. Bankole, as the eldest Black man traveling though not yet converted to Earthseed equalizes Earthseed with other religions. He tells Lauren, "All religions change. Think about the big ones. What do you think Christ would be these days? A Baptist? A Methodist? A Catholic? And the Buddha—do you think he'd be Buddhist now? What kind of Buddhism would he practice?" He smiled. "After all, if 'God is Change,' surely Earthseed can change, and if it lasts, it will."[28] This is the first scene that compares Earthseed to Jesus Christ, the central figure of Cone's definition of Black liberation theology. If the variables of society and human experience can shift, or *change*, then Bankole's philosophical debate about how religions adapt suggests that Christianity and Earthseed are cyclical responses to sociopolitical shifts that determine society's recurring lapses in and out of prosperity and demise. In essence, belief systems can be viewed as interrelated and fluid.

One consideration is whether or not Earthseed is the product of Lauren's biblical revelation. She quotes biblical scripture all along, so that Earthseed offers alternative earthly understandings of the relationship between humans and God, but it aims to coexist with Christianity, thus remaining Black liberation theology and introducing responses to futuristic social contexts that Cone did not witness or respond to during his era. Although fiction, Butler's story challenges organized Black religion to consider its adaptability in an age where social unrest prohibits preachers, churches, and congregations from assembling in conventional ways to do its organized version of God's will. *Parable of the Sower*'s content, then, is not as heretical as it first appears, and it can be taken as a speculative fictional account questioning the life of the church in a context that negates all aspects of traditional worship and organization. Lauren's and Earthseed's continued emphasis on biblical scriptures suggests that spirituality is constant, while cycles of social rest and unrest may determine which practice of spirituality is most effective. The victims of Hurricane Katrina who spent their Wednesday (a customary Bible study night) and their Sunday morning (a customary Sunday worship moment) stranded on a dry, thirsty, hungry, highway overpass are better equipped to survey the deeper meanings of Lauren's version of spirituality through Earthseed. For them, it could indeed make sense to metaphorically define God as "Change." In one entry, Lauren writes, "I wonder if the people on the Gulf Coast still have faith. People have had faith through horrible disasters before."[29]

For Lauren, society's shifts toward mass poverty cause her to ignore traditional Christianity or her father's version of Black liberation theology. She confesses: "When my father . . . disappeared . . . it was Earthseed that kept me going. When most of my community and the rest of my family were wiped out, and I was alone, I still had Earthseed. What I am now, all that I am now is Earthseed."[30] In essence, after her religious leader (her father), her worldview, and her community disappear—all elements that supported the system of Christianity—Earthseed becomes Lauren's inheritance. The existence in which she finds herself is sustained by a liberation theology that does not depend on a physical building, a specified place, and a specified community for its identity. Perhaps these ideas influence the Earthseed verses that introduce the chapter detailing the destruction of Lauren's community and the murder of her family. She likens her path to the phoenix rising from the ashes. Thus, Earthseed is the phoenix rising from Black liberation theology's Christian ashes, burned to the ground during social upheaval, demanding newness for survival.

Lauren even admits Earthseed's similarity to and relevance to other religions. She insists that Earthseed will one day have a permanent base or site as home. This assumption that a religion thrives and grows when its members have a physical site or foundation supports the contention that the destruction of Lauren's family home and compound is what caused Black liberation theology to transform from its Christian agency into Earthseed.

When the travelers reach Bankole's land in upstate California—Humboldt County—they accept the responsibility to set up an Earthseed community. The community's first sacred act is to hold a ceremony for their dead. When Lauren's father went missing in 2025, she delivered a sermon in his place, choosing to preach from the New Testament's gospel of Luke (chapter eighteen about the importunate widow) in his honor. At this ceremony in the new Earthseed community, Lauren again chooses a passage from the gospel of Luke, reiterating the Bible's, specifically the New Testament's, relevance to the group's past religious history and life experience, which was formerly based on Christianity. The passage, from St. Luke 8:5–8, known as the parable of the sower, is directly related to Earthseed and to Lauren's role as a new messiah or religious leader nurturing fruitful ground. This ceremony and the familiar Biblical scripture suggests a transition from traditional Black liberation theology to Earthseed liberation theology, and the selected passage embodying metaphors of sowing seeds is a final statement on the adaptability of Black liberation theology into a liberation theology for the synthesized racial masses.

Earthseed's members are diverse yet mostly people of color, and they are committed to each other's survival beyond the racial loyalties that are the striking feature of Black liberation theology. Butler has already proven to be prophetic in her fictional account of the results of the nation's poor economic policies, corporate greed, and exploitative and reckless domestic policies that, in the novel, are catalysts for mass poverty across racial lines and new slavery for whites. In her vision of the United States in 2027, the nation has regressed nearly 200 years, with slavery being a phenomenon that affects much of society, regardless of race.

This model of explicating the Black nationalist and historical–experiential practice of Black liberation theology is an outcome of contemporary Africana grounding in the multidimensionality of the discipline's subject areas. It differs from literature and culture-based studies on spirituality in fiction because it speculatively deciphers the applied possibilities of Butler's message. In *The Cambridge Companion to the African American Novel* (2004), Maryemma Graham's introduction confirms the role of literature in the lived experience of the Black community. She writes, "For many an African American author, the act of writing is part of a larger process of cultural revisionism, of redefining history and historical memory, and of confronting the past in innovative and provocative ways that are intentionally self-reflexive. To change the future is to give meaning to a common past in new ways." [31] In the *Cambridge Companion*'s chapter addressing the novel and popular culture in the discussion of Butler's craft in the *Parable* novels, Susanne B. Dietzel writes that the novels "deal with the establishment of new social orders and communities based on equality, social justice, and religious freedom. Her leaders or protagonists are almost exclusively black women who transcend slavery—mentally and physically—and who move on to create community and generations." [32]

There is room in Dietzel's overview, particularly in her mention of religious freedom, to shift toward the novel's intersection with Black liberation theology, but it is subtle. However, merging Dietzel's reminder of Butler's writing of Black women protagonists and in the case of *Parable*, their participation in religion, introduces an extended pairing of Butler's novel with womanist theology. Stacey M. Floyd-Thomas's chapter on "Womanist Theology" in *Liberation Theologies in the United States* (2010) updates traditional Black liberation theology with Black women's perspectives from traditional liberation and freedom discourse, religious exposés and preaching, Black feminism, and womanism. Her essay narrates the depth of the tradition of Black women's spiritual leadership and vision beginning with Pauli Murray's question, "Is God calling women to reassert prophetic leadership and ministry before it is too late?"[33]

Much of the language Floyd-Thomas introduces in womanist theology applies to Lauren Olamina and enhances an Africana-based literary reading of *Parable*. Lauren certainly exhibits prophetic leadership as she epistemologically approaches the problem of survival through studying geography, topography, agriculture, human nature, and religion in terms of what Floyd-Thomas calls "knowledge production"[34] and what Katie Cannon in the seminal womanist theology text *Black Womanist Ethics* (1988) describes as Black women's "rugged endurance."[35] This is consistent with Alice Walker's itemization of womanism, and Floyd-Thomas further describes womanist theological agency in terms of how Black women "self-define and self-determine both themselves and the discourses to which their destinies are delineated and affixed."[36] Floyd-Thomas's emphasis on the "organic discourse" of womanist theology which "is faithful to the church while also seeking to remake the institution"[37] characterizes Lauren's religious accomplishment in creating Earthseed. Butler does not construct Lauren Olamina's characterization as overtly feminist, but Lauren's womanism develops along the lines of Clenora Hudson-Weems's definition of Africana womanism.[38] Lauren is aware of social and familial expectations and the hurdles of being a daughter, of bodily threats and vulnerabilities to rape and being physically overpowered by men and thieves, yet her activism is gender complementary. She works on behalf of her community, draws from her familial and broad historical racial-cultural traditions, even impersonates a man for a strategy of protection, and maintains an open humanism toward all ethnic groups in her quest for survival. She maintains a balance of strength, femininity when needed in romance, and, borrowing from Floyd-Thomas's itemization of womanist theology, "moral wisdom and experience of the divine."[39] The richness of both traditional Black liberation theology and the more recently defined womanist theology critically enhances an Africana-based explication of Butler's novel and is ideal required reading in such an Africana critical approach to *Parable*. Floyd-Thomas's emphasis that womanist theology is not "innovation" but is "continuation" helps readers to remain located in explicating this dystopic novel, in which it is an intriguing approach to characterization to consider Lauren to be a theologian whose creativity in the verses of Earthseed is literary and whose futuristic approach reflects a version of the African worldview.[40]

NOTES

1. Octavia Butler, *Parable of the Sower* (New York: Warner Books, 1993), 48.

2. Tuire Valkeakari, *Religion Idiom and the African American Novel, 1952–1998* (Gainesville: UP of Florida, 2007).

3. David Morris, "Octavia Butler's Evolutionary Movement for the Twenty-First Century," *Utopian Studies: Journal of the Society for Utopian Studies* 19.3 (2015): 270–88.

4. Clarence W. Tweedy III, "The Anointed: Countering Dystopia with Faith in Octavia Butler's *Parable of the Sower* and *Parable of the Talents*," *Americana: The Journal of American Popular Culture* (1900-Present) 13.1 (2014): [no pagination].

5. Octavia Butler, "Science Fiction Writer Octavia Butler on Race, Global Warming and Religion," https://www.democracynow.org/2005/11/11/science_fic-tion_writer_octavia_butler_on (Accessed December 13, 2016).

6. See Giulio Prisco, "Octavia Butler's Fictional Religion of 'Earthseed' Inspires Real Religious Movement," http://ieet.org/index.php/IEET/more/prisco20140620 (Accessed December 13, 2016).

7. Bernard W. Bell, *The Contemporary African American Novel: Its Folk Roots and Modern Literary Branches*, (Amherst: University of Massachusetts Press, 2004), 344.

8. Gates and McKay, *Norton*, 2515.

9. James Cone, *A Black Theology of Liberation* (Maryknoll, NY: Orbis Books, 1990), 4–5.

10. Ibid.

11. Ibid., 5.

12. Ibid.

13. Ibid.

14. Butler, *Parable of the Sower*, 206.

15. Ibid., 158.

16. Ibid., 1.

17. Ibid., 20.

18. Ibid., 23.

19. Ibid., 47.

20. Ibid., 48.

21. Ibid., 70.

22. Ibid., 111.

23. Ibid., 176.

24. Ibid., 186.

25. Ibid., 200.

26. Ibid., 213.

27. Ibid.

28. Ibid., 234.

29. Ibid., 13.

30. Ibid., 235.

31. Maryemma Graham, ed., *The Cambridge Companion to the African American Novel* (Cambridge, UK: Cambridge University Press, 2004), 5.

32. Susanne B. Dietzel, "The African American Novel and Popular Culture," in *The Cambridge Companion to the African American Novel*, edited by Maryemma Graham (Cambridge, UK: Cambridge University Press, 2004), 164.

33. Qtd. in "Womanist Theology," in *Liberation Theologies in the United States*, edited by Stacey M. Floyd-Thomas and Anthony B. Pinn (New York: New York UP, 2010), 37.

34. Ibid., 45.

35. Qtd. in Ibid., 47.

36. Ibid., 44.

37. Ibid., 37.

38. Clenora Hudson-Weems, *Africana Womanism* (Troy, Michigan: Bedford Publishers, 1994).

39. Floyd-Thomas, "Womanist Theology," 46.

40. Ibid., 37.

Chapter 9

Self-Eulogy as Prophetic Afrofuturism in Narratives of John Henrik Clarke and Malcolm X

In the original African homelands, prior to the enslavement experience, African people were stabilized by a god-concept in their own image, by a collective cultural worldview reflecting familiar landscapes and experiences, and by the spirit force of ancestors who were virtually present among them, remembered and chronicled through place, naming, and physical resemblance. The rituals and ideas about the sacred that early Africans brought with them to the Americas were transformed, adapted, and even forgotten, and a new challenge of both spirituality and religion faced them, as they navigated through and synthesized their beliefs of the traditionally African with European, and even Middle Eastern, elements of religion. Some refused Western religious forms altogether and practiced personal and cultural forms of spirituality on their individualized terms. From an institutionalized Africana Studies perspective there is a multidimensional set of data on how people of African descent have culturally and creatively met the challenges of articulating their spiritual worldview, particularly based on sources that record reflections on anticipated or impending death, or on inevitable transition from life to death.

This chapter is a study of two African American transition narratives as literary primary documents. John Henrik Clarke's self-eulogy—part of his "initiation into eternity"—is an example of the paradigm shift from traditional African American Christian cosmological ideologies to contemporary Africana spiritual transitions, and Malcolm X's narratives of self-eulogy comprise a different, Islamic-grounded synthesis of warrior-based martyrdom on behalf of African-American, African, and eventually human, concerns. Malcolm's narrative is significantly different from Clarke's narrative which represents the plight of an elder who transitioned peacefully.

This is an exploratory engagement of African American transition ideologies and practices that range in classification from funeral, obituary,
dirge, mourning, eulogy, elegy, ode, requiem, and memorial, to reflection.
These diverse terminologies help to describe the cultural artifact created
when a transitioning individual or responsible agent offers written or oral
reflections to be shared with family, friends, and the public as a type of
affirmation of life, consolation, or spiritual testimony aimed at forging a
continuum between the past, present, and future. Of the many choices,
self-eulogy offers the most clarity. This content analysis and comparative analysis of these two forms of pre-death narrative aims to interpret
the cosmological practices of *transitional Africana spirituality* that are
synthesized in African American Christian and Muslim autobiographical
narratives.

The practices of liberation self-eulogy and impermanent mortality[1]
(willingness to be a martyr to ensure gains for future generations) have the
potential to inspire a paradigm for ancestral transition that contributes to
creatively developing African-derived rituals for use in diaspora transition
worldviews and practices. This reading of self-eulogy is attentive to the
pre-death speculation of the afterlife, and this aspect links the two narratives to prophetic Afrofuturism, which is an expanded reading in self-eulogy
studies. In addition, a futuristic lens toward impermanent mortality, which
is a conceptual precursor to what becomes martyrdom, relates to Afrofuturism in several contexts. Alondra Nelson defines Afrofuturism as "African
American voices with other stories to tell about culture, technology, and
things to come,"[2] (italics added), which I interpret here as a cultural vision
of the afterlife. Reynaldo Anderson and Charles E. Jones add that "the first
Afrofuturistic dimension of metaphysics includes and energizes ontology or
the meaning of existence," which relates to this study's interest in "spiritual
practices."[3] Exploring innovative dimensions of African-centered practices
of ancestor acknowledgment and memory contributes to a modeling of Africanity in death and in the afterlife. Afrofuturism's shifting definition has
always meandered between descriptions attempting to capture the meaning
of waves of contemporary enhancements in technology, art, and music and
their transformative effects on the Africana worldview in life and in the cultural imaginary. Anderson and Jones announce, "Afrofuturism is now a Pan-
African project,"[4] and this study on Clarke and Malcolm X is an exploration
of the peace and resolve of conceptualizing the process of living toward a
Pan-African vision of afterlife.

Transcendence is based on a phenomenological approach to Africana Studies that highlights critical possibilities of approaching the genre of eulogy,
which is structurally inexact, using markers from two forms of pre-death
narrative. Africana phenomenology is:

the treatment of events, episodes, challenges, and revisionist interpretations relevant to the African-derived experience within a framework that prioritizes world views and critiques from a perspective of authority derived from cultural experience, self-determination, self-actualization, and intergenerational value. It is an African agency-driven epistemological approach to understanding social behavior, identity formation, events, and trends as they relate to people of African descent who are engaged as subjects of their experience.[5]

Africana phenomenology accounts for the African-centered critical impulse responsible for an Africana orientation toward an iconic funeral program as a cultural artifact. Clarke transitioned in June of 1998 and Malcolm in February of 1965, and their funerals, like those of many revered African American icons, were highly respected sacred events with representation from the generation's most prolific and accomplished scholars, activists, and community organizers.

Obituary and eulogy as genres have cultural legacies in funeral and spiritual practices representing elements of West African to early African American ontologies and cosmologies such as the dirge, praise poems, memorials, odes, and more. Western literary guides do not sufficiently provide background, context, and examples for this multidimensional African-centered phenomenon. Creative literature has taken considerable license to weave spirituality, epic memory, and the broadly supernatural in narratives, duly noted by literary critics such as Georgene Bess-Montgomery in *The Spirit and the Word: A Theory of Spirituality in Africana Literary Criticism* (2008) and Carol P. Marsh-Lockett and Elizabeth West's *Literary Expressions of African Spirituality* (2013). Thus, the collective vision of Africana Studies multidimensionality prepares an Africana reader-responder to be attentive to numerous cultural impulses of literary texts, in this case, merged forms of obituary and eulogy. The two central African American literature anthologies, *Norton* and *Riverside*, sample sermons, autobiographies, and other self-reflective works to prepare society to think broadly about the genre of personal narrative.

As a godfather of Africana Studies Clarke gifted the discipline and society with a spiritual legacy through his funeral program, which is a cultural artifact. It is not widely available (except for personal copies and its preservation in Clarke's archive). The quotidian critical process of the Africana reader's acknowledgment of and itemization of the features of this document's transcendent value is a demonstration of the effect of Africana disciplinary cognitive impulses applied naturally to Africana letters. It reflects the intersection of the worldviews and practices of the transition from life to death in traditionally documented formats, and the transcendence is also the layering of Black nationalism, impermanent mortality, and spirituality in an expanded (or transcendent) model of prophetic Afrofuturism.

Black nationalism is a key concept of African agency, particularly in the Americas, where African survivors of enslavement demarcated central differences of worldview and societal well-being between European American members of society and themselves. The Black nationalist tradition anticipates ideal criteria of a healthy Black nation or a nation-within-a-nation. This includes African-centered self-determination, protection and security for the community's or region's borders, economic self-sufficiency, an educational curriculum that centers African agency, the right to self-name, and the right to worship a Black/African image of God. Merging Afrofuturism and impermanent mortality produces a framework that liberates thinkers from being confined by linear realism, and it encourages innovationist and revisionist approaches to static assumptions about the domains and possibilities of Black life and afterlife.

Exploring Clarke's transition narrative from the points of view of a type of Afrofuturist Black nationalist model of impermanent mortality is transcendent in many ways. First, it expands our thinking about the genres of obituary and eulogy. Theatre scholar Keith Kirk's study on self-eulogy and commemoration in the civil rights era differs from Mushira Eid's genre-based study of obituary, and neither reaches the conclusions generated in this Africana reader-response exploration of Clarke's document. It is compelling how Kirk expands the narrative with an emphasis on pairings ranging from Emmett Till and Medgar Ever, Malcolm X and Martin Luther King Jr., to Rosa Parks and Coretta Scott King. In a departure from Kirk, this chapter's pairing of Clarke and Malcolm X contrasts a Christian self-eulogy with a Muslim assisted self-eulogy.

Liberational *self-eulogy* is a feature of transitional Africana spirituality in which the autobiographical and even biographical narratives of the deceased reveal a pursuit of victorious consciousness as an objective of the individual's memorial legacy. It also supports a paradigm for the cosmological rituals for ancestral transition and ceremony. The critique of apparent and imbedded *spiritual texts* culled from funeral programs and autobiography is an academic intersection of history, religion, spirituality, aesthetics, worldview, and culture. Clarke's and Malcolm's examples are prototypes that enable the exploration of new dimensions of African-centered practices of ancestor acknowledgment and memory that are significant because they are models that demonstrate a cognitive and even psychic level of Africanity in death. These models emerge as archetypes of the African American activist tradition, which extends the realist functions of obituary and eulogy toward literary genre, compatible with Africana versions of odes, elegies, memorials, and commemoratives.

Frameworks of obituary and eulogy/self-eulogy as genres inform this chapter's idea formation. Mushira Eid's *The World of Obituary: Gender Across*

Cultures and Over Time (2002) presents multiple variables related to the act of self-narrated eulogy which has points of intersection with obituaries. Eid is attentive to the role of obituaries, their communicative function, their conceptual frameworks, and how obituaries are "situated in cultural space and time of the social realities outside them."[6] His study highlights aspects of memory, legacy, and constructions of identity, including those in which the deceased is the author. Authors' selection of what is to be included is "based on their perception of value."[7] These criteria suggest what Clarke and Malcolm X want us to know, and what they expect of their legacies. Eid notes, "Understanding the relationship involved in authorship (the creation of a text), the nature of the genre within which the text is written, and the expectations of its audience provide yet another perspective on the role of obituary writers."[8] Naturally, as Eid offers, obituaries are nonfiction, but he adds, writers of obituary "are expected not to use their imagination in constructing identities and events nor to create an imaginative world but a real one where content matches the realities of the world outside."[9] Eid also notes that obituaries reflect "an ideal or perfect world" in which "conflicts are resolved."[10] It is upon these two descriptions of the idealism and imaginativeness of obituary that this chapter pivots, because Clarke's obituary/self-eulogy does indeed have elements of the creative and imaginary. In fact, these are attributes which support the intersection of spirituality (or a spiritual eulogy narrative) and Afrofuturism.

Kirk's study is on eulogy, including the self-eulogy of Martin Luther King Jr., and he describes the funerals of King and of Malcolm X as the "iconographic funerals of the civil rights movement."[11] Clarke's funeral, though on a smaller scale, was also iconographic, for inheritors of the Black Studies Movement. Both Barbara Eleanor Adams in *John Henrik Clarke: Master Teacher* (2000) and Ahati N. Touré in *John Henrik Clarke and the Power of Africana History: Africalogical Quest for Decolonization and Sovreignty* (2008) confirm Clarke's centrality to the origins of the discipline. As a journalist and historian Clarke was aware of the extraordinary cultural value of both King's and Malcolm X's funerals and was aware of both the self-eulogy in Malcolm X's Alex Haley-assisted *Autobiography*, as well as King's sermon, "The Drum Major Instinct," in which King writes, "And every now and then I think about my own death and I think about my own funeral."[12] Much is written on King's reflection. This chapter limits its domain to Clarke's and Malcolm's self-eulogies as representative of two different religious practices—Christianity and Islam—and two iconic lives that directly inspired the Black Studies Movement from which contemporary Africana Studies evolved.

An assumption of this critical engagement is that the African American transition narrative—in its many literary and public forms—functions as a *cultural text*. There is a cultural storehouse of African American funeral programs, self-eulogy, self-obituary, and transition narratives housed in Black Bibles and church clerk offices that can provide raw data to help us identify additional characteristics of Africana spirituality. And there is even more data to be found in the public, festival-like, transition ceremonies of Black cultural pioneers such as James Baldwin, Toni Cade Bambara, Katherine Dunham, Alvin Ailey, and Maya Angelou. The community is a repository of data, and it would not be difficult to access these indigenous cultural sources.

Born in 1915, John Henrik Clarke was "an Alabama sharecropper's son whose thirst for unfettered knowledge led him to hop a freight train to New York and transform himself into an African history scholar who helped spur the development of black studies."[13] He passed away on July 16, 1998, and the "Service of Commemoration and the Initiation into Eternity" was July 21, 1998. Attached to the commemoration program was a nearly three-page narrative written by Clarke and dated July 16, 1998, the day he died. The narrative is entitled "From SBA to SIA: A Great and Mighty Walk," and it functions as both traditional self-eulogy and Africana spiritual narrative. As self-eulogy, his document includes an autobiography, an auto-obituary as he speaks of his oldest daughter who preceded him in transition, a statement of his life's mission, an appeal to his younger children, a list of relatives who survive him, a bibliography of his fiction and nonfiction writings, an acknowledgment of close friends.

As an Africana spiritual narrative, it includes a Black Nationalist affirmation, an ancestral litany noting on whose shoulders he stands, a reminder of how he summoned African ancestral power to anoint and lay hands on his children, and a reminder that the African image of God is not the same as the colonized image Europeans presented to Blacks. It also provides a historical account of European oppression of African people, a corrective on how to honor an ancestor in order to give him peace, a list of his former contemporaries who are now ancestors, and a statement of transition. Additionally, Clarke publicly bequeaths his library to African American archival institutions and affirms that he will be spiritual protection for his close friends. His final testament is concerned with ancestry. He shares a vision of him being beckoned by the ancestors, an affirmation of his ongoing spiritual presence alongside his wife, an affirmation that his spirit is literally in the "cool breeze," an acknowledgment that Christ is Black, and an acknowledgment that both Christ and Kwame Nkrumah are meeting him in this new place (heaven).

From Clarke's document, key features of Africana spirituality emerge, and this chapter introduces them as usable criteria for measuring Africana spirituality. Its attributes include several affirmations and acknowledgments:

- Africans and African Americans are inextricably interrelated as ancestors.
- The God of Africans is anticipated to be African in appearance.
- The ancestors are attentive to what takes place on earth.
- Transition is communal among recognizable Africans and African Americans who have gone before.
- Being an ancestor unifies us with the elements of nature.
- There is no contradiction between being Christian and African.

From Clarke's self-eulogy, there emerges a working definition of Africana spirituality as *a cosmological process that links African Americans to their African ancestors and gives African Americans the agency to integrate elements of their African diasporic or Pan-African cultural worldview into their individual and community consciousness at the juncture of passing from life to the afterlife, in spite of the fact that they no longer practice the traditional African religions on which this cosmological process is partially based.* This phenomenon suggests that the cultural activism responsible for Africana Studies has not only academic, practical, community, and policy priorities, but also spiritual priorities expressed in the discipline's emphasis on cosmology. It is plausible that the pursuit of the discipline of Africana Studies has an inherent element of spirituality related to the primacy of the ancestors in the inspiration for the creation of knowledge.

Clarke is one of the early elders of the discipline of Africana Studies to transition expectedly because of old age, which gave him an opportunity to personalize the meaning of his life in an African-centered context as a gift of legacy to present and future generations. Other pioneers and elders of the discipline such as Vivian Gordon, C. Tsehloane Keto, and Asa G. Hillliard III passed suddenly and unexpectedly and did not leave legacy statements that corroborate the link between their cosmological worldview and their intellectual activism in the discipline of Africana Studies. Clarke's legacy and elder status within the discipline of Africana Studies make his transitioning relevant in a unique and applied way.

The discipline of Africana Studies is based on the legacy of ideas, practices, consciousness, and activism that preceded the formal academic establishment of university departments, and there is a host of African Americans who articulated early elements of what is embodied in Clarke's model of transitioning into Africana spirituality. This section shifts to introduce, for future research directions, the examples of African Americans who anticipated their deaths within a context of spirituality, which may also include levels of African-centered spiritual consciousness in their accounts. As exploratory research, its methods could extend to numerous sources such as autobiographies and personal narratives of African Americans who wrote their narratives as elders anticipating certain death, as activists compelled by a sense of impermanent mortality, and as thoughtful cultural philosophers coming to terms with potentially terminal illness. This set of works could easily include George Jackson's *Blood In My Eye* (1972), Mumia Abu Jamal's *Live From Death Row* (1995), David Walker's *Appeal* (1829), the speeches of Henry Highland Garnet, the *Cancer Journals* (1980) by Audre Lorde, and a host of late-life Africana autobiographies. Such a study of autobiography and personal writing framed within the Africana literary enterprise is transcendent and is a discipline-specific expansion of the genre of spiritual narrative. Such an extended study would yield dynamic and multidimensional reflections on the meaning of Africana transitioning and spirituality wherein the agents directly anticipate their death in a broad Africana cultural context.

The spiritual transition worldview of Malcolm X is an Islamic model that contrasts with Clarke's Christianity. Malcolm was born in Omaha, Nebraska on May 19, 1925 and witnessed both Black nationalism and the alarming effects of racialized violence against his family at an early age. Similar to many marginalized Black males of his era, he explored a life of crime and hustling that landed him in prison, before he transformed into a spiritual, activist leader representing, first, the Nation of Islam, and later, his own organization, the Organization of Afro-American Unity (OAAU). Malcolm's process of transitioning into Africana spirituality is unique because he was Muslim, not Christian, and he merged his Muslim faith with imperatives for his African "fatherland."[14] In searching his record for the ideology that he embraced in anticipation of his death, there is a single, neat section of his *Autobiography*—chapter nineteen, entitled "1965" that best parallels Clarke's reflection and is Malcolm's self-eulogy.[15] However, the account is not as directly spiritually reflective as is the Clarke self-eulogy model. Malcolm suspected that he would not be allowed to die of natural causes; in 1965 he lived with constant death threats and attempts on his life. His identity as a leader, social activist, and fearless proponent of Black human rights placed him in a different, though still spiritual, category.

Malcolm's self-eulogy chronicles primarily history and confession, and these contribute to a comprehensive transition narrative. There are many categories in Malcolm's narrative, including autobiography and legacy correctives, the historical–political context of his final days, a global Africanist vision and worldview, comparative attributes of Christianity versus Islam, and predictions of his death. Malcolm left enough self-eulogistic perspectives for his legacy to be reflected on his own terms, and his corrective begins with an evaluation of how the white press deliberately misinterpreted his message and ideas. It offers a statement of the autobiography's truth of testimony, and places his experience as a "ghetto" story identical to that of many disenfranchised youth. It gives an admission that his major flaw was his lack of formal education.

The narrative verifies that his revised message is for Black people around the world in the context of human rights for all, and he frames the United States as an interruptive agent for Black progress with liberal evidence. He gives a reminder of the brutal, violent origins of the United States, and the absurdity that this violence is exalted, and he prophecies possibilities for how the United States will atone for its racism. The United States' sociopolitical context includes Malcolm's contrasting encounters with both good and narrow-minded white men, an African American–centered analysis of the 1964 U.S. presidential election. He also explains the philosophy that Whites should advocate among whites, not Blacks. The text highlights Malcolm's intellectualism—his interest in studying all knowledge in "ranging study" in spite of how the United States treats Blacks as if they only have knowledge about racial issues. The chapter even differentiates between Malcolm's goals and tactics and those of Martin Luther King Jr. as it makes two central legacy and prophetic points—affirmation of his support for both Black nationalism and true cross-racial brotherhood and the dream that it will be Malcolm's voice that might save America from a grave racial catastrophe.

In contrast to the critique of the United States, the narrative frames a relationship with Africa as a powerful extension of agency. It chronicles Malcolm's meetings with African world leaders from Egypt, Tanzania, Nigeria, Ghana, Guinea, Kenya, and Uganda. Additionally, it chronicles Malcolm's global reputation as a human rights ambassador. Another confession of a deficit is his lamentation that he could not communicate in African dialects when he visited the continent of Africa.

The next distinguishing feature of the transitional narrative from Malcolm's *Autobiography* is his comparison between Christianity and Islam. The text notes that Christian African Americans reject his leadership because he is Muslim. He evaluates Christianity's use of violence and its support of white supremacy as a form of false spirituality. Malcolm predicts the end of Christianity as people of color turn to Islam, Hinduism, and Buddhism, and spends much of the narrative itemizing the virtues of Islam. He surveys the lessons he learned in the *Koran* and as part of the Nation of Islam, noting Islam's value to solving the race problem because it is a "true religion—of the spirit."[16]

Clarification of his dedication to Islam frames the chapter's orientation toward his sense of impermanent mortality—that death is imminent and that his deeds will benefit future generations. He gives credit to Allah if his death brings change or exposes light and truth. He speculates on his death, explaining why his beliefs will prevent him from dying of old age. He warns readers to beware of how the United States will continue to manipulate his image and the meaning of his life after death. Finally, he gives a direct prophecy that he will die before his autobiography appears in print.

Compared to the structure of the self-eulogy of Clarke, Malcolm's Islam-inspired narrative and its context of direct warrior activism invoke a different sense of Africana spirituality. Clarke did not wear his Christianity on his sleeve, but his Southern roots, being a writer, and being the author of the classic short story, "The Boy Who Painted Christ Black" (1949), contribute to aspects of his identity inextricably tied to Christianity. Clarke also practiced a form of Black nationalism that was not radical enough to reject Christianity.

While all categories of Malcolm's self-eulogy are not representative of Clarke's model of transitioning into Africana spirituality, there are several formal characteristics of Malcolm's approach:

• Christianity is a substandard orientation to a life of spiritual engagement of humans.
• Islam, as religious practice, naturally embodies practical, daily spirituality.
• Activist agency on behalf of people of African descent, in particular, and of humanity, in general is automatically spiritual because it is an act of love.
• Black activism on a global scale is a radical act of martyrdom that is for the glory of Allah.

This model of transitioning into Africana spirituality is a radical version of Black nationalism made radical most explicitly because Malcolm does not romanticize the fact that freedom requires bloodshed. He does not focus on the mortal aspects that his daughters will be fatherless and that his wife will lose her husband. In the dedication of his autobiography, he gives credit "to my beloved wife Betty and to our children whose understanding and whose sacrifices made it possible for me to do my work."[17] This dedication has a loving and sentimental offering in it, even though he affirms that his calling as a liberator competes with his role as a family man. In addition, Malcolm does not anticipate his death as a peaceful transition whose circumstances will comfort and affirm those left behind. However, in response to the abruptness and violence of his transition, Black Arts writers complete his memorial cycle of consolation through performing a virtual funeral dirge to elevate him to ancestor status.

Since Malcolm's self-eulogy does not reveal an identical set of elements related to Africanity and ancestor-status as does Clarke's, it is helpful to explore several additional sources that also chronicle Malcolm's anticipation of death. Clarke had the luxury of living to be eighty-three years old and dying peacefully of old age, while Malcolm died at thirty-two at the imperative of the assassin's gun. A complete vision of Malcolm's transitional context would be incomplete without the inclusion of several pertinent observations that help to construct a fuller survey. In an interview with Gordon Parks he says, "It's a time for martyrs now. And if I'm to be one, it will be in the cause of brotherhood. That's the only thing that can save this country."[18] Malcolm also shared, "I live like a man who's already dead . . . I'm a marked man . . . It doesn't frighten me for myself as long as I felt they would not hurt my family . . . No one can get out without trouble . . . and this thing with me will be resolved by death and violence."[19] His concern is for his family, though he does not detail a version of protective spiritual transcendence here. In his autobiography he states, "It has always been my belief that I, too, will die by violence. I have done all I can to be prepared."[20]

In the words of Omar Osman from the Islamic Center of Switzerland and the United States, the sense of Malcolm being a living ancestor is determined by Muslim doctrine, rather than by Malcolm's Africanity. He states, "The highest thing that a Moslem can aspire to is to die on the battlefield and not die at his bedside. . . . Those who die on the battlefield are not dead, but are alive!"[21] Thus, Malcolm's Islamic religion, in the interpretation of Osman, unlike Christianity, permits a sense of life beyond death in its version of a warrior transitioning into the afterlife. Alex Haley, as autobiographical assistant to Malcolm X, uses language that also suggests a transition, rather than a death. He writes, "I still can't quite conceive him dead. It still feels to me as if he has just gone into some next chapter, to be written by historians."[22]

In Malcolm's model of Africana spirituality African identity is understated, but other observers relate to Malcolm's death as an African concern. The Nigerian press described Malcolm as "a dedicated and consistent disciple of the movement for the emancipation of his brethren. . . . He will have a palace of martyrs."[23] The Ghanaian press "added his name to 'a host of Africans and Americans' ranging from John Brown to Patrice Lumumba 'who were martyred in freedom's cause.'"[24] Haley also reprints a *New York Times* (London) reporter who noted that "a London group calling itself the Council of African Organizations has violently attacked the United States over the murder. . . . A press release described Malcolm as a "'leader in the struggle against American imperialism, oppression and racialism.' It said, 'the butchers of Patrice Lumumba are the very same monsters who have murdered Malcolm X.'"[25] Thus, journalists and observers list Malcolm alongside a highly regarded and mourned African leader of the Congo, which satisfies a memorial linkage to Africa enough to include him in the history of leaders who transitioned into Africana spirituality. At another point, Haley describes Malcolm as a spirit, suggesting that "the ghost of Malcolm X was in the coliseum" at the annual Nation of Islam's Saviour's Day convention following Malcolm's death.[26]

Molefi Kete Asante projects Malcolm in identical cultural terms that leave space for the assumption of his spirituality based on morality. He writes:

There is a reason that African Americans felt that Malcolm X brought the persona of morality when he entered a room. The meaning of this is that he brought with him the full complements of blackness, and expected rhetoric against oppression, the optimism of victory over evil, courage to speak his mind, and the validity of struggle for a good cause. It was often said that Malcolm X was the fulfillment of the culture of the African American because he was immersed in an environment of consciousness of all forms of humanity. Every thought, action, and motivation appeared to be connected to the totality of the people's will and desire.[27]

Asante's overview of Malcolm includes spirituality through an assumption of the ethical and moral standard of Malcolm's fusion of cultural behaviors with religious and social leadership. Malcolm himself said, "I'm a religious leader, yes. But religion is not enough."[28] Malcolm also insisted that spirituality gives moral discipline.[29] This is similar to Clarke's integration of Christianity with African politics and African global history as core aspects of his activism and craft. Asante also provides an overview of Clarke, reminding us of Clarke's insistence that "we were Africans who retained much of Africa even through the slavery institution and we also were deeply affected by Europe in America, but we remained Africans."[30] Asante also credits Clarke with leading the "chorus of scholars" who helped to engage, spread, and popularize the findings of the Senegalese scholar, Cheikh Anta Diop, whose reconstructive work on the African origins of civilization is central to the Africana Studies enterprise.[31]

Concluding the comparison of the Africana spiritual transition narratives of Clarke and Malcolm X in their visionary, prophetic, Afrofuturistic, and noble inspirations compels us to also acknowledge how both men function as forefathers of the discipline of Africana studies. Their narratives are still literary, and they reiterate the diversity of ideas and critical methodologies aligned with the literary enterprise that illuminate new constructions of knowledge and cognitive strategies to improve the life chances and life experiences of people of African descent. The primary documents reflecting Clarke's and Malcolm's self-eulogies reflect layers of critical possibilities for a paradigm of transitional Africana spirituality.

NOTES

1. See Christel N. Temple, "The Cosmology of Afrocentric Womanism," *Western Journal of Black Studies* 36.1 (2012): 23–32. In a discussion of immortalization theory related to Maria Stewart, the author introduces the concept of impermanent mortality.

2. Alondra Nelson, *Afrofuturism: A Special Issue of Social Text* (Book 71) (Durham: Duke University Press, 2002), 6.

3. Reynaldo Anderson and Charles E. Jones, *Afrofuturism 2.0: The Rise of Afro-Blackness* (Lanham, MD: Lexington Books, 2016), x.

4. Ibid., ix.

5. Christel N. Temple, "Communicating Race and Culture in the Twenty-first Century: Discourse and the Post-Racial/Post-Cultural Challenge," *Journal of Multicultural Discourses* 5.1 (2010): 49.

6. Mushira Eid, *The World of Obituary: Gender Across Culture and Over Time* (Detroit: Wayne State University Press, 2002), 273.

7. Ibid., 276.

8. Ibid., 276–77.

9. Ibid., 277.

10. Ibid., 275.

11. Keith B. Kirk, "Eulogy as Mass Mobilization Narrative: Performing Commemorative Discourse in African American Civil Rights Funerals," (PhD diss., Northwestern University, 2013), 108.

12. Martin Luther King, Jr., "The Drum Major Instinct," in *Martin Luther King, Jr. and the Freedom Struggle* (Website/online encyclopedia). http://kingencyclopedia.stanford.edu/encyclopedia/documentsentry/doc_the_drum_major_instinct/index.html (Accessed January 28, 2017).

13. See the formal obituary from the *New York Times* by Robert McG. Thomas Jr., titled "John Henrik Clarke, Black Studies Advocate, Dies at 83," July 20, 1998. http://www.nytimes.com/1998/07/20/arts/john-henrik-clarke-black-studies-advocate-dies-at-83.html (Accessed June 30, 2017). The obituary was also duplicated in the preface of the funeral program before Clarke's self-eulogy.

14. Malcolm X, *February 1965: The Final Speeches of Malcolm X.* (New York: Pathfinder Press, 1992), 255.

15. Malcolm X, *The Autobiography of Malcolm X as told to Alex Haley*, 1964 (New York: Ballantine Books, 1992), 364–82.

16. Malcolm X's Autobiography—*The Autobiography of Malcolm X As Told to Alex Haley* (New York: Pathfinder Books, 1964), 424.

17. From the autobiography section of Clarke's funeral program.

18. Malcolm X, *Final Speeches*, 231.

19. Ibid., 171.

20. Malcolm X, *Autobiography*, 2.

21. Ibid., 453.

22. Ibid., 456.

23. Ibid., 447.

24. Ibid.

25. Quoted in Malcolm X, *Autobiography*, 448.

26. Ibid., 449.

27. Molefi Kete Asante, *An Afrocentric Manifesto* (Oxford: Polity, 2007), 154.

28. Malcolm X, *Final Speeches*, 182.

29. Ibid., 125.

30. Asante, *Manifesto*, 36.

31. Ibid.

Chapter 10

Maat and the Psychology of Justice in the Morrisonesque Community of *Perfect Peace*

Nobel Prize–winning author Toni Morrison is a highly canonized author, and this chapter stresses the legacy of her contribution to constructing symbolic characters and textual communities whose traumas and insularity enable Black communities to deal with crises without outside interference. Daniel O. Black's novel *Perfect Peace* (2010) utilizes this Morrisonesque technique perfected in the novels *Sula* (1973), *Paradise* (1997), and *Home* (2012) to isolate twenty-first-century variables related to gender and gender orientation. This chapter's approach moves beyond Uzzie T. Cannon's research on the novel's gender fluidity and Black masculinity.[1] Black's use of Morrison's canonical variables of storytelling even function as a form of metafiction, especially "psychological representation and regard for the intertextual dependence of [his] writings on earlier black texts."[2] He expands the meaning and implications of Morrison's gendered trope of ugliness woven throughout *The Bluest Eye* (1970) as well as the theme of communal scapegoating, present in several of Morrison's novels, including *The Bluest Eye* and *Sula*. The central anthologies on African American literature have both anthologized Morrison's writings. *Norton* excerpts *Song of Solomon* (1977) and *Riverside* (1998) reproduces *The Bluest Eye* in its entirety. Because of the pervasiveness of Morrison's prolific writing of independent, regularly taught texts that are also anthologized, the public should quickly recognize Black's reliance on Morrison for the characterization of Emma Jean Peace and for his thinly veiled borrowing of Morrison's "Bottom" community (from *Sula*) as his "The Bottoms."

Perfect Peace is an allegorical novel about a mother's choice to disguise her male child as a female for the first eight years of its life. In addition to tackling a complicated gender orientation discourse, Black reveals the tensions between ethical and moral pursuits of justice. African-centered, or

Black, psychology and the Africana ethical and moral principle of Maat stabilize this chapter's deconstruction of the characters' convictions about justice, morality, and order that emerge from Black's symbolic textual community. The transcendence of this chapter is highlighting literary analysis grounded in concepts from studies of Afrocentric anteriority merged with profiles from Africana behavioral sciences.

Sexual orientation and parent-driven activism for gender-choice identity are contemporary politicized topics with precedents and conflicts requiring judicial input. The topics' seriousness appears in debates about parent and child rights, choices, and justice. The interest of Black's novel is more basic—a Black woman who has borne six sons earnestly desires a daughter in order to heal the wounds of maternal abuse sustained during her childhood. When her seventh child is, instead, a boy, she solves this problem by disguising him and raising him as a girl. The text shifts attention from Black's storytelling to the sociopolitical questions of ethics and morality related to research on parental or motherly influence on child identity development, which usually pertains to issues of gender identity, biracial identity, post-adoption identity, sex typing, and psychological androgyny.[3] Black chooses to imagine an extreme tale of desire for "gender sway"[4] gone awry, and the novel's characterizations capture diverse judgments and interpretations of gender identity within a microcosm representing the African American community.

Black shifts the discourse away from its contemporary legal jurisdiction and relocates it to the isolated, insular, and rural 1940s Black Arkansas village of Swamp Creek. Constructing setting and environment is Black's first innovation. Unlike the contemporary national terrain's experience with primarily White over-policing and discriminatory racialization in the execution of the law, Swamp Creek behaviorally enacts a distinct performance of *law* that bears its own functional philosophies and logics.

The Swamp Creek community, which aspires to incorporation as a Black town, has routines and rituals that order social interactions with the predictability of law, and the village manages its own traditions and systems of morality, ethics, and civility without white American interference and hegemony. In addition, members of the community trade roles of judge, witness, jury, executioner, and pardoner over the twenty-five-year span of the novel's plot. Because of the private familial domain, the communal town setting, and the complicated outcomes of the novel's central conflict of passing a boy child off as a girl, the text is a rich narrative of cycles of offense and reconciliation. The most useful ethic from which to assess these Black community behaviors is the ethical and moral ideal of Maat. Maat is the foundational, ancient African norm of civic behavior guiding positive personal relationships and has seven principles: truth, justice, balance, order, harmony, reciprocity, and righteousness/propriety. Denise Martin's study of Maat supports this chapter's literary use of Maat because she "tests its conceptual elasticity" as "an analytical tool" in cosmological, religious, and philosophical realms and "extends the concept of Maat beyond ancient Egyptian civilization."[5] She defines it as the ancient Egyptian principle that members of society "were expected to embody in their daily actions toward family, community, nation, environment, and god."[6] The Afrocentric paradigm, which reinforces the natural process of using all relevant cultural traditions to inform transgenerational knowledge related to Africans in Africa and the diaspora, equips us even for the literary enterprise, with concrete cultural norms from which to measure and assess variables of Africana behavior and worldview. In the characters' varied pursuit of "doing what's right," it is character motive, informed by strong assumptions of the domains of masculinity and womanhood—in spite of their behaviors being confounded by personal crises and competing personal logics—that defy easy and conventional assumptions of morality. Thus, it is the moral ideal of Maat, not simply law (including even de facto law), that is the most appropriate lens from which to decipher acts within the narrative that range from abomination to the iconoclastic.

As a second innovation to characterization is the unquestioned punishment of Emma Jean Peace, the mother, as views from reader-response, including compassion, understanding, and the logic of forgiveness, pale in comparison to the novel's congruence of blame on Emma Jean, while other criminals escape similar consequences. Black usurps shock away from the conservative's disgust with the alleged abomination inherent in manipulating biological identity and later, of same-sex desire and fluid gender identity by redirecting the reader's appall to Emma Jean, the matriarch who dares to pass off her seventh son as a girl until he is eight years old. Black reserves the novel's most significant wrath and punishment for Emma Jean because of the power and guile she assumes by playing God and by allegedly destroying a male-child's gender identity. Society punishes this offense among many other offenses (murder, extreme child abuse, vanity, and child abduction/illegal adoption) most severely because the imagined community of Swamp Creek perceives virile masculinity as divinely ordained and untouchable.

Black's third innovation is that the text uses the characterization of the exile or the escapee to offer pivotal post-climactic context. Emma Jean's second-born son Solomon (Sol) goes away to study psychology at a Black college and returns with an informed understanding of his home environment. He serves as the exile who balances intimate knowledge of the community with his training. As a returnee and as an observer with a therapist's lens, he diagnoses the village's competing ideals of justice within a framework linked to the field of Black psychology.

Black's Swamp Creek community is religious but not righteous. The church serves a social and entertainment function with limited impulses to sustain the African American community's spirituality. Black uses dialogue strategically, cornering deacons' exchanges on sexuality and on the merits of beating one's wife in the perimeter of the sanctuary, yet the dialogues could be equally eavesdropped on in the juke joint. The female dialogues in the sanctuary and on the church steps are the cultural hazing of African American mean girls and adult female rhetoric of gossip and backstabbing. Black's decentralizing of religion as a compelling moral and ethical impulse is another attribute of the narrative that demands the new critical tool of Maat.

In majestic opposition, Black differentiates between a religious imperative for morality and spiritual grounding with a focus on ritual cleansing and healing. This aspect of the narrative is one of its most compelling cultural cosmological feats. The Peace family patriarch Gustavus (Gus) and his sons practice a ritual release—one originating from Gus's youth experience with gender role conflict and the other based on the beauty and pathos of African American aesthetics of song, that cleanse their souls and purge the conscience and spirit of the rather raucous, meddling, socially competitive, rural working-class community. Both Gus as patriarch and Emma as matriarch are responsible for blurring gender role expectations. Internalizing assumptions that men are not supposed to cry, Gus ritualistically awaits the cloak of the first thunderstorm of the harvest season to veil an annual ritual of release, as he cries and wails under the cover of nature's loud, natural storm. Emma Jean methodically raises a girl, satisfying her need for intergenerational female companionship and nurture in the absence of having sisterhood or mother-daughter intimacy. The novelist's art responds to his society, and one cannot read Black's novel without acknowledging it as allegory signifying on both the lack of tolerance and the rigidity of society's judgments about its members' gender-related choices, behaviors, and inheritances.

Swamp Creek is a cultural public—an African American niche of church, a school room, neighborhoods, and families mapped away from white American sheriffs and jails that so often loom as haunting specters double-guessing Black behavior and intent or waiting to spring on the Black community's minor offensives. Law in Swamp Creek is familial and private, yet it is also locally public. Because of this, acknowledgment and punishment of crimes or unjust acts is irregular, as age, nepotism, class, religion, education, secrets, and a diversity of private opinions replace law. Different sectors interpret right and wrong from distinct worldviews, and community-based powers and influences further affect such localized interpretations of right and wrong.

The history of Maat relates to the maintenance of law as its "discourse was addressed to the monarchs of the time with the intention of taming absolutism and transforming it into a tolerant and enlightened form of centralized government."[7] Thus, Maat's itemization of ethical variations—truth, justice, balance, order, reciprocity, harmony, righteous/propriety—emerges as a set

of variables associated broadly with a hierarchy of moral behavior that critically informs what transpires in Swamp Creek. The townspeople demonstrate
flawed and localized approaches to communal virtual governance, and they
even manipulate reason and cause-and-effect logic in enactments that are
antithetical to Maatic categories of ethics.

The plot introduces several key conflicts that it challenges the reader to
arbitrate. The first is Gus's fight to be a male who has the right to cry. He is
creative in managing this right, first "without fear of his father's reprisal,"
and later as an act of release and repentance for verbal and physical abuses
from his family. [8] Another conflict is his anger at Emma Jean for getting
pregnant a seventh time. "He would love the baby, he resolved, but he would
never forgive Emma Jean. Never."[9] This is ironic because Emma Jean's
parental gender-choice decision for her disguised daughter/son Perfect/Paul
becomes a larger transgression that requires additional forgiveness from not
only Gus but also from Perfect/Paul, the midwife—Henrietta—whom Emma
Jean blackmails to keep her secret, and her other sons whom she places in
uncertain predicaments. Emma Jean participates in multiple textual conflicts,
beginning with her decision to act in response to God's alleged unfairness
in denying her a girl child. The text offers many examples of her sense of
being a victim of injustice. Her action represents her need for vindication
and revenge-through-healing against her mother's abusive parenting. She
wonders, "How would she ever spite her mother without a daughter of her
own?"[10] Readers are in suspense and in problem-solving mode working to
figure out, along with Emma Jean, how she should best conceal or reveal the
secret. The final significant conflict is the text's severity of consequences for
Emma Jean. Black has constructed an intriguing story with many complex
cultural features of interest to the Africana literary enterprise. Because one
of the novel's most transcendent features is its application of Morrisonesque
tropes and techniques, this chapter primarily engages the problematic of
Emma Jean's decision with a Maatic lens of the multiple principles related to
human ethical behavior.

Inevitably, Emma Jean is an adult embodiment of the race- and gender-
traumatized Pecola Breedlove from Morrison's *The Bluest Eye*, and Black
lures readers into a realization of how the legacy of Pecola's trauma is antithetical to Maat. Emma Jean is fixated on having a girl because she seeks,
as Morrison's *The Bluest Eye* diagnoses as a cure for the Breedlove family's ugliness, "to contradict" this imposed identity.[11] Gracie, Emma Jean's
light-skinned sister who tries to mend Emma Jean's relationship with their
dying mother, Mae Helen, surmises, "A child's hurt obviously evolves into
an adult's resentment."[12] Emma Jean's preoccupation differs from Pecola's
interest in blue eyes. Instead, she wants someone to tell her she is pretty.
Her light-skinned sisters, Gracie and Pearlie, also cultivate the self-hatred

Mae Helen teaches. When Emma Jean asks them "'cain't chu be dark *and* pretty?' The sisters frowned and said in unison 'No.'"[13] The severity of Mae Helen's motherly damage is evident in Emma Jean's inability to consent to her father Claude Lovejoy's request for custody. Complying with a further Morrisonesque influence, Black names Lovejoy's community "the Bottoms" and defines it as a racially healthy neighborhood full of dark-skinned people who feel proud and beautiful. This is a merging of the dark-skinned, prideful characters and aesthetics from Morrison's *Sula* and *Paradise*.

Black's narrative challenges the meaning and the philosophy of truth as a character-based orientation to stories and motives. At Perfect/Paul's birth, Emma Jean shares her philosophy of truth. She says, "a child gon' believe whatever you tell it. As long as she thinks she's a girl, that's what she'll be. So that's what she is now."[14] She adds, "Most folks *look* like a boy or girl, but you don't *know* for sure what they is, do you?"[15] Here, Emma Jean gives a 1940s voice to the history of transgender identities, that though they were not as central to the public domain's discourses, the community was aware of them. Here the elements of truth represent a duality in which Emma Jean draws from random humanistic truths of a population peripheral to her world-view in order to justify a homemade and imposed version of transgender identity. She aims to justify choosing her child's gender by concealing his sex through appropriating a transgender discourse, in which she is not invested, in support of her action. This randomness problematizes contemporary discourses on gender identity, almost by reversing the way diversity, civil rights, affirmative action, and under-representations are appropriated politically to support adjacent struggles. Emma Jean's parallelism is inauthentic.

For Henrietta, readers struggle with understanding how she is able to pardon her own lie about stealing her sister's baby while punishing Emma Jean's lie about Perfect's biological sex. However, the novel, perhaps as polemic, favors Henrietta's interpretation of truth. Henrietta states her truth of Emma Jean's offense against her, but it is not credible in a psychological understanding of truth and human responsibility for their own actions. Truth has consequences, and Henrietta is selective about who deserves consequences. In her interpretation, stealing her deceased sister's baby from her grieving brother-in-law is not a crime, yet Emma Jean's choice is worthy of punishment. Henrietta could have sacrificed and accepted the consequences of her own act that defied truth, but instead, she chose self-preservation and redirected blame to Emma Jean. Henrietta's admission blurs responsibility for her deeds in light of Emma Jean's blackmail. In an example of the Maatian principle of order—the proper alignment of things—Henrietta admits that she should not have feared the truth.

Emma Jean has a valuation of Henrietta's relationship to truth, as well. She asks Henrietta, "So, how is the preacher's daughter?" and follows it with a

challenge, "So, did you ever tell her the truth?"[16] Henrietta rejects this possibility of truth and insists "it ain't the same thing."[17] Emma Jean's response
suggests an interpretation of the Maatian principle of balance when she tells
Henrietta, "Well, every woman gotta fight for whatever piece of life she gon'
have. You fought for what you wanted, and so did I, so let's just leave things
be."[18]

The novel's gender identity constructs show gender-related complications
of truth, as the community's assumptions about sex and gender include con-
tradictory prophecies and expectations about Perfect/Paul. Henrietta accuses
Emma Jean, asking, "How do you just ignore truth and create the reality you
want?"[19] Henrietta is troubled because she assumes that Paul's first eight
years as a girl will negatively influence his future relationships. She asks,
"And what if that boy get married one day and then start thinkin' 'bout boys?
Ain't you gon' blame yo'self?"[20] Emma Jean's response has a level of realism
and assumption of order when she retorts with confidence that he will be true
to whatever vow he makes.[21] This topic under the tutelage of Paul's age-mate
Eva Mae suggests a sense of the Maatic principle of harmony, and she helps
Paul understand by challenging him to learn and then synthesize his personal
truths on a spiritual level.

Even more than itemizing the debates and considerations of how gender
functions and includes a narrative of trauma in society, the narrative structure
relies on youth dialogue to mirror the primer of society's simplistic expectations of how biological males and females should behave in society. Early in
the narrative, Perfect's brothers debate about the rules governing the behavior
of boys and girls, framed around the reasons why Emma Jean will not allow
them to see their little "sister" naked. The young boys' dialogue frames the
truth of sex and gender as they confer about gender difference, marriage,
domestic roles, and anticipatory parent role-play with dolls. The dialogue
then shifts to an interpretation of male identity as the boys interrogate the
requirements for being a daddy. This role is based on a male capacity and
expectation to work, ideally as a provider. The boys conclude that they would
rather be boys based on the community's Biblical rendering of gender roles.

In addition, Black borrows the language and terminologies of "coming
out" and of transgendering, both of which are deliberate acts of social agency
and of self-determined identity pioneering, when the helpless, eight-year-
old Perfect Peace, a girl, begins to reinvent as Paul Peace, a boy—against
her will. This shift and renegotiation of gender identity intent is a situation
that Perfect/Paul inherits, rather than chooses, and it is another socio-literary
rupture that Black uses to force readers to consider the hegemony inherent in
judging non-heterosexual gender orientation. In other words, because Black
characterizes Perfect/Paul as an innocent whose path to gender ambiguity
or duality is circumstantial, the fictive Swamp Creek as well as the realistic

readership cannot legitimately punish or reject Perfect/Paul's gender predicament. The dilemma has a concrete truth and cause–effect about its origin that
is less mysterious and less ambiguous than many of society's examples of
gender shifts. Black measures the Swamp Creek community's tolerance and
by extension, he measures readers' tolerance. The community feverishly
dialogues about Perfect/Paul's gender inevitabilities because it is allegedly
self-fulfilling that being a girl for eight years will never permit him to be a
"normal" man. Many in the village persecute him, even though, they cognitively understand his conundrum.

Some readers consider the novel's ending to be ambiguous—that there is
no final word on whether or not Paul Peace behaves as a heterosexual adult
male. In the future, he emerges as a fashion designer in New York. However,
the text does not reveal what happens before then, for after Emma Jean's
death, Paul takes Eva Mae (possibly as a love interest) by the hand en route to
Henrietta the seamstress's shop to learn the trade that accelerates his mother's
madness.

The narrative introduces "justice" by name, first regarding Gus's crying,
noting, "Had he known words like 'injustice' or 'inequity' he might've been
able to translate his feeling into words, but with a third-grade vocabulary, it
was out of the question. All he knew was that he cried when things weren't
right."[22] The eight-year-old Emma Jean considers that justice would be suicide or for God to "taker her away."[23] Henrietta asserts an expectation of
spiritual justice that Emma Jean will "answer to God" for her choice, and
Henrietta's psychology of justice appears as selective, which is a conflict
that the reader seeks to reconcile even after the novel's ending.[24] She sought
to torture Emma Jean by conscripting her to sewing in servitude.[25] Initially,
readers expect that the most significant consequence of Emma Jean's choice
is when her dress catches fire shortly after her community learns of her son's
masquerade. Gus's words, "God was going to have his say," suggest that this
was *the* punishment for her choice.[26]

The novel frames much of its orientation to justice as something measured
by God. When Emma Jean fails to reproduce a fine three-piece suit for Paul
to wear to the school dance with Christina, she considers God's role in her
failure—"God was laughing out loud, she told herself. He always gets the last
word. She thought He'd forgiven her, but maybe forgiveness doesn't mean
you don't pay."[27] Eva expects that God requires further penance in the form
of her having to beg Henrietta to help her perfect Paul's suit, however, the
bargain she must strike with Henrietta inevitably costs her life. Henrietta's
narrative makes reinforces this. She snickers, "I been wonderin' how de
Lawd was gon' make you come back to me, and now I see."[28] She adds, "You
made me agree to destroy somebody's life. . . . But you gon' pay. You gon'
wish to God you had let that boy be a boy."[29] Henrietta is convinced that God

favors her interpretation and that she is a victim. She adds, "I was mad at you for years 'cause seem like God wunnit gon' do nothin', then all o' sudden, you show up on my doorstep."[30] The intended ethical assumptions of the Maatian variable of justice are warped in this episode of *Perfect Peace*, and the Africana-trained readership pursues the discrepancy. Henrietta "laughed hard" in her realization that "He may not come when you want Him, but He's always right on time," and she celebrates this African American religious adage about how God provides, with a selfish context of revenge rather than justice.[31] The novel presents many binaries and opposites in the characters' appropriations of ethics and logic, often toward self-serving ends.

Paul looks like "a handsome, black prince" in the tailored suit, and in exchange for giving Paul a glorious, well-dressed night to prove to Swamp Creek that "Paul had evolved into one of Swamp Creek's gems" Henrietta requires Emma Jean to become her slave.[32] To give Paul this gift, Emma Jean had already considered, "If she had to pick cotton again, which she swore she'd never do, she'd do it."[33] When Henrietta said, "I want the rest of your life" and "I don't want no one-time payment. I want you to work for me. For free. For the rest of yo' life," Emma Jean became bound by a different type of debt slavery.[34]

Perfect/Paul's best childhood friend Eva Mae's "retaliation plan" for the Redfield brothers' physical and sexual assault on Paul is a central critical event of the novel.[35] The novel's seeming acceptance of Eva Mae's covert act of retribution as unpunishable further suggests Black's effective use of Morrisonesque literary features such as how characters justify the use of fire, reminiscent of Eva and Plum in *Sula* and of righteous avenging by the group Seven Days in *Song of Solomon* (1977). There are also similarities between the character Shadrach from Morrison's *Sula* and Black's character Sugar Shack, who is a savior to several characters and, like Shadrach, is a benevolent misunderstood community outsider. Paul first suspects that Sugar Shack set the fire, but Eva Mae watches from the woods in satisfaction. Her version of justice is "retribution," as she thinks "those boys had to pay. It was only right. They had violated her best friend . . . and it was her job to make them pay."[36] The narrative emphasizes the words "justified" and "deserved," and Eva Mae inevitably indicts the Redfield parents, whose deaths she did not intend, because they did not raise their boys to be kinder. Her final justification reads like scripture or a prayer—"So she sent them all to hell forever, amen," which is similar to the accusations the community leveled against Emma Jean who allegedly acted like God in choosing her child's identity.[37] At the funeral, Eva Mae describes herself as a servant of God, thinking— "Someone had to submit themselves as a vessel in the hands of the Almighty God."[38] In fact, Sugar Shack interprets the fire as "God was collecting His debt" and "it had to be paid" as, he considers, "God was punishing their wrong."[39] The matter of justice appears in many relationships. Paul observes that if the fathers were to catch Johnny Ray and Mister together "they would have hanged them."[40] These are all individual, subjective character interpretations and manipulations of truth, justice, balance, order, reciprocity, and righteousness—the principles of Maat—even though the characters do not have formal authorized ethical or moral authority.

Gus's annual, cyclical watershed of crying, performed with his sons Blind Bartemeus and King Solomon singing, is a ritual of cleansing and renewal that merges balance and harmony. As a remedy for the chaos of conflict that distorts justice in the lives of Swamp Creek the family's act benefits the wholeness of the community. Even Emma Jean's descent into madness, an adult version of what Morrison creates with the character Pecola Breedlove from *The Bluest Eye*, and her subsequent suicide in the community's Jordan river "promised an imminent transformation."[41] Emma Jean's subconscious taunts her until she admits that her choice to disguise Perfect/Paul was a mistake. In the afterlife, she fulfills a hope for "perfect peace."[42]

The Morrisonesque narrative traits cue readers to interpret Emma Jean as a new embodiment of Pecola, emphasizing her prettiness, and in Emma Jean's prayer, a supplication for "God not to make her so dark this time that her mother would beat her for it."[43] This passage explains one function of Black's allegory, which is exploring additional iterations of the effect of ugliness and abuse that Morrison defines as a source of African American female trauma in the seminal *The Bluest Eye*. Eventually, Black's novel excuses the cowardice of Henrietta, who eventually admits to Gus, "I know it [concealing both her and Emma Jean's lies] was wrong, but I felt like I didn't have a choice."[44] The narrative admits that Henrietta is guilty of her own injustices of stealing her sister's baby and forcing Emma Jean's servitude. However, the fact that *Perfect Peace* unfolds with Emma Jean as the primary character with consequences suggests that Black's objective may really be to pay tribute to Morrison's character Pecola Breedlove by examining her psychological trauma through the adult configuration of Emma Jean. As the adult embodiment of Pecola Breedlove, Emma Jean can only be a flawed character who experiences redemption and peace after death. This reading of *Perfect Peace* equates the Maatic principle of order with Black's interpretation of destiny.

The relationship between destiny and proper order is often culturally, religiously, politically, or economically defined. Chester Peace, Gus's father, believes in male authority distinct from the female trait of "emotional fragility."[45] In an African-centered view, the sacredness of childbirth is the assumption that the child emerges from the realm of the ancestors who participate in ordering the child's destiny. Emma Jean's choice to play God interrupts this "order," and the Maatic sense of what is order could account for why Emma's choice looms as the most serious abomination within a narrative that also introduces homicide, domestic abuse, and other offenses.

The meaning of reciprocity shifts in the narrative because while there are anticipated episodes in which characters benevolently and expectedly meet each other's needs, often in their most dire and low moments, there are also episodes in which characters manipulate reciprocity as forms of blackmail and revenge. The latter is the context for the relationship between Emma Jean and Henrietta. On the one hand, the women agree to keep each other's secrets—Henrietta reluctantly (and with a curse of revenge) agrees to corroborate Emma Jean's decision to present her child as a girl. Paul and Eva Mae, his childhood friend and confidant, have a relationship that reflects a level of reciprocity even though Eva Mae is more visionary and protective of Paul, whose identity is emergent. Sugar Shack makes serendipitous appearances, in spite of the negative community lore about his character, and layered with his role as the novel's prophet, these appearances support mutual understandings between him and Gus, Paul, and Eva Mae, reminiscent of the communion between Shadrach and Sula in Morrison's *Sula*.

The diversity of opinions and rationales from the Swamp Creek community corroborates why the seven principles of Maat are well-suited for the text's critical orientation, which additionally familiarizes contemporary readers with Maat as a legacy tool that reminds us of African moral and ethical contributions to the world's philosophical systems. The theoretical innovation of fine-tuning Western notions of "justice" into Afrocentric clarity from an anterior ethical ideal—that of Ancient Kemet—is not new. In addition to Martin's study, scholars and activists have utilized Maat in conceptual understanding of hip-hop values[46], for training urban African American youth[47], and for its uses in school forums.[48]

In addition to advancing Maat as a context for understanding *Perfect Peace*, the topic of the psychology of justice *in literature* borrows from its treatment in the fields of Psychology and Justice Studies. The concepts associated with studies on the topic of *social psychology of justice* are relative depravation, distributive justice, procedural justice, and retributive justice as well as group processes in social psychology. The field is attentive to individuals' "subjective view" and "subjective understanding of the world."[49] Specifically—"As increasing attention was paid to people's thoughts about their social experiences, it was discovered that people are strongly affected by their assessments of what is just or fair in their dealings with others. This recognition has led to a broad range of studies exploring what people mean by justice and how it influences their thoughts, feelings, and behaviors."[50] Considering that psychology refers to people's thoughts, feelings, experiences, and behaviors[51], society's collective responses confirms a belief that "conduct ought to be

influenced by justice criteria derived from logical analysis" and this includes
"criteria of fairness."[52] *Perfect Peace*'s narrative of fairness, justice, and logic
within an African American community exposes the caveat that Western
antecedents of justice studies do not include the African-centered ethical ideal
of Maat, which for Africana-trained readers is a logical anteriority. In *Social
Justice in a Diverse Society* Tyler et al. summarize the antecedents of justice
studies as a Western phenomenon:

> Throughout history, the writings of philosophers, theologians, and social theo-
> rists as diverse as Aristotle, Kant, Marx, Plato, and Rawls have been shaped
> by efforts to define how individuals, groups, and societies should or ought to
> behave. Although diverse in many respects, all of these efforts have in common
> the argument that both people and societies should be governed by standards
> of conduct beyond simple deference to the possession of power and resources.
> The use of terms such as "right and wrong," "ethical and unethical," "moral and
> immoral," and "just and unjust" connotes that conduct ought to be influenced
> by justice criteria derived from logical analysis; the works of religious, political,
> or legal authorities; and many other sources. In other words, there is a widely
> shared belief that societies ought to be constructed in ways that reflect what is
> just, and social theorists have devoted considerable energy to defining what is
> just in objective terms.[53]

In spite of the fact that this landscape of justice does not include specific
African-derived contributions that Africana-trained scholars know should
be part of the universal bibliography on justice, ethics, and morality, *Social
Justice in a Diverse Society* offers helpful definitions that are important as we
move toward a microanalysis of African-derived justice-related variables of
Maat and Black psychology. For example, the volume mentions the notion
of "subjective justice," which is a relevant framework for what happens in
Perfect Peace, and it is identical to the itemization of the seven principles
of Maat as a norm to discern the behaviors, expectations, worldviews, and
agency of the people of African-descent in Swamp Creek. Tyler et al. also
clarify the "social consequences" of society's behaviors related to justice and
injustice, particularly with respect to entitlement, anger, envy, depression,
moral outrage, self-esteem, interpersonal perceptions, political attitudes, and
prejudice.[54] They write that "justice standards are a socially created reality.
They have no external referent of the type associated with physical objects.
Instead, they are created and maintained by individuals, groups, organizations, and societies. Justice judgments are central to such a social reality
because they are the 'grease' that allows groups to interact productively without conflict and social disintegration."[55] They add: "This subjective sense of
what is right or wrong is the focus of the psychology of justice . . . Subjective

feelings about justice or injustice are not necessarily justified by reference to particular standards of authority. Our concern in exploring subjective justice is with understanding what people think is right and wrong, just or unjust, fair or unfair and with understanding how such judgments are justified by the people who hold them."[56] Literature and its plot elements of cause, effect, and consequence of human behavior benefits from a reading of subjective justice, and it is well-suited in particular to Black's use of allegory to represent contemporary gender debates.

From an Africana cultural point of view, there are African-derived antecedents that are rich and suitable for contextualizing justice. Maulana Karenga's comprehensive volume *Maat: The Moral Ideal in Ancient Egypt* (2006) is the final word on the deeper philosophical meanings and implications of the moral and ethical idea. Roderick Watts's study on social justice and Black psychology introduces an additional dimension that helps frame the interpretations of justice in *Perfect Peace*. Watts draws from Karenga's introductory Africana text (not the *Maat* volume) that presents the categorization of a "radical school" of Black psychology that notably includes feminists and Black nationalists who participate in what Watts views as liberational psychology. Watts's focus on a valuation of "population-specific psychologies" or "worldview" is the precise fine-tuning needed to inform the African-centered contexts of Black's novel *Perfect Peace* as well as the shift from Western justice definitions to the Kemetic moral ideal of Maat for greater cultural agency in this example of literary criticism.[57] Watts describes this approach as "conceptual scaling" wherein scholars can value the Western definitions and orientations to the psychology of justice but have the freedom to rehabilitate it toward an African-centered function (in this case by layering it with Maat).[58]

Even though Black's novel is recent fiction, it is a text that represents much of the African American literary tradition, and it is ideal for canonization. It challenges the Black community, in particular, and readers, in general, to itemize their cultural—and by extension socio-political—views on gender identity. At a minimum he invites society into a discursive encounter by creating hyperbolic characters and situations that compel readers to argue and debate aloud with the narrative as a tactic to find their voice, to declare or strengthen an opinion or position, or to rehabilitate empathy. It emerges as a final textual confession that perhaps the purpose of Emma Jean's life was "to show people what *not* to do," and this cues readers further to consider the literary and ethical traditions with which the characterization of Emma Jean Peace is conversant.[59] Finally, the novel invokes wonderment about legacies and practices of African American and African networks of ethics and morality that extend to questions of aesthetics and beauty, whose contestations are outcomes of racism.

NOTES

1. Uzzie T. Cannon, "Tears, Fears, and Queers: Transgendering Black Masculinity in Daniel Black's *Perfect Peace*," *College English Association, CEA Critic* 78.1 (2016): 45–58.

2. See Wilson Napier's description of metafiction as he reviews Madelyn Jablon's *Black Metafiction: Self-Consciousness in African American Literature* (Iowa City: University of Iowa Press, 1996) in *MELUS* 23.4 (1998): 216–18.

3. In particular for Allen C. Harris's study on "African American and Anglo-American Gender Identity: An Empirical Study," *Journal of Black Psychology* 22.2 (1996): 182–94.

4. No author. "Parents Try to 'Sway' Gender of Children," *Telegraph*. December 30, 2014. http://www.telegraph.co.uk/news/uknews/11316977/Parents-trying-to-sway-gender-of-children.html (Accessed January 14, 2017).

5. Denise L. Martin, "Maat and Order in African Cosmology: A Conceptual Tool for Understanding Indigenous Knowledge," *Journal of Black Studies* 38.6 (2008): 951, 952.

6. Ibid., 951.

7. Jan Assman, Introduction, *Maat: The Moral Ideal in Ancient Egypt* (Los Angeles: University of Sankore Press, 2006), xviii.

8. Black, *Perfect Peace*, 1.

9. Ibid., 5.

10. Ibid.

11. Morrison, *The Bluest Eye*, 39.

12. Black, *Perfect Peace*, 51.

13. Ibid., 55.

14. Ibid., 15.

15. Ibid., 16.

16. Ibid., 274.

17. Ibid.

18. Ibid., 275.

19. Ibid., 274.

20. Ibid.

21. Ibid.

22. Ibid., 2.

23. Ibid., 21.

24. Ibid., 17.

25. Ibid., 303.

26. Ibid., 164.

27. Ibid., 268.

28. Ibid., 270.

29. Ibid., 273.

30. Ibid.

31. Ibid.

32. Ibid., 277, 266.

33. Ibid., 267.

34. Ibid., 270.

35. Ibid., 250.

36. Ibid., 285, 284.

37. Ibid., 285.

38. Ibid., 286.

39. Ibid., 285.

40. Ibid., 280.

41. Ibid., 332.

42. Ibid., 353.

43. Ibid., 333.

44. Ibid., 314.

45. Ibid., 11.

46. Jawanza Kunjufu, *HIP-HOP v. Maat: A Psycho/Social Analysis of Values* (Chicago: African American Images, 1993).

47. Suzanne Miles, "Turning in: The Impact of Inner Resource Training on African American Adolescent Males," (PhD diss., Pacifica Graduate Institute, 2012).

48. Derrick C. Lewis, "Maat, Egyptian Concept Inspires Schools Forum," *Michigan Citizen*. February 16, 1991.

49. See Tom R. Tyler, Robert J. Boeckmann, Heather J. Smith, and Yuen J. Huo, *Social Justice in a Diverse Society* (Boulder, CO: Westview Press, 1997), 1.

50. Ibid.

51. Ibid. See the variables of the conceptual model on page 7.

52. Ibid., 3.

53. Ibid.

54. Ibid., 6.

55. Ibid.

56. Ibid., 4.

57. Roderick Watts, "Integrating Social Justice and Psychology," *The Counseling Psychologist* 32.6 (2004): 857.

58. Ibid., 858.

59. Black, *Perfect Peace*, 332.

Chapter 11

Beyoncé? No. Lauryn Hill? Yes

Interludes of Womanist Hip-Hop and the Traditional Activist Genre

Scholarly iterations attempting to legitimize "Beyoncé feminism" have blurred the lines between popular culture and activism, as scholars make exceptions for the artist's contradictions in order to claim her cultural production as an ongoing contemporary manifestation of the Black female voice. Nathalie Weidhase categorizes the myriad interrogations neutrally as "tensions" that reflect the fact that capitalism, performance, voice, Black women's bodies as texts, and informal versus academic expectations of gender labels complicate easy assumptions.[1] The recent trends include a set of nonacademic and blogosphere responses to Beyoncé Knowles's release of the video album *Lemonade*, her 2016 Super Bowl Performance infused with Black Panther-inspired symbolism, and her performance in front of the word "feminist" at the 2014 MTV Video Music Awards. The popular culture reactions—much of it as acritical praise—bestow all sorts of unearned epistemological credentials upon the songstress. Some prioritize gender-based ideas, and others interpret Knowles's contributions to an emergent *southern* Black women's studies and even respectability studies. These trends, however, often overlook the documented chronological traditions of African American women's public performance and voice that reflect linearity—deliberate, chronological, and clarified narratives about the relationship between voice and the privileges of performance—and a tradition of a more humble and less capitalistic response to having access to a hungry Black nationalist audience.

This chapter's transcendence is the act of excavating Maria W. Stewart's superlative early-nineteenth-century models of public address for theorization as a tool to provide historical stability to the continuum of African American women's presentations of cultural and sociopolitical worldview. As a refinement and corrective in the genealogy and historicization of the Black womanist tradition in which Knowles seeks to participate, this chapter reintegrates the voices of nineteenth-century abolitionist speaker Maria Stewart and contemporary rap/hip-hop artist Lauryn Hill into the rhetorical Black nationalist and Black consciousness canon that intersects with nonfiction and lyrical sources anthologized in both the *Norton* and *Riverside* anthologies. The caveat is that while Hill is a musical performer, she participates with Stewart in the African American women's speech tradition more through the impromptu commentary she inserts between songs in a seminal recorded live performance.

Both the *Norton* and *Riverside* anthologies naturally feature the speech and oratory genre as a key literary contribution to the canon. Additionally, *Riverside* has a discussion of rap/hip-hop music and its consistencies and innovations as an oral/aural literary form and excerpts rap and hip-hop with critical explanation for their vitality.[2] *Norton*'s companion compact disc includes spoken word texts such as Grandmaster Flash & the Furious Five's hit "The Message" (1982) and the song "Dancin' in the Street" by Martha and the Vandellas (1964). The latter is a female group performance that "coincided with the 1960s urban race riots" and that "was often taken to indicate a call for direct political action, city by city."[3] In fact, even the *Norton* inclusions of gospel, folkloric, juke joint, and blues lyrics performed variously by Mahalia Jackson, Clara Ward, Bernice Johnson Reagon, Zora Neale Hurston, Ma Rainey, and Bessie Smith are part of the tradition of African American women's lyrical and oratorical voices of worldview, social concerns, and protest. And foundational Africana disciplinary texts such as Karenga's *Introduction to Black Studies* and *A Turbulent Voyage* edited by Floyd Hayes address how to critically maneuver through emergent contemporary forms of popular culture and music.

Beauty Bragg's *Reading Contemporary African American Literature* (2015) also helps to contextualize the merit and effect of this type of historical-popular comparison and how it successfully challenges possibly artificial or reductionist notions of canon. She studies nontraditional Black women's literary creative production from the post–civil rights era to the present to consider "several distinctive ways their work makes important contributions to public discourse," namely how they "foreground gender in ways that are frequently missing from other modes of discourse on contemporary black experience."[4] Bragg's historical periods overlap with this chapter, and parts of Bragg's analysis are in direct conversation with the agency Hill's hip-hop contribution assumes when placed in the continuum of Stewart's legacy as a pioneer. Bragg acknowledges the deficit that African American women have not been "well-positioned to shape the conversation on the nature of black culture to which critiques of hip hop culture are often linked,"[5] but perhaps working from Hill's agency captured in her Interludes is a step in that direction. This becomes particularly hopeful through Bragg's affirmation that "each historical moment produces an engagement of black female experience in a relation to a specific set of discursive conditions"[6] that I contend are functional and active in the continuum of dutiful comparative survey that bridges the contemporary and the historical, however meandering.

This chapter is not intended to be a feature study of Knowles's music and film. Instead, it reorients us toward the womanist intellectual tradition of orality and performance in order to offer a critical benchmark from which to more fruitfully engage with products of popular culture. The chapter relies on content analysis, historical-biographical interpretation, interdisciplinary Black women's gender theory, and African-centered interpretations of gendered cultural legacy in oral performance to introduce several theoretical orientations to assess and measure the consistencies in the Black women's voice and activist agenda over time. The chapter's emphasis is on the theory of immortalization per Stewart's model and the practice of confessional transformation based on Hill's model of using performance to cleanse and heal wounds of the past through public testimony.

Exploring the critical value of one of Knowles's performance precursors, Lauryn Hill, fills a gap in scholarship for how to measure womanist/feminist art and consciousness in popular culture. Hill's second solo project is a live album whose ratings suffered because of its confessional didacticism and unfamiliar musicality, but it is methodologically brilliant because of what Hill introduces as *Interludes*. These interludes are transitional, confessional conversations that Hill shares with the audience between songs in order to contextualize the music. The linearity and critical communication does not leave the lyrical performances' interpretations to chance. In addition, the interludes provide first-person artistic data that helps align the popular culture production with theoretical womanist counterparts, such as Maria Stewart, in spite of the distance in time and era.

La Marr Jurelle Bruce studies Hill's album and its interludes to "carefully watch and listen for madness," even though the author does acknowledge "the significance of Hill's black womanly command of 'genius' and 'prophecy' within racist/sexist pop cultures and public spheres in America."[7] While the emphasis is on Hill's "journey to madness," Bruce gives Hill credit for the types of womanist Black nationalist features that compel this chapter's comparison of Hill's concerns with Stewart's over a century earlier.[8] In fact, the author's interest in Hill as a larger critical project is in how she utilizes madness as a tool for radicalism. Bruce writes, "Hill's commentary is dense with womanist, Afro-affirmative, antimisogynist, antiracist and anticolonial insights. She cites a centuries-long history of epistemic violence, and spiritual assault endured by black women."[9]

There are striking similarities between Stewart's authentic voice and Hill's transformed voice—a voice that emerged once she removed herself from the cycles of negativity and defeat that confronted her in the entertainment industry. Hill's retreat from the materialism and puppetry of the rap/hip-hop industry permitted her to emerge as a more traditional Black female intellectual, and the unity of concerns between Hill's *Interludes*, or lectures, and Stewart's formal speeches and writings suggests that the Black woman's activist voice is stable, consistent, and functional over time within the Black woman's experience in the United States. The consistency of Black female responses to oppression over time, indicated by comparing the methods and ideas of Stewart and Hill, which reflects a time differential of 171 years (1831–2002), reveals a resurrectionist artistry in Black women's experience.

The oral tradition from which rap and hip-hop emanate is a cultural, literary, and even political tradition that can embody ancient to modern traditions of divine speech, performance hermeneutics, culturally identifiable language, culturally thematic validation in which content transmits the values and morés of the group, and speech performance paradigms in which positive audience reception affirms the appropriateness, value, and beauty of the work. These conditions reflect descriptions of functionality, which is a standard measure of the value of a work in African-centered paradigms of Africana Studies whereby literature and rap/hip-hop lyrical performance would fall under the category of creative production.

As a comparative study of the Black female voice in two genres of literature—the abolition speech and rap/hip-hop—the concern is to address each lyrical artist's contribution based on her usage of the spoken/written word. Specifically, this is a comparative study of the essays, speeches, and theory of immortalization of the first Black female abolition orator, Maria Stewart and of rapper/vocalist Lauryn Hill's confessional musical document, *Lauryn Hill: MTV Unplugged 2.0* (2002) that introduces a transformative paradigm for the direction of the contemporary Black female voice in rap/hip-hop.

This chapter addresses the question "What do Black women orators do when they have the opportunity to speak to the Black community?" Many people take the activism of voice for granted, but it has not always been this way. The activist critique of the primarily *negative* role and image of Black women in contemporary rap and hip-hop—a critique prioritized both by an early-twenty-first-century *Essence Magazine* campaign and by a host of Black feminist and cultural critics—is an indicator of the need for this exploration of the history, the cultural norms, the value, and the power of the Black female voice, even in the blurred realm of musical entertainment. An additional indicator of the differential between the contemporary negative constructs in rap of the Black female voice and the positive and progressive phenomena of the Black Women's Movement (which by the year 1970 saw the publication of Toni Cade Bambara's *The Black Woman* and Toni Morrison's first novel, *The Bluest Eye*) is the prologue to Toni Morrison's novel, *Love* (2004), that offers a renewed critique of the negative transformations of the Black female experience since even before the Black Women's Movement. These contexts validate a comparison between the nineteenth-century representative works of Stewart and the twenty-first-century creations of Hill.

Rap has emerged as a modern genre that is capable of expressing the Black female voice, and viewing the history of the Black female voice demonstrates that rap/hip-hop, as a synthesis of authentic cultural expression (which is progressive) *plus* its marketing as a capitalist commodity in a racist world that embodies female stereotype, exploitation, and over-sexualization (which is negative), is inadequate. Charting the legacy of the Black female voice from Maria W. Stewart to Lauryn Hill is a critical exercise that permits the Black female voice to be explored in a dialectical manner. A comparison of these two voices reveals a usable standard set of attributes that can be criteria for assessing the function of Black women's civic discourse. Interpreted from the ideas of Stewart and Hill, the attributes reflect: a dimension of spirituality, a concern for freedom, an articulated concern to break the chains of literal or virtual slavery (or enslavement), a commitment to be a role model for righteous living, an understanding that the act of expressing the female voice is an act of leadership, a decisive articulation of the responsibility that comes with leadership, advocacy for positive change through activism, promotion of a functional hero dynamic, and concerns for immortalizing Black women.

It is expected that Stewart's work, created within an abolitionist platform, would exhibit these admirable parameters that are the foundations of the Black female public voice. However, Lauryn Hill's articulation of identical parameters within the genre of rap/hip-hop comes as a surprise. Inevitably, Hill's cyclical return to and emphasis of a type of functional Black female discursive foundation suggests that the negativity experienced by women within the structure of rap/hip-hop is not permanent. Hill's transition into what she jokingly describes as a "hip-hop folk singer" introduces a functional yet eclectic creation and performance paradigm that is so profound that it emerges as a distinct creative form.[10] The cover for Hill's performances generically describes her impromptu speeches before and between songs as interludes. They are not her songs or her lyrics, but they are her personal confessions and testimonies that contextualize her experience as a performer. The live format of *MTV Unplugged* gave Hill space and license to project her Black female personhood through a transformative performance, and it is a rich document revealing an organic Black female voice. In fact, there are incredible similarities between Hill's ideas in the songs "Mystery of Iniquity," and "I Get Out" and Stewart's 1831 to 1833 speeches. Thus while Stewart pioneers a womanist *discourse on immortalization*, Hill, in a similar act of verbal creation, demonstrates a womanist process of confessional transformation that has implication for the Black family as a holistic unit.

The intellectual tradition from which this study on Stewart's and Hill's discourses emerges is catalogued by the critical anthology, *Women in Africa and the African Diaspora: A Reader* (1996), edited by Rosalyn Terborg-Penn and Andrea Benton Rushing. As a seminal volume that emerged from proceedings of an interdisciplinary conference sponsored by the Association of Black Women Historians, its contexts are timeless, as it emphasizes the need for "theories that focus on the way black women define their experiences through various genres."[11] It calls for theories, research methods, and techniques that are effective because they "require understanding the cultural context and acknowledging black women's definitions of themselves, as well as their means of expression."[12] In *Reading Contemporary African American Literature*, Bragg also relies on an older, but seminal, source in her argument of how popular culture is of "importance in the cultivation of the public sphere."[13] The late-twentieth-century perspectives of the historians who contributed to Terborg-Penn's and Rushing's seminal collection are particularly relevant in aiding this chapter's emphasis on continuum. The authors reiterate that the Black woman's role traditionally includes the vital duty of being a "reproducer of lineage groups."[14] Both speaker-writers engage their Black female realities and artistries from the perspectives of nurturing, guiding, advising, and mothering. The anthology's call for scholarship and interpretation of the diversity of Black female experience validates the creative license to theorize the spoken and lyrical creations of Stewart and Hill.

Black women's creations are permanent parts of the intellectual heritage of Black women, and it is the cultural and literary critic's task to further illuminate and decipher their contributions so that posterity may better take notice. Rushing states it well in the introduction to *Women in Africa and the Diaspora* when she identifies the task as creating scholarship that shifts us away from viewing ourselves as "victims," acknowledges "strategies for adaptation, autonomy, woman-to-woman cooperation, and subversion," and contributes to "expanding the quilt that bravely recovers and analyzes, creates and theorizes about women of African descent."[15]

While the objectives of the conference that produced *Women in Africa and the Diaspora* are important to this chapter, one essay of the collection is central to supporting the framework for the comparison of Stewart and Hill. Historian Darlene Clark Hine offers a discussion on "To Be Gifted, Female, and Black" that indicates the barriers erected to limit the impact of the Black female voice. She writes:

> A deep, pervasive, and centuries-long conspiracy of silence surrounds the creative expressions, strivings, and struggles of the African-American woman. A shroud of virtually impenetrable ignorance enveloped the black woman and gave rise to racial and sexual stereotypes which distorted her image—indeed,

buried her from view. Unable to break through the derogatory images created and sustained by the mass media, the creative black woman has labored and suffered in isolation. Convinced that the struggle against racism was of paramount importance, the African-American woman spoke for decades with muted voice of her own sexual oppression.[16]

This description of constraint is most applicable to Stewart's life experience but in a disappointing cyclical way, it also emerges through Hill's experience as a modern woman. Hine writes of Black women who "refused to allow a deprecating society to stifle their creative impulses to give voice, vision, and sound to their condition as black women in white America," and she insists that "an accurate social history of America cannot be written or understood until the artistic, literary, and musical aspects of the cultural tradition relentlessly created by African-American women are revealed."[17] Hine sets a standard when she writes, "it is crucial that we begin to see [Black women] as agents of social change as one of the pivotal forces in the creation of culture of the black community. These things must occur in order that the black women's culture—the meaning of being gifted, black, and female—can be known and interpreted."[18] These critical observations that highlight the relationship between Black women's history, voice, and creative production, are sufficient theoretical foundations from which to proceed to the comparative study of the works of Stewart and Hill.

In *Maria W. Stewart: America's First Black Woman Political Writer: Essays and Speeches* (1987), Marilyn Richardson describes Stewart as "likely the first black American to lecture in defense of women's rights."[19] Stewart was born in 1803 in Hartford, Connecticut and was orphaned without siblings at age five, married at age twenty-three, and widowed three years later. She was swindled out of her husband's estate and inheritance, and she responded to her newly found destitution with a vocal prowess and activist zeal that supported a divinely inspired mode of self-preservation. She used her status as a widow as a way to liberate her from the silence, passivity, and domestic confinement that characterized the lives of her female peers. Richardson's pioneering study of Stewart confirms:

> Stewart constructed a spirited series of arguments citing feminist precedents drawn from biblical, classical, and historical sources. A bold and militant orator, she called on black women to develop their highest intellectual capacities, to enter into all spheres of the life of the mind, and to participate in all activities within their community, from religion and education to politics and business, without apology to notions of female subservience. Her original synthesis of religious, abolitionist, and feminist concerns place her squarely in the forefront of a black female activist and literary tradition only now beginning to be acknowledged as of integral significance to the understanding of the history of black thought and culture in America.[20]

Stewart's contribution, which begins in 1831, sets the standard for the Black woman's activist voice in immortalization discourse, an Ebonic use of heroes, and formulating Black women's heroic prowess.

Stewart challenges Black women to pursue supernatural and divine objectives for future generations of African Americans. In a tract on "Religion and the Pure Principles Of Morality, The Sure Foundation On Which We Must Build" (1831), Stewart speaks directly to Black women about securing their legacy. She writes, "O, ye daughters of Africa, awake! Awake! Arise! No longer sleep nor slumber, but distinguish yourselves. Show forth to the world that ye are endowed with noble and exalted faculties. O, ye daughters of Africa! *What have ye done to immortalize your names beyond the grave? What examples have ye set before the rising generation? What foundations have ye laid for generations yet unborn?*" (emphasis added).[21] This is a profound declaration of African cosmological sensibility found in early African American women's writing, whereby a Black woman acknowledges the supernatural process of ancestor creation and articulates the Black woman's potential for eternal effect. This statement is the foundation of Stewart's discourse on immortalization that she poses as a solution to the oppression of her era. Later in the essay, Stewart reiterates in a prayer that God "grant that every daughter of Africa may consecrate her sons to thee from birth," which is another call for Black women to take advantage of a divine relationship that has the potential to positively influence destiny and the broader future of African Americans.[22]

A premise of the discourse on immortalization that I credit to Stewart is an assertive belief in the empowerment of Black women. Stewart believes in the capability of Black women, and she admonishes women to pursue their strength. In "An Address Delivered Before the Afric-American Female Intelligence Society of America" (1832) Stewarts proclaims, "O woman, woman! Upon you I call; for upon your exertions almost entirely depends whether the rising generation shall be anything more than we have been or not. O woman, woman! Your example is powerful, your influence great; it extends over your husbands and your children, and throughout the circle of your acquaintance."[23] In this sense Stewart attests to the power and potential of Black women.

Another facet of Stewart's discourse on immortalization is the process whereby Stewart deliberately immortalizes herself into the public and historical record as a response to mistreatment and disregard by her Washington, D.C. community that knew her in her poverty-stricken and geographically isolated old age, rather than in her militant youth. Stewart's essays and speeches were originally published in 1835 and then again in 1837 in Boston. However, after nearly forty-five years of a life of struggle and/or poverty in New York City, Baltimore, and particularly Washington D.C., where Stewart lived out her final days, Stewart republished the intellectual accolades of her young adult career as a way of cementing her legacy. One can speculate that Stewart knew that her days were numbered. Stewart lamented the disregard with which she was treated in Washington, D.C. in her later years. The fact that Stewart's Boston public speaking legacy survives today is testament that Stewart was successful in deliberately immortalizing herself through the republication of her 1835 volume. Inevitably, Stewart deliberately perpetuates her own legacy in a discursive act of self-preservation. Self-preservation into posterity is not disreputable, and Lauryn Hill's hip-hop folklore and "Interlude" lectures perform a similar function.

Stewart further immortalizes herself by summoning historical precedent and using rhetorical structures of indirection and hypothetical associations to elevate herself as a supernatural, godly representative, similar to a high priestess. In "Mrs. Stewart's Farewell Address to Her Friends in The City of Boston" (1833), after chronicling the ancient record of women's rights and acknowledgment, she warns her listeners:

> And in the most barbaric nations, all things that have the appearance of being supernatural, the mysteries of religion, the secrets of physic, and the rites of magic, were in the possession of women.
>
> If such women as are here described have once existed, be no longer astonished then, my brethren and friends, that God at this eventful period should raise up your own females to strive, by their example both in public and private, to assist those who are endeavoring to stop the strong current of prejudice that flows so profusely against us at present. No longer ridicule their effort, it will be counted for sin.[24]

Stewart's indictment in this passage should summon fear in listeners. She elevates herself to a supernaturally divine Black female status and then issues a warning to those who oppose her power. The discourse on immortalization embodied in this passage historically affirms characterizations Black women writers have cultivated in Black women characters with such powers. Alice Walker's character Celie, from the novel *The Color Purple* (1985), first comes to mind, particularly the repeated curses that Celie places on her husband Albert, drawing a direct relationship between his lack of goodwill toward women and his future failures. The power that Celie exhibits is compatible with the Black female divine that Stewart constructs in her speech, and Henry Louis Gates Jr. relates this to a continuum between Zora Neale Hurston and Alice Walker.[25]

The examples Stewart offers to justify her right to speak and to be heard as a Black woman are not necessarily examples of Black achievement. However, since Stewart was a lone female activist, not involved in organizations of white women activists at the time, her usage of these models fits into her uniquely constructed paradigm for the uplift of solely, *Black*, women. From this commitment emerges an *Ebonic use of heroes* reflected in her pantheon of examples. *Ebonic use of heroes* refers to how Stewart compels the only history available—European/Eurocentric history, United States current events, biblical history, and scattered realms of Black Ethiopianism—to function toward her African-centered freedom objectives. In essence, she transforms European women into models for Black progress without featuring their European-ness as a condition to be emulated.

Stewart best uses this device in her "Farewell Address." With respect to biblical examples, she prioritizes her identity as a Black woman when she suggests that if the apostle Paul knew the plight of Black women, then he would not have objections to a woman's gospel voice. She writes, "Did St. Paul but know of our wrongs and deprivations, I presume he would make no objections to our pleading for our rights."[26] Prior to this, Stewart offers a roll call of biblical heroines to support the cause of Black women's freedom and rights to a public platform. She summons biblical women, namely Deborah, Esther, Mary Magdalene, and the woman of Samaria, as ancestors to the Black woman's cause.

Stewart's "Farewell Address" is rich in comparative metaphors for Black female success, but her use of the example of a young lady of Bologne from the thirteenth century leaves a lasting example of her *Ebonic use of heroes*. Stewart offers a lengthy paragraph describing this young woman's advancement from student, to funeral orator, to earning a Doctor of Laws degree, and to practicing as a public speaker. Stewart poetically concludes her description of the young woman, saying, "She joined the charms and accomplishments of a woman to all the knowledge of a man. And such was the power of her eloquence, that her beauty was only admired when her tongue was silent. What if such women as are here described should rise among our sable race?"[27] Stewart does two things here. First she mocks her disapproving audience by subtly pointing out the balance between her personal intellect and physical beauty. Stewart is earlier described as "one of the most beautiful and loveliest of women," but she points out that she is not just another pretty face.[28] She seeks to be defined by her intellect, not her beauty. The second thing Stewart does by analyzing the thirteenth-century young woman of Bologne is that she offers another example of an *Ebonic use of heroes*. It does not matter that her heroine is European, but Stewart always reinforces the fact that she is concerned with the achievement of her own "sable," or Black race.

Stewart's *Ebonic use of heroes* represents one type of prowess—she is more direct about the need to exalt legends of the Black experience. She was a personal friend of abolitionist activist and writer David Walker, who was killed, and her treatment of his memory indicates a practice of remembrance. She writes, "But where is the man that has distinguished himself in these modern days by acting wholly in the defence [sic] of African rights and liberty? There was one, although he sleeps, his memory lives."[29] It is memory that sustains heroics, and Stewart's act of public memory represents a much more lasting phenomenon than that for which she receives credit. Stewart engages the culture's heroic prowess and achievement to Haiti as well, noting, "And the Haytians [sic], though they have not yet been acknowledged as a nation, yet their firmness of character, and independence of spirit have been greatly admired, and high applauded."[30] She even mentioned Egyptian women in her "Farewell Address."

Stewart rhetorically and masterfully enlivens legendary historical awareness related to a vision of more formal achievement for the race. In "An Address Delivered At The African Masonic Hall" she laments: When I cast my eyes on the long list of illustrious names that are enrolled on the bright annals of fame among the whites, I turn my eyes within, and ask my thoughts, 'Where are the names of our illustrious ones?'"[31] She ponders further, "Where can we find among ourselves the man of science, or a philosopher, or an able statesman, or a counsellor [sic] at law? Show me our fearless and brave, our noble and gallant ones. Where are our lecturers in natural history, and our critics in useful knowledge? There may be a few such men among us, but they are rare."[32] She acknowledges that enslavement has hindered the elevation of Black men and women consistently to such rank, but her words, as a form of *nommo*, summon and predict such accomplishment into existence. Stewart's legacy is rich, and her collective contribution to defining the foundations of Black activist womanhood is a model for exploring the contemporary Black female activist voice exhibited by Lauryn Hill.

Lauryn Hill's artistry presents the practice of confessional transformation. This practice is the enactment of a personal paradigm shift, a turning-point transition in the style of spiritual or religious rededication, and public confession as a way to better society by modeling change. From her first solo album (as well as her previous well-known work with the group the Fugees) to her 2002 live performance on *MTV Unplugged*, Hill transformed from a rapper/hip-hop artist into a vocalist intent on using her voice to critique a "decaying social system."[33] Her change reflects the transformation that is required in order for women to be true to themselves in an age of popular, media-instigated deception.

The fact that Black female rappers do not flourish as profitably as their male counterparts is not only a testament to the sexism of the trade but also to the fact that much of the thematic demands of the material for capitalist consumption and mass marketing are antithetical to the nurturing of Black life. The crisis in the Black female rap tradition is that the commercialized rap industry generally promotes a Black female identity that is in opposition to traditional and progressive definitions of Black female personhood.

Stewart is a credible forbearer of Hill because, as Richardson writes, "Within a year of its appearance [Stewart's published work] other women, black and white, following the dictates of mind and conscience, began to emerge from the shadows and, taking the path she had opened, walked up the steps to the podiums of churches and meeting halls throughout the land to proclaim the social gospel of liberation and justice for all."[34] Hill includes speeches within her *Unplugged* performance, and this is another structural consideration that places her within a continuum of Stewart's tradition. Her speeches are called "Interludes" and last up to thirteen minutes. The creations of Hill and Stewart are compatible with respect to theme and ideology. Hill's words are powerful because she offers a critical, comparative analysis of her old versus her new self, and the editorial comments she presents in her interludes demonstrate that her rap/hip-hop and now folkloric artistry exist within a functional, evolved paradigm of Black female personhood. In her own words, Hill addresses this by saying, "Fantasy is what people want. Reality is what they need. It's just I've retired from the fantasy part."[35] Hill's Interludes emerge as more important than her copyrighted music and rap lyrics. The "Interludes" are *critical monologues* of her Black female consciousness, and similar to Stewart's speeches, they embody significant elements of the Black female voice. Hill earned this voice through a type of womanist resurrection and admits, "I had to do some dying and be who I am. When we submit our lives to someone else's opinion, we die."[36]

In the "Intro" Hill refers to the power of the spoken word. She says, "It's just very important that you listen to the words . . . and if you're having a hard time hearing what I'm saying please just raise your hand, you know, something, object or whatever." Hill lets the audience know that the evolved person they are witnessing on stage (and in audio) as she sings "new" songs is a product of forces beyond human control. She refers repeatedly to God in religious terms, and she also admits an ancestral component of her process when she says, "I'm talking to people in my head, too." Hill does not cite Maria Stewart as an ancestor, but it is possible that Stewart is one of the anonymous guiding voices in Hill's cultural psyche or epic memory. Hill's sacrifice of self for the greater good is identical to Stewart's legacy. Hill verbalizes this, saying, "The more I focus *less* on myself, the more I realize I can be used to spread a message."[37]

A distinction between the entertainment persona the MTV audience expected and the one they received is that Hill uses only an acoustic guitar (compared to a twenty-piece band) as backup for her live performance. Her intention is to have the audience regard her words as primary without the distraction of stylized sound. This is ironic in an era of rap/hip-hop where consumers make excuses for negative ideologies in the music because the rhythm and beat are so dynamic. Hill's reduction of instrumentation for a nearly two-hour concert was unprecedented and signaled a new artistic paradigm.

Hill's leadership call for revolt is similar to Stewart's when Stewart writes, "Shall Afric's sons be silent any longer? Far be it from me to recommend to you either to kill, burn, or destroy. But I would strongly recommend to you to improve your talents; let not one lie buried in the earth. Show forth your powers of mind."[38] Hill makes a confession about the song "I Find It Hard to Say," which she wrote in response to the 1999 Amadou Diallo police brutality tragedy in New York City.[39] The refrain of the song is "What I got to say is rebel" [as an action verb], however, Hill did not release the song for several years. She realized the power of her song, and believed that people might take her incitement to "rebel" literally and take to the streets. After years of reflection, Hill discovered that singing is a responsibility and that she must "be a living example." Thus, she took responsibility for the authority that she has as a role model and an artist. She had to put the song back on the shelf until she understood her impact and her power as a womanist voice in the public domain.

Both Hill and Stewart acknowledge that their respective eras present real life-and-death struggles. Hill's song "I Get Out" expresses life, death, sacrifice, and martyrdom sensibilities identical to Stewart's address when Stewart wrote:

> Many will suffer for pleading the cause of the oppressed of Africa, and I shall glory in being one of her martyrs; for I am firmly persuaded, that the God in whom I trust is able to protect me from the rage and malice of mine enemies, and from them that will rise up against me; and if there is no other way for me to escape, he is able to take me to himself, as he did the most noble, fearless, and undaunted David Walker.[40]

Stewart reiterates Walker's martyrdom for Black freedom, and Hill does the same thing in her song "So Much Things to Say" when she mentions Jesus Christ, Marcus Garvey, and Paul Bogle.[41]

Hill's approach to hero dynamic diverges from Stewart's because Hill is concerned with healing male-female relationships and perfecting the "self." However, they both consider the psychic and tangible value of God. A primary feature of Hill's *Unplugged* performance is that she is openly spiritual. She quotes biblical scripture, repeats "Praise God," and speaks freely of being "blessed" by God. Her spiritual relationship with the Creator is a foundation of her emergence as a visionary. Stewart is a forbear in this arena, as well. She writes:

> I suppose many of my friends will say, "Religion is all your theme," I hope my conduct will ever prove me to be what I profess, a true follower of Christ; . . . Do you wish to become useful in your day and generation? Do you wish to promote the welfare and happiness of your friends, as far as your circle extends? Have you one desire to become truly great? O then become truly pious and God will endow you with wisdom and knowledge from on high.[42]

The spiritual liberation that Stewart promotes is documented in Hill's *Unplugged* performance. In the song, "You Are My Peace of Mind," Hill's discourse on confessional transformation is at its clearest as she breaks down into tears during the repetition of the song's praise line, "Oh what a merciful . . . merciful, merciful, God." Hill's weeping during her performance is symbolic of a ritual cleansing and demonstrates the depth, conviction, and spiritual element of her humanity and artistry. Stewart also references weeping in her rhetoric when she writes: "at times I have felt ready to exclaim, O that my head were waters, and mine eyes a fountain of tears, that I might weep day and night [Jeremiah 9:1], for the transgressions of the daughters of my people."[43] Hill also uses liberal biblical references and quotations of scripture in her performance, or what she calls her "sharing."

Stewart mentions that her objectives are on behalf of Black people. She refers to Ethiopia as a trope designating the global Black race, when she writes, "Truly, my heart's desire and prayer is, that Ethiopia might stretch forth her hands unto God. But we have a great work to do. Never, no, never will the chains of slavery and ignorance burst, till we become united as one, and cultivate among ourselves the pure principles of piety, morality, and virtue."[44] There are similarities between Stewart's words here and Hill's rhetoric. Hill references Ethiopia figuratively in the song "The Conquering Lion" that refers to Rastafarianism, which is based on African bonds of brotherhood divinely inspired by Ethiopian Haile Selassie and associated divine miracles. In Hill's song, she duplicates Stewart's rhetoric as she sings, "The conquering lion shall *break every chain*! Give him the victory again and again and again." It is an identifiable tradition that in both 1831 and in 2002 Black women lyrically offer similar protests against "the chains of slavery." Although Black women respond to the oppression of their respective eras, the activism they counter with their voice seeks solutions to the problems that apparently span nearly two hundred years in the history of Black women. Hill does not mention Stewart as an intellectual ancestor, but the connection is indisputable. Hill's paradigm for *Unplugged* is also concerned with piety, morality, and virtue. In the "Intro" when she says, "I'm talking to people in my head too," it indicates that Hill is in tune with the voices of the ancestors.

In "Interlude 5" Hill states, "I don't have to slave anymore. . . . Music was my love and because of everything that I thought had to accompany my music, it became my burden . . . it just got stolen from me." She then concludes, "We were each created to be individual standards," which counters the deception in society that Black women have to fit into an outsider-defined mode of existence. Stewart's speeches and writings are compatible to Hill's explanation of the Black woman's struggle for an independent identity.[45] When Stewart offers her "Farewell Address" she articulates her right to be free as a self-determined woman. In many respects, Hill's public transformation witnessed in the *Unplugged* performance is structurally similar to Stewart's "Farewell Address." Both women use a public venue to expose their Black female personhood, in spite of the fact that their respective societies resisted their rights to such self-definition.

Perhaps the most striking similarity between Stewart and Hill is that they deliberately use the spoken word—the speech tradition—to enact change. Hill claims that her new paradigm is a response to learning some "wonderful life lessons that aren't easy to come by."[46] In the same vein, Stewart's widowhood, her exploitation by her husband's business partners, and her grief over the murder of David Walker, inspire her "thus publicly to express my sentiments before you."[47] This deliberate, verbal act of self-creation is the legacy that remains the most profound as these two Black female activists affirm the primary role of the Black women's voice in immortalizing and transforming the race into its expected greatness.

Thus, in the twenty-first century when society interprets an accolade in Beyoncé Knowles's visual and lyrical format of the 2016 Super Bowl halftime show or the subsequently released *Lemonade*, it can be mindful that there are indeed precursors. The critical explosion over *Lemonade* confirms that society is aware of how the twenty-first century continues to stress the valves of the African American community, including its forms of womanism that balance women's performances reflecting desires for justice and equity for both Black people and Black women. This chapter's discourse analysis intervenes to temper the contemporary trend of over-anointing Knowles with social and academic activism that is both unearned and declared without proper intellectual precursors. Of course, Knowles's primary innovation is largely concerning the Black woman's body, and perhaps society is merging her achievement about the body with her recent compelling symbolic gestures toward intellectualism. The transcendence is how the *texts* of both Stewart and Hill have the power to challenge and temper social assumptions of tradition, consciousness, intellectualism, and innovation in the African American womanist speech tradition as a form of both political and popular culture that, in Hill's genre, intersects with music and filmic performance.

NOTES

1. Nathalie Weidhause, "Beyoncé Feminism and the Contestation of the Black Feminist Body," *Celebrity Studies* 6.1 (2015): 128.

2. Hill, *Riverside*, 1363, 2039.

3. Gates and McKay, *Norton*, 2752.

4. Beauty Bragg, *Reading Contemporary African American Literature: Black Women's Popular Fiction, Post-Civil Rights Experience, and the African American Canon* (Lanham, MD: Lexington Books, 2015), xi.

5. Ibid., xvii.

6. Ibid., xviii.

7. La Marr Jurelle Bruce, "The People Inside My Head, Too": Madness, Black Womanhood, and the Radical Performance of Lauryn Hill," *African American Review* 45.3 (2012): 371.

8. Ibid., 385.

9. Ibid.

10. Hill, *MTV Unplugged*, Interlude 4.

11. Benton Rushing, Andrea. Introduction to *Women in Africa and the Diaspora: A Reader*, edited by Rosalyn Terborg-Penn and Andrea Benton Rushing (Washington, DC: Howard UP), xix.

12. Ibid., xx.

13. Bragg, *Reading Contemporary Black Literature*, xiii. Here Bragg notes that Mae Gwen Henderson's 1989 essay "Speaking in Tongues" "is as much in evidence today as it was in the period she initially explicated it" (p. xii.)

14. Ibid., x.

15. Ibid., xi.

16. Darlene Clark Hine, "To Be Gifted, Female, and Black," in *Women of Africa and the Diaspora*, edited by Rosalyn Terborg-Penn and Andrea Benton Rushing (Washington, DC: Howard UP, 1996), 181.

17. Ibid.

18. Ibid., 182.

19. Marilyn Richardson, *Maria W. Stewart: America's First Black Woman Political Writer: Essays and Speeches* (Bloomington: Indiana UP, 1987), xiii.

20. Ibid., xiii–xiv

21. Maria W. Stewart, "Religion and the Pure Principles of Morality, the Sure Foundation on Which We Must Build," in *Maria W. Stewart: America's First Black Woman Political Writer: Essays and Speeches*, edited by Marilyn Richardson (Bloomington: Indiana UP, 1987), 31.

22. Ibid., 34.

23. Maria Stewart, "An Address Delivered Before the Afric-American Female Intelligence Society of America," in *Maria W. Stewart: America's First Black Woman Political Writer: Essays and Speeches*, edited by Marilyn Richardson (Bloomington: Indiana UP, 1987), 55.

24. Maria W. Stewart, "Mrs. Stewart's Farewell Address to her Friends in the City of Boston," in *Maria W. Stewart: America's First Black Woman Political Writer: Essays and Speeches*, edited by Marilyn Richardson (Bloomington: Indiana UP, 1987), 69.

25. See Henry Louis Gates, Jr.'s essay "Color Me Zora: Alice Walker's (Re)Writing of the Speakerly Text," in *Alice Walker*, edited by Harold Bloom (Broomhall, PA: Chelsea House, 2002), 118.

26. Stewart, "Farewell Address," 68.

27. Ibid., 70.

28. Richardson, "Introduction" to *Maria Stewart*, 3.

29. Maria W. Stewart, "An Address Delivered at the African Masonic Hall," in *Maria W. Stewart: America's First Black Woman Political Writer: Essays and Speeches*, edited by Marilyn Richardson (Bloomington: Indiana UP, 1987), 57.

30. Stewart, "Afric-American Female Intelligence Society," 54.

31. Stewart, "Masonic Hall," 56.

32. Ibid., 57.

33. Hill, "Unplugged," Interlude 1.

34. Richardson, "Introduction" to *Maria Stewart*, 27.

35. Hill, *Unplugged*, "Intro."

36. Ibid., "Interlude 1."

37. Ibid., "Interlude 2."

38. Stewart, "Religion," 29.

39. Amadou Diallo was from Guinea and resided in New York City. His highly publicized tragedy is based on the fact that police shot him an excessive forty-one times as he, though innocent, reached for his wallet for identification.

40. Stewart, "Religion," 30.

41. Paul Bogle is a national hero of Jamaica who led an 1865 protest.

42. Stewart, "Religion," 32.

43. Ibid., 30.

44. Ibid.

45. Hill, *Unplugged*, "Interlude 5."

46. Ibid., "Intro."

47. Stewart, "Religion," 28.

Chapter 12

Broadway as *Text*

Africana History on Stage in
Hamilton *and* Aida

Broadway, as an American theatrical cultural product, is a seminal site of African American performance history, but Broadway musicals are not critically engaged in the Africana literary canon with the same treatment as plays.[1] This chapter's analysis transcends the assumption that a Broadway performance of a play, such as a published and available dramatic literary text like August Wilson's *Fences* (1986) or Suzan-Lori Parks's *Topdog/Underdog* (2001), is different from a Broadway performance of a musical. Specifically, this chapter contends that musicals such as *Hamilton* and *Aida*, representing elements of African-derived storytelling, demand the same acute criticism as the early-twentieth-century, Black, but questionable-in-context breakthrough musical *Shuffle Along* (1921). Looking back, the latter seems to have a more complex historical genealogy emerging from the minstrel tradition; however *Aida* had its own contemporary racialized challenges. This genealogy challenges folkloric and creative authenticity, particularly because the root tale of the show is adapted from a more ancient African legacy whose storytelling is interrupted by colonialism. This chapter engages in the Afrocentric pursuit of balancing tradition and innovation. The methodology suggests that contemporary cultural phenomena emerge, to an extent, from past ideas and artifacts, but the new cultural product must be ethically accountable for the interpretive shifts that it introduces. The analysis of the acclaimed Broadway show *Aida* reveals narrative contradictions and the need to reconstruct literary and performance histories not customarily included in the canon but relevant nonetheless.

Racial bias and hegemony are regularly infused into popular culture, and approaches to deciphering the heritage of cultural products must be an investigative process that requires research into European as well as African and diaspora histories and narratives. In order to assess cultural bias or

163

reproduction of hegemony in contemporary cultural production, scholars must study the origins of contemporary cultural artifacts. Like drama, Broadway represents a *text*, and in many ways it merges the power of creative literary genres with elements of dynamic, and in this case, musical stage performance.

The question at hand is about the historicity and the historiography of the texts presented in Broadway performances, particularly those related to the African American experience. *Aida*'s four-and-a-half-year run from April 2000 to September 2004 represented a racialized Broadway moment whose oversights were lost on viewers. In the current September 2015–November 2017 run of the hit Broadway show *Hamilton*, whose cast is primarily performers of color, matters of race, cultural performance, and representation are also central in the analysis, and as Anthony Tomassini and Jon Caramanica convey, it is "steeped in heritage."[2] These contemporary informed and historical critiques represent the type of cultural competence that Africana reader-response (also viewer-response) anticipates. Tomassini and Caramanica speak of "hybridization," "technical fluency," and "storytelling" in their observations that *Hamilton* is a "position statement" on American history, through the artistic choice of a hip-hop aesthetic as collaborative metaphor, that addresses "the unrelenting whiteness of Broadway." Their dialogue examines matters of structure and form with matters of content, or the historiography of not only Alexander Hamilton's and Aaron Burr's interpersonal and political conflicts but also of the hip-hop genre. The *Hamilton* Broadway moment indicates society's capacity to historicize the text of a popular form of entertainment and performance. In addition to critical praise, *Hamilton* is also under scrutiny for what Lyra D. Monteiro describes as "its silencing of the presence and contribution of people of color in the Revolutionary era."[3] In essence, the musical obscures the presence of enslaved Africans, and Monteiro's review of the actual script attests to this. Her review essay's critique is identical to critiques of the earlier *Aida* when she notices that the nonracially exact casting still associates skin color with genre, as cast members who appear white sing white genres; those who look Black sing the Black musical genres; the hip-hoppers are Black and Latino; and the star—Hamilton—and his understudy are cast as Puerto Rican/Caribbean. This chapter only stresses *Hamilton* for comparison's sake, as the chapter's focus is measuring the dearth of a similar historicization in *Hamilton*'s precursor *Aida*. The objective is to tell a broader story about Africana interests through locating Broadway's cultural productions as viewable/readable texts.

Harold Cruse observes that African American writers need to explore ancient African mythology, legend, and history as sources for new and dynamic literary themes. He writes:

One prominent indicator of the serious intellectual lag in the Afro-American creative tradition is the absence of original fiction and drama depicting African antiquity, which remains wide open for the fictional recreation of everything William Leo Hansberry or Chancellor Williams ever contrived to put in print. Beginning with Shakespeare down to the present day, the white writers have repeatedly recreated myths, the facts, the fictions of Ancient Greece, Rome, Persia and Egypt in novels and dramas. Despite the fact that African antiquity cries out for the same treatment, the creative intellectuals of the "African People" produce nothing (even "Roots" is not much of an exception).[4]

By comparison, writers such as Ghanaian Ayi Kwei Armah and African American science-fiction writer Octavia Butler have demonstrated how writers can be historical, authentic, creative, and political by using ancient Kemetic principles, settings, and contexts for functional literature.

For example in *Osiris Rising* (1995), Armah's African protagonist, Asar, lists the objectives for his country's newest university. The list includes a provision for "placing a deliberate, planned and sustained emphasis on the study of Egyptian and Nubian[5] history as matrices of African history instead of concentrating on the European matrices, Greece and Rome."[6] Armah knows that both Egypt and Nubia are Black lands, but Britain and the United States continue to wage war against African history in the most peaceful, public, and artistic front in America—Broadway.[7] In the opera-turned-musical *Aida*, which ran successfully (earning over $800,000 per week) on Broadway and in national tours from 2000 to 2004, all of the Egyptians are cast as white, and all of the Nubians are of African descent. Broadway and American media have sung praises of the "multicultural" cast of the show, only to shock Black consumers of the arts into realizing that the show is just another attack on foundations of the Afrocentric enterprise.

Disney's *Aida* is a story about a Nubian princess, Aida, who is the daughter of the Nubian king Amonasro. Aida is captured by the Egyptian army led by a young general, Radames, with whom Aida falls in love. However, Radames is engaged to the Egyptian princess, Amneris. The tale is one of the princess Amneris's jealousy of Aida, and of her rejection by the General Radames. The tale is also about love between enemies, a love that causes both Aida and Radames to appear as traitors to their warring countries. In the end, Aida escapes and encourages Radames to move to Nubia so they can be together. Their plan is foiled, and Radames is sentenced to death. The Egyptian princess Amneris pleads for his life, to no avail, and prays to the gods to protect him. In the meantime, Aida hides in the death chamber so that she and Radames can die together in love.

The Broadway show reignites Africana interest in the tale's origins. *Aida*, the opera, was first performed at the Cairo Opera House I, on December 24,

1871. The opera is set in "The Age of the Pharoahs" in the cities of Memphis and Thebes. In Verdi's opera, the resolution that Aida and Radames seek is for Radames to flee to Ethiopia, Aida's homeland, and she welcomes him saying, "And my gods shall be your gods. Home is where one loves."[8] The Broadway interpretation imposes modern racialism onto the Egyptian past. It is steeped in the racialism and skin color divisions per American and European contexts, beginning with Verdi's watered down version of the cultural identity of neighboring, yet warring countries.

Aida has always been regarded as an "exotic showpiece" of "Egyptian authenticity" based on elaborate costuming and settings approved by the Khedive of Egypt in 1871.[9] Allegedly, a Frenchman, Camille du Locle, gave Verdi ideas for this opera creation. Du Locle sent Verdi a synopsis of an idea for a play based on a story he learned from a French Egyptologist named Auguste Marriette. Marriette held the title of "Bey," which was given to him by the Khedive (or viceroy) of Egypt, Ishmael Pasha, and he persuaded the Khedive to commission a European opera to celebrate the opening of the Suez Canal. The opera was completed too late to actually celebrate the canal's opening.

The theme of tragic, or star-crossed, lovers has been witnessed in literature all over the world. However, Mariette's authorship of the story of Aida is questionable. Marriette was a prominent nineteenth-century archaeologist who uncovered "temples and tombs of the Pharoahs at Giza, Abydos, Sakkara and Thebes."[10] His brother claims to have written a developing story similar to what emerged as *Aida*. The brother suggests that August Mariette plagiarized his story to come up with the basis for *Aida*. The premises of *Aida* are likely drawn from Egyptian legend or an old historical event and the history and interaction between Egypt and Ethiopia leave ample room for the possibility. Osborne writes:

> The conflict between Egypt and Ethiopia extended over several hundred years. Around 1000 B.C., the time of the *Aida* story, Ethiopia gained an upper hand, only to be defeated again, for a period, by the Egyptians. Both countries at the time worshipped Amon, the Sun God, and many of the names of the royal personages began with the sacred prefix "Am." Thus, in Mariette's synopsis, the Egyptian princess Amneris and the Ethiopian king, Amonasro.[11]

In *Opera as Drama* (1957), Joseph Kerman suggests that the plot for *Aida* was from a libretto called *Nittiti* written by a composer named Metastasio who lived from 1698 to 1782. Metastasio credits his storyline to "historical facts which are to be found in Herodotus and in Diodorus of Sicily" regarding "Apries, a Pharoah of the twenty-sixth Dynasty and his General, Amasis."[12] In this story, the king asks his general to find the real princess, who has been lost. The acting princess is really a shepherd's daughter. The general

promises that once he finds her, he will give her to his son in marriage so that
the king's and the general's families can rule Egypt together. However, the
general's son is really in love with the shepherd's daughter. The real princess
is scorned, and many of the final events unfold similar to *Aida*. The theft and
manipulation of the story is credited to the Frenchman, Du Locle. In summary, Osborne observes:

> The sounds [Verdi has] created are not picturesquely Egyptian: Verdi has cre-
> ated his own Egypt just as surely as his beloved Shakespeare did in *Antony and
> Cleopatra* . . . and in Amneris, who almost steals the opera from Aida, he has
> created perhaps the greatest of his mezzo-soprano characters. Both in its spec-
> tacular and its intimate aspects, *Aida* is a triumph of the creative imagination.[13]

The history of the original opera reveals important information about the
story's origin, and this knowledge deconstructs our attachment, as people of
African descent seeking to embrace mythologies of our past, to the story of
Aida as a tale that is distinctly Egyptian. It is an ongoing endeavor for scholars to identify and reclaim the genre of Egyptian lore and legend. Armed with
an accurate history of the tale's origin, African-centered consumers of the arts
learn of the European contexts of the transmission of the tale, which inevitably, according to Osborne's research, is a Frenchman's synthesis of scenes
from "Metastasio, Racine . . . and several other dramatists."[14]

In Marlon Riggs's *Ethnic Notions* (1987), a documentary of America's
racism and stereotype of African images, one of the commentators (Lenny)
describes the minstrel tradition as a formula of Black people "impersonating
the impersonator." *Aida*'s run on Broadway parallels this cycle of racialized
adaptation and influence. By the time Broadway finished with its racialist
Euro-American interpretation of Verdi's *Aida,* it was a cultural catastrophe
because it was an already manipulated version of ancient Egypt now juxtaposed with even more deliberate and aesthetically racist hierarchy. In Broadway's *Aida* the Egyptian conquerors are white "rock n' roll" singers while the
Nubian "slaves" are gospel and soul-singing Black characters. There is even
a moment in the opera when Radames threatens the insolent Aida with rape,
similar to the fate that befell enslaved African women who resisted the domination of the white enslaving class of men. The aesthetics—the dress, hair-
dos, make-up, and extravagant fashion of Princess Amneris compared to the
drab, sack-like, brownish clothing and ethnic hairstyles of the Black Nubian
slaves—parallel American plantation dynamics between the coddled white
women who lived in excessive luxury and the oppressed African women who
were required to serve them.

Amneris responds to rejection with a jealous rage, and because skin-color
dynamics are so heavily juxtaposed on stage, the racial dynamics of the story
mimic the oppressive power plays and racial passions that plagued Africans

during American enslavement. Enslavement narratives consistently chronicle antebellum white women's violent and raging reactions to the fact that white men favored women of African descent.

The Broadway *Aida* phenomenon and now the *Hamilton* phenomenon as well compel such critical analysis because Broadway advertises the productions as landmarks of multiculturalism, and this manipulative advertising and propaganda is consistent with companies like Disney Corporation's (a proprietor of *Aida*) marketing of difference. In the early twentieth century, the cartoon form played an influential role in transmitting racism to the impressionable minds of children. Disney continues to project a-historical, white feel-good interpretations of history. Critics responded vehemently to the Disney version of *Pocohontas*, which glorifies British imperialism against Native Americans and makes the Native American heroine look like a voluptuous, scantily clad, Playboy version of womanhood. *The Lion King* is Disney's attempt to treat African culture among its pantheon of image-making. Disney chose to use animals to symbolically represent African subjectivity, while movies documenting European-derived cultures generally exhibit human characters to represent agency. Amy Cappiccie et al. find it necessary to apply critical race theory tools to deconstruct Disney's microaggressions, "indirect social slurs," and Americanization of the core cultural narratives they exploit in the creation of "*The Lion King, Mulan,* and *Pocahontas*."[15] Dorothy L. Hurley's study of princesses in Disney's fairy tales approaches reader-response to Disney as a matter of critical literacy skills.[16] The author contextualizes the problem and offers beneficial strategies "to weaken the negative impact of a literature that is laced with White privileging and or with a binary of color symbolism that associates white with goodness and black with evil."[17] Scholars assertively critique Disney's collective effect on social consciousness primarily for the benefit of children and to prevent media from negatively affecting their development. Lisa Renée Tanner et al. highlight the need for parents to engage children about the social messages they encounter in feature animated films.[18] The assumption is that parents are equipped with the types of cultural competency transmitted through antiracist, pluralistic, or Africana points-of-view and training, which is not necessarily so, and is evidenced by the off-centered and largely absent critiques of *Aida*.

There is also a problematic conflation of race-based critiques of the Disney creative enterprise which ironically challenges Disney's oversights while participating in stereotyping African American culture. Rebecca Rabison's report on the topic of deviance in Disney representations operates on questionable assumptions in the discussion of Disney's over-whitening of cartoon criminals. The author makes qualitative observations that the films convey "that crime is unrelated to social conditions such as race" and "Disney's representations of criminals and their motivations mask the reality of crime and its deep association with race." [19] This is a bizarre claim. Recent studies reveal that over the past fifteen years of data, there is less than a three percent difference between Black and white incidents of crime (featuring homicide).[20] The 2016 election cycle initiated a robust debate over the meaning of racial crime statistics that were misrepresented and overgeneralized in damaging stereotype. The author's conclusions imply that Disney should permit more of its deviant characters to be culturally non-white in order to convey a more realistic image of crime and deviance in the United States population. The application of such assumptions in a critique of Disney reiterates the need for layered qualitative and quantitative research data when dealing with real populations, particularly in an Africana Studies context that merges academic and practical effects of knowledge creation.

Finally, among the many subtle, cartoon attacks on other cultures, Disney's animated film, *Hercules*, was directly offensive to African origins of civilization. The early media trailer advertising the cartoon movie *Hercules* was a manipulation aimed at Black audiences. At a special pre-screening of the movie *The Preacher's Wife,* starring Whitney Houston and Denzel Washington, it was assumed that the audience would stay behind to watch an approximately five-minute trailer/animated music video for Hercules. The theater had a primarily Black audience, and it was expected that the audience would not critically analyze the stereotyped, overtly sexual, antics of the trailer. The animated music video featured the film's set of five muses, drawn as voluptuous and curvy Black women, clad in skimpy togas, who sang bluesy, soulful, gospel praises of the Greek hero, Hercules. In their cheeky banter, they proclaim themselves as his greatest fans. The animated Black women gyrated and sashayed around Hercules, singing about his dominant role in classical Greek and world civilization. It was an insult to the audience, yet this version of racially juxtaposed black-and-white images embodies Disney's Eurocentric definition of multiculturalism. Disney's antics in the creation of Princess Tiana (first Black Disney princess) and the conceptual dimensions of her storyline in *The Princess and the Frog* (2010) presents even more significant challenges ranging from blatantly racist secondary characters to denying a pairing with an authentically *Black* male prince. Disney and many of the power brokers of popular culture make deconstructionist moves against Africana agency, and the manipulation covers history, music, images, and entertainment. It is an ongoing critical endeavor to analyze the subtle ways in which popular culture is infused with layers of racism.

Amos Wilson's *The Falsification of Afrikan Consciousness* (1993) is an important guide to study occasionally in dutiful survey to keep our wits sharp about the war people of African descent fight against forms of oppression. Africana reader-response is attentive to what in society transmits history, and Wilson emphasizes that everything has a history. In the projection of institutions and policies assumed to be socially neutral, there is actually a historical foundation being emphasized. This historical foundation, or premise, is a tool for maintaining the status quo. Relevant to this study of *Aida*, Wilson writes:

> They all have one thing in common in a Eurocentric oppressive system—to maintain the status quo and to maintain Afrikan people in oppression. We must keep this in mind. It is not so much what they say or don't say they represent. It is how they function that is of importance. The European writing of history is in tandem with everything else European and its purpose is ultimately the same: to maintain European power and domination.
>
> European historiography does this by a number of means. It may do this by pure falsification and concealment of history, by omission and by commission. It may do it by what I call a "theft of history." We, in studying Egyptology, are trying to take back what European historiography has stolen, completely falsified; to erase the new false identities it placed on the Afrikan Egyptian people. Or when there isn't a direct lie we get a history book that's written about Egyptians without any reference to ethnicity. We have an unwritten rule which says that if ethnicity is not mentioned then we are talking about White-folks. That rule has been so deeply ingrained within us that we can read history about ourselves in great detail but project *whiteness* right into it and "whitewash" our own identity . . . In other words, historiography can create an outright lie (as it often does), or present itself "neutrally," "non-ethnically," and achieve deceptive ends since it has already set us up to misperceive reality and truth. The European historiography so "beautifully" sets us up that we *supply* the lie while looking directly at truth.[21]

Wilson also writes about how society is trained to equate the word "slave" with African people.[22] Conceptually, the producers of Broadway's *Aida* cannot deny this sensibility. A White reviewer of the opera admits: "There is an essay on racism and Aida in my head that I want to put into words, but I'm too emotional now to write anything coherent."[23] The writer spoke these words in response to the opera *Aida*; however, in spite of negative criticism, the critics are fascinated and titillated with the Broadway musical's brilliant costumes, lighting, and the Egyptian Princess Amneris's fashion show.

Black, or rather, interracial observers on a website dubbed as "Your Interracial e-Mag" with the motto "Love yourself, love each other" are, ironically (and paradoxically), preoccupied with Broadway's *Aida* as an interracial love story. The reviewer observed, "As with many ancient stories, interracial love ends badly, and it ends badly here. But I applaud Disney for casting a beautiful black woman (not by show business standards—she is dark-skinned with short hair) and a handsome white man wrapped up in each other's arms for all to see. It's a start."[24] Indeed there is a paradox. Disney commissions a British pop singer and an American Broadway box-office producer to rework an opera written by an Italian who lived from 1817 to 1901, in the age of imperialism, enslavement, and colonialism. He writes the opera in 1872 at the request of a Eurocentric Egyptian Khedive, who wants to make a grand showing to European investors at the inauguration of a new opera house in Cairo. Disney advertises its Broadway version as multicultural, and school systems even earned grants in excess of $50,000 to create programs where school-age children could meet the multicultural cast of actors to discuss diversity. Yet, the ancient Egyptian setting where individual identities reflected culture and nativity, rather than skin-color or race, is altered so that the alleged "multicultural" musical is actually a musical about interracial love within the mythical hierarchy of race where whiteness is empowered and dominant. A note on *Hamilton* is relevant here because even though *Hamilton* can be considered to show signs of historical accuracy, it is at the expense of people of African descent. Monteiro exposes a similar set of service and philanthropic assumptions that children and students of color benefit from Broadway's forays, however compromising they are to the ethos of the Black experience in the United States. Her final observation is worth repeating: "But reviews of the show regularly imply that what is powerful about the show is how it brings *history* to life. So I ask again: Is this the history that we most want black and brown youth to connect with—one in which black lives so clearly do not matter?"[25] The impact of such white Americanized Broadway musical narratives on youth is contested in advanced critical reviews by scholars such as Monteiro, who works from a History and American Studies background, as well as those in and aligned with Africana Studies perspectives.

There has been an attempt to critique the racialized premises of the story of *Aida* set in ancient Egypt. The African American opera diva, Leontyne Price, performed the opera, *Aida*, since the late 1950s. She published a children's version of the story, using the illustrations of famed African American children's literature artists Leo and Diane Dillon. In Price's storybook, all the characters are of visible African descent. The images are powerful and political, although the author, Price, as well as critics, are relatively silent on the differences between Price's vision of the princess Aida and everyone else's versions. For example, in the "Storyteller's Note" after the body of the children's book, Price shares:

> She [Aida] was my best friend operatically and was a natural for me because my skin was my costume. This fact was a positive and strong feeling and allowed me a freedom of expression, of movement, and of interpretation that other operatic heroines I performed did not. I always felt, while performing Aida, that I was expressing all of myself—as an American, as a woman, and as a human being.[26]

Price is confusing, at least, or political, at best. She identifies with the character Aida because "my skin was my costume," which refers to the fact that Aida is African. However, when Price defines herself, she mentions nothing about being of African descent. Instead, she defines herself as "an American, as a woman, and as a human being."

An original review of the children's book in *Publisher's Weekly* is equally political. The reviewer observes, "The art [by Dillon and Dillon] focuses on overall action, not individuals."[27] Consumers deny the racial-cultural contradictions of the tale, including the fact that Price's version is deliberately historical, meaning that all the characters are African. Curiously, while the Broadway version as well as opera productions tend to ignore the biological and cultural similarities of the regions in the play's conflict, German producer Weiland Wagner, with his 1961 production of the opera in West Berlin, did not hesitate to fit the opera into a colonialist mentality, describing it as an "African mystery."[28] Specifically—"The West Berlin triumphal scene was quite ethnocentric. Ethiopian slaves lugged enormous totemic objects and African sculptures across the stage as part of the victors' booty. Suddenly we were in the deepest Congo. Nothing was left of Egyptian artwork."[29]

In *Opera, Sex, and Other Vital Matters* (2002), Paul Robinson considers whether or not *Aida* is an orientalist opera. He suggests that "opera weds music to language and hence to literature—and often to politics as well."[30] In this equation, is it a wonder, then, what it is that Broadway creates when it attempts to interpret opera and engage in cultural politics disguised as high art? In this essay, Robinson exposes the possibilities of racial and imperialistic meaning of *Aida* through analysis of critic Edward Said's contention that "the whole of Europe's culture is deeply tainted with invidious representations of the non-European other."[31] Robinson's essay provides useful background on the politics involved in the creation of *Aida*. He writes:

> Crudely put, Verdi's opera was to form part of the cultural superstructure of the European presence in Egypt, a presence that reached back to Napleonic invasions at the end of the eighteenth century and that, by the time of *Aida's* premiere in 1871, had transformed Egypt into a semicolony. Indeed the opera, as Said rightly says, was intended as "an imperial *article de luxe*," purchased to entertain the European population of Cairo, a population whose real purpose was to administer Egypt as a piece of Europe's overseas empire. . . .
>
> At the same time, *Aida* was, of course, an opera about ancient Egypt and, as such, was intended by Ismail to serve as a significant piece of nationalist propaganda. Verdi seems to have cared nothing for this objective, and, as far as anyone has been able to tell, he never expressed an opinion about modern Egypt, although he was told that his opera would do much to advance its cultural consciousness.[32]

Quoting Robinson at length is a means of reinserting the *political* back into the discussion of *Aida*. In *Politics and Opera* (1992) Anthony Arblaster writes that "music, and therefore opera, played a central role in creating a sense of national identity and rallying people to the national cause in the various European countries."[33] Broadway wants to convince society that its objectives and performance of *Aida* are a-political, but they are actually cultural attacks on African-centered consciousness. Without the types of critical arguments fashioned from African agency-driven training such as an Africana Studies curriculum, society is ill-equipped to properly assess Broadway as *text*. As an aside, the Italians were overtly political when they staged *Aida*. It did not go unnoticed that "when Fascist producers staged *Aida* in Mussolini's Italy, they often presented a blackshirted Radames subduing Amonasro's Ethiopian hordes, and Amonasro himself became an obvious stand-in for Emperor Haile Selassie, engaged in a bloody anticolonialist war against contemporary Italy."[34]

The challenges with representation and racial-cultural accuracy also appear in other forms that transmit the tale of *Aida*. Leontyne Price's children's storybook on *Aida* is described in the library card catalog with bias. The description conveys that *Aida* "relates the story of Verdi's opera in which the love of the enslaved Ethiopian princess for an Egyptian general brings tragedy to all involved."[35] This description blames the Ethiopian princess for the tragedy that ensues when she decides to fall in love, as if the love was one-sided. The values of the tale are also in question, and they exhibit not only a cultural attack, but also a gender attack.

A consistent corrective from the field of Black psychology is for cultural observers to be mindful that African Americans have been rewarded by European American society for using the side of the brain that relates to music, dance, and sports, and punished for using the side of the brain that handles critical thought and intellectualism. White America's desire to consume blackface minstrelsy was the origin of the modern theater, and *Shuffle Along* was the turning point of the modern Broadway musical, as African Americans, though entering the theater from the back door, showed America how to sing and dance to mesmerize an audience.

The Africana literary critique of a basic, representational application of multiculturalism by hiring a racially diverse cast invites a layering of subject areas that even permits the literary to intersect with qualitative or quantitative survey research. Similar to chapter 6 in which Lorraine Hansberry's *A Raisin in the Sun* benefits from being integrated with applied possibilities from an innovative use of the Worldview Analysis Scale (WAS), scholars could also study the worldview and opinions of casts of contemporary Black actors about the realities of a non-African-centered approach to multicultural casting. A survey or ethnography would likely uncover a narrative strain that problematizes the way both *Hamilton* and *Aida* may juxtapose modern racism onto colonial and ancient history, respectively, through manipulations of cast and color.

Playwrights such as August Wilson were adamant about the misapplication of color-blind theater, based on the assumption that multicultural casting continues to defy historical and cultural agency. This elevates the conflict between African-centered or Afrocentric worldviews and liberal American beliefs about what constitutes, as the critic above described, "modern multiculturalism?" In fact, while the prologue scene of the musical *Aida* exhibits contemporary diversity, segregation supersedes this in the flashback tale. The modern day prologue scene shows many ethnicities wandering through a museum exhibit on ancient Egypt. The individuals, moved by the tragedy of the love between Aida and Radames told from the perspective of the jilted white Egyptian princess, eventually pair off as a Black-white interracial couple, an Asian-white interracial couple, and a lesbian couple. This opening theme is multicultural, if you will, but the ensuing history that the musical presents is an antebellum version of racism and imperialism. Broadway's *Aida* is a figurative attack on African historical agency and a literal attack on African American historical memory, all in the name of multiculturalism.

The challenges of Broadway are canonized in the African American literary tradition in the 1930s by the Langston Hughes poem, "Note on Commercial Theatre." He writes, "You've taken my blues and gone / You sing 'em on Broadway."[36] Yet, the conclusion of the poem is confidence that even though African American culture is infused with European symphonies and even though its cultural genealogy is blurred, "But someday somebody'll/Stand up and talk about me." This chapter's transcendence is demonstrating how to reconcile intellectually—using historical and popular research sources—the extra-literary or anti-historiographical elements of viewings of popular musical performances. For *Aida*, which, at its mysterious and uncertain core, is an African story, the Africana literary corrective is layering evidence and perspectives from multiple subject areas—history, performance, children's literature, film, psychology, etc.—and modeling a method of culturally aware consumer inquiry that interrogates even popular forms that liberally accost Africana historical sensibility by manipulating cultural non-negotiables. There are parts of the African American narrative that should not be imaginatively exploited even as trope. In the contemporary Broadway moment, public awareness of *Hamilton*'s racial-historical variables is more promising than it was over a decade ago during *Aida*'s run. But as more viewers trained with an Africana reader-response approach experience the performance, they will be seeking to better understand the ways public storytelling reduces historical agency. This chapter is a reminder that viewers are not required to check their critical Africana consciousness at the door and blindly consume popular stage shows, or visual and musical *texts*, falling into a cultural entertainment trap disguised as the arts.

NOTES

1. This chapter is a revision and update of "Broadway's *Aida*: Deconstructing the Spectacle of an Aggressive Popular Eurocentrism" previously published in *Africalogical Perspectives* 2.2 (2005): 44–58.

2. Anthony Tomassini and Jon Caramica, "Exploring 'Hamilton' and Hip-Hop Steeped in Heritage," *The New York Times*. August 27, 2015. http://www.nytimes.com/2015/08/30/theater/exploring-hamilton-and-hip-hop-steeped-in-heritage.html?_r=0 (Accessed January 2, 2017).

3. Lyra D. Monteiro, "Race-Conscious Casting and the Erasure of the Black Past in Lin-Manuel Miranda's Hamilton," *The Public Historian* 38.1 (2017): 90.

4. Harold Cruse, "Contemporary Challenges to Black Studies," *The Black Scholar* 15.3 (1984): 47.

5. Nubia is defined as the desert region and ancient kingdom in the Nile valley of South Egypt. Leontyne Price and others use Ethiopia interchangeably. Ethiopia is a country in Northeast Africa. It borders the eastern coast of modern day Sudan and the Red Sea.

6. Ayi Kwei Armah, *Osiris Rising* (Pompenguine: Per Ankh, 1995), 104.

7. Butler, in *Wild Seed, The Parable of the Sower*, and other works, highlights a continuum of African humanity that acknowledges African identity through time and the power of the ancestors.

8. Charles Osborne, *The Complete Operas of Verdi* (New York: Da Capo Press, Inc.), 374. See also Ama Ata Aidoo's Play *Dilemma of a Ghost* (Accra: Longmans, 1965) in which an African man marries an African American woman and then takes her to his West African homeland, and makes use of the same line. The *heroine*, Eulalie, asks her husband Ato if "your gods will be my gods" and "your ma and pa mine too." Scholars have not widely linked *Dilemma* to *Aida*. The difference is that *Dilemma* rejects becoming tragedy because there are matriarchs who can implement the heroine's transformation.

9. A. M. Nagler, *Misdirection: Opera Production in the Twentieth Century* (Hamden, CT: Archon Books, 1981), 88, 87.

10. Osborne, *Complete Operas*, 378.

11. Ibid.

12. Qtd. in Ibid. See Joseph Kerman, *Opera as Drama* (New York: Knopf, 1957).

13. Ibid., 393.

14. Ibid., 382.

15. Amy Cappiccie, Janice Chadha, Muh Bi Lin and Frank Snyder, "Using Critical Race Theory to Analyze How Disney Constructs Diversity: A Construct for the Baccalaureate Human Behavior in the Social Environment Curriculum," *Journal of Teaching in Social Work* 32.1 (2012): 49.

16. Dorothy L. Hurley, "Seeing White: Children of Color and the Disney Fairy Tale Princess," *The Journal of Negro Education* 74.3 (2005): 229.

17. Ibid.

18. Lisa Renée Tanner, Shelley A. Haddock, Toni Schindler Zimmerman and Lori K. Lund, "Images of Couples and Families in Disney Feature-Length Animated Films," *The American Journal of Family Therapy* 31.5 (2003): 355–73.

19. Rebecca Rabison, "Deviance in Disney: Of Crime and the Magic Kingdom," in *Debating Disney: Pedagogical Perspectives on Commercial Cinema*, edited by Douglas Brode and Shea T. Brode (Lanham, MD: Rowman and Littlefield, 2016), 200, 201. This chapter was originally an undergraduate honors thesis from a psychology department student. While it has thoughtful premises of exploring the difference between deviance in Disney films and deviance in reality, its assumptions about crime statistics and the role of prison industrialization complex in the African American community are also stereotypical.

20. Matthew Cella and Allen Neuhauser, "Race and Homicide in America by the Numbers," *US News and World Reports*. September 9, 2016. Online. http://www.usnews.com/news/articles/2016–09–29/race-and-homicide-in-america-by-the-numbers (Accessed January 03, 2017).

21. Amos Wilson, *The Falsification of Afrikan Consciousness: Eurocentric History, Psychiatry and the Politics of White Supremacy* (New York: Afrikan World InfoSystems, 1993), 26–27.

22. Ibid., 27.

23. Donna Christensen, "Ogling Olga" www.cafemo.com/donna/ogling.html/ (Accessed February 28, 2005).

24. Yvette Walker Hollis, "Movies and More," Your Interracial e-mag: Love Yourself, Love Each Other. http://newpeople.weblogger.com/movies (Accessed February 28, 2005).

25. Monteiro, "Race-Conscious Casting," 98.

26. Leontyne Price, "Storyteller's Note," in *Aida: As Told By Leontyne Price* (New York: Harcourt Brace Jovanonich, 1990).

27. "Editorial Reviews," *Aida: As Told by Leontyne Price* (New York: Gulliver Books, 1990). https://www.amazon.com/AIDA-Leontyne-Price/dp/015200405X/ref=sr_1_2?ie=UTF8&qid=1485829327&sr=8–2&keywords=aida+leontyne+price (Accessed January 30, 2017).

28. Alan Nagler, *Misdirection: Opera Production in the Twentieth Century* (Hamden, CT: Archon Books, 1981), 89.

29. Ibid., 90.

30. Paul Robinson, "Is *Aida* an Orientalist Opera?" in *Opera, Sex, and Other Vital Matters* (Chicago: University of Chicago Press, 2002), 124.

31. Ibid., 124. This is Robinson's definition of Said's theory of orientalism.

32. Ibid., 124–25.

33. Anthony Arblaster, *Politics in Opera* (London: Verso, 1992).

34. Robinson, "Orientalist Opera," 127.

35. Description of *Aida* (1990) as told by Leontyne Price, from http://amazon.com

36. Langston Hughes, "Note on Commercial Theater," in *The Collected Poems of Langston Hughes*, edited by Arnold Rampersad (New York: Vintage Classics, 1995), 215–16.

Chapter 13

Image and Verse, Music and Media
Diasporic Performance of Cultural Memory

Lyrics and music appear in the literary canon in the folk origins of African verse, work songs, spirituals, blues, and jazz as expressions of a literary and aesthetic ethos of survival. This legacy continues in the lyrics and music of rap/hip-hop. In an additional formation, the literary intersects with popular culture, autobiographical living history, and shared diaspora heroics. Prioritizing the African-centered framework that considers Pan-Africanism—unity, cooperation, and mutual identification—as a functional and meaningful practice in contemporary Black life, this chapter is a media and communication-framed content analysis of the cross-fertilization of autobiography and heroics between Black America, the Caribbean, and France regarding Malcolm X as an icon in music beyond the canon's sense of his poetics. Stimulated by Afro-European rap music's postmodern addition of symbolic visual imagery to lyrics, this chapter is a study of the diasporan implications of shared heroics. It encourages an exploration of practices of Pan-Africanism and transnationalism that account for similarity as well as difference in the cultures, languages, and philosophies of the diaspora, and the research explores the cross-fertilization of legacy, heroics, and ancestors sustained by images and lyrics of rap/hip-hop performance with chartable paths between Africa, the Americas, and Europe.

Scholars such as Marc Perry have comprehensively articulated this phenomenon from the vantage point, not of Africana Studies literary and textual aesthetics, but from anthropology and hip-hop performance studies. This chapter is in conversation with Perry's observations about the cache of hip-hop in the "international marketplace [and how] it has retained a critical capacity to convey a signifying blackness of aesthetic form and emotive force."[1]

Perry's approach is not antithetical to traditional literary categorizations of lyrics and performance. *Call and Response: The Riverside Anthology* (1998) includes not only the raw forms of contemporary lyrical traditions such as proverbs, epic narratives, praise poems about epic heroes, and toasts, but also lyrics from rhythm and blues and rap. "Rap Lyrics" appear in the section representing 1960 to the present under the description "Folk Call for Social Revolution and Political Strategy." *The Norton Anthology of African American Literature* (2004) includes some of these lyrical forms under the heading "Secular Rhymes and Songs, Ballads, Work Songs, and Songs of Social Change" with less emphasis on specific African lyrical forms in its narrative. *Norton* also has a section on hip-hop included in its sampling of "The Vernacular Tradition." Linking contemporary categories of rap and hip-hop included in the canon by two major literary anthologies, Africana Studies introductory volumes such as Manning Marable's *The New Black Renaissance: The SOULS Anthology of Critical African American Studies* (2005) devotes a section to "The Hip-Hop Nation" whose conversations on U.S.-based rap and hip-hop are even extended in discussions that appear in the collections section on "Transnational Blackness." There is no doubt that the contemporary musical genres are documented in the literary canon and as a core topic in the discipline of Africana Studies.

The transcendence of this chapter is its capacity to extend the transnational discourse on African American vernacular and lyrical traditions with two interventions. The first is the addition of visual imagery that symbolizes features of the African American literary canon including what both the *Riverside* and *Norton* anthologies categorize within frameworks of the social, political, revolutionary, and change-oriented traditions. The second is the addition of the transnational with respect to borrowed and shared traditions. These culminate in the uses of the persona of Malcolm X, who Joanne V. Gabbin in her entry to the genre of African American poetry in *The Oxford Companion to African American Literature* (1997), highlights as a catalyst for a "furious flowering" that is now both national and international. In these contexts of the canon and its shifts as the discipline's approach to the literary enterprise opens up new and expanded spaces to accommodate layered discourses, the French-Haitian rap artist Kery James's music video for the song "A L'Ombre du Show Business" (translated as "In the Shadow of Show Business") initiates a conversation in which the literary intersects with media, popular culture, autobiographical living history, and shared diaspora iconography and heroics.

The world knows Malcolm X. He is an icon. In the French-language music video for James's song "A L'ombre" featuring Charles Aznevour, a frame of the video flashes the image of Malcolm X. In the United States as well as abroad, popular songs with popular music videos receive consistent and cyclical air time. In the case of James's video, it received significant air time during its prime, and it became a phenomenon to African American visitors to Paris who kept seeing the image of Malcolm X flash across the television screen. The image of an African American heroic figure in a Haitian-French music video suggests a space for inquiry about the transmission of hero dynamics between regions of the diaspora, in this case from the United States to Europe. There is already a significant sharing of Pan-African legacy figures such as Toussaint Louverture, Marcus Garvey, Claude McKay, Josephine Baker, Bob Marley, and Haile Selassie, who are classic and pervasive traditional representatives of the African world in spite of geographical distances between Africa, the Caribbean, the United States, and Europe. Thus, in the traditional engagement of a synthesis of lyrics, music, and images, there is a precedent for international, transatlantic, or Pan-African shared iconography that is an expansion of rhetorical and literary discourses as well as sociopolitical activism.

Another variable is the fact that the African-French populations represent France, the Caribbean, Canada, and Africa, so charting the routes of icon influence may not be a concise exercise. Interrogating routes and the meaning of borrowed icons is based on studies on and applications of representation, migration, globalization, cultural production, national character, and cultural signifying. This project has comparative potential for other regional points of view and relies on multi-modal research to excavate sources and data. Thus, the methodology for this is an exploratory survey of written and oral historical, cultural, popular historical, media, and film sources on the African European diaspora that insinuates a sense of intersection with Africana traditions ranging from the literary, to the cultural, to the sociopolitical.

Malcolm X is a figure in Black cultural memory whose heroic ascendancy is widely documented. Generations have used their literary art forms to capture and perpetuate Malcolm's legacy. Scholars view Malcolm's legacy as the embodiment of an African American retention of the West African funeral dirge tradition. These types of contemporary theorizations of the diaspora's memorialization behaviors align with the intellectual genealogy of cultural and scholarly iterations of Malcolm's appeal and value. Joanne V. Gabbin emphasizes Larry Neal's observation that Malcolm,

> touched all aspects of contemporary Black nationalism, and his life became a symbol and inspiration.[2]

She adds,

> With his words resonating in their consciousness and his image inspiring a revolutionary world vision, poets such as David Henderson, James A. Emmanuel, Robert Hayden, and Etheridge Knight paid tribute to him after his death.[3]

Malcolm's image as *symbol* continues to have a pronounced national and global appeal in the contemporary era.

Malcolm's appeal is about the power his legacy holds for modes of story-telling that are deliberate practices of immortalization. Malcolm's image and story are powerful because they are reminders of a chronicle of the hero's path from unfavorable or negative responses to oppression to his transformation into a nobler, more effective consciousness of revolutionary and honorable behavior and activism.

The artist Kery James's use of Malcolm X as a *visual* indicator, and the discovery of his and other French rappers' inclusion of Malcolm X in their diasporic memorial repertoire to the extent that they include him as a reference and resource in their contemporary modes of oral storytelling, are reinforcing additions to lyrical, performance, and popular culture intersections of the literary canon. They help to extend the range, scope, and application beyond original U.S.-based cultural and geographical frames of reference.

Alix Mathurin, the Guadeloupan-born rapper of Haitian parents, known since 1992 as Kery James, was raised in the Orly suburb of Paris. He has participated in the French rap scene since the age of thirteen and has been considered the country's premier rapper. Raised in a largely Muslim suburb, James converted to Islam shortly after his close friend La Montana was shot and killed. Although he took a brief hiatus from rap music, he returned in 1999 with a solo album. Over his three solo albums, his themes range from topics concerning his African roots, society's problems, moral values, politics, and the Iraq war, to the media. He is generally characterized as having a militant side, even though he has also shown a milder side, collaborating with popular French performers in nontraditional musical alliances. For the track "A L'Ombre du Show Business" he collaborates with Charles Aznevour, an elderly French chanson star who echoes James's lamentation that show business, with its market concerns and exploitative nature, stunts the creativity and poetics of passionate artistic youth and performers.

Andre Prévos describes the nature of show business in the context of 1990s French rap. As of 2001, French and Francophone rap were "well into its second decade," and Prévos characterizes its three phases as (1) borrowing from African American rap forms and distribution models in the suburbs of Paris; (2) adopting "most of the attitudes, repertoires, and musical and performance techniques" of U.S. models; and (3) adopting *some* of the "ideals, theories, and techniques" of the African American model.[4] His observation that French rappers "saw themselves as voices of criticism of French society at large and of the establishment" informs his impression that "their search for social relevancy and artistic activism . . . made them aware of the dual role of the media. Television and show business have seldom helped rap artists, tending instead to favor more popular forms of musical entertainment."[5] James's "L'Ombre" is an accusation of these practices.

Felicia McCarren deciphers the unique history of hip-hop dance in France, which is state supported, and she suggests an emerging commercialization. There is no dance in James's 2008 video that decries the commercialization of the youth's performance aspirations, but McCarren's review of the stages toward commercialization is informative. She writes:

> Discourses articulated in the ongoing debates surrounding hip-hop always engage the vocabulary of social action, antidiscrimination, cultural cultivation of the working class, and elaboration of a popular form into art, revealing dance's place in French culture as something crucial to political and social well-being, capable of doing social good and worthy of tax dollars. With a very different ambiance from U. S. rap music and its commercial culture, it provides a site for refection and discussions about race and class, opportunity and hard work, and professionalism and the right to artistic self-development; and it is only now beginning to be exploited for its commercial possibilities.[6]

The seven to seven years between McCarren's observation and James's "L'Ombre" apparently reflect a period of greater exploitation of rap and hip-hop for commercial possibilities, and Aznevour's corroboration and encouragement within the song are testament that the pairing has the objective of inspiring greater artistic freedom for French youth. T. Cokes's (1996) digital video "No sell out (overture): I wnt 2 B th ultimate commodity/ machine," though a U.S.-based analysis, describes Malcolm X as "the serialized signifier that sparks problematic readings and profits in rap music, political art, and fashionable sportswear," which could be related to James's symbolic use of Malcolm's image in his scathing critique of show business, and this is related to James's critique in "L'Ombre."[7] An updated description of his projects describes it as follows: "Using a pulsing rock soundtrack and music video-style editing, Tony Cokes combines archival footage of Malcolm X, advertisements, and corporate logos in *No Sell Out* to provide a scathing commentary on commodity culture."[8]

The lyrics of "L'Ombre de Show Business" indicate a passion and fervor that relate to the legacy of Malcolm X, who is also a frequently mentioned and powerful ancestor in the U.S. rap tradition.[9] In "L'Ombre" James sings about rappers being "heirs" of a universal, urban, and human poetry and of a memory archive bearing witness to the present as well as the past. His references to the urban ethos and to the linkages to the past summon the spirit of Malcolm. The image invoking Malcolm (appearing at 1:09/4:07 of the video) is an imitation of a classic photograph of Malcolm X taken in 1964 by John Launois of Black Star enterprises. When James features Malcolm's trademark image in his video, it accompanies a lyric that speaks about the artist's ability to practice a sad and infamous art whose music enables the ghetto to rise up. This chapter contends that such an image as media is simultaneously text, history, a postmodern image as code, rap symbolism, musical sound, and an abstract reference to cultural memory interpreted by diverse global citizens who are acquainted with Malcolm's formal and informal life narratives. As the final chapter of this book, such an analysis is a propos in its merging of traditional and contemporary forms of texts.

Scholars characterize Malcolm's value based on his standard of using "language and logic" in a poetic, revolutionary way. In *Kawaida and Questions of Life and Struggle* (2008), Maulana Karenga writes: "It is Malcolm who taught that the logic of the oppressed cannot be the logic of the oppressor if liberation is to be achieved (Malcolm X, *Lectures at Harvard*) . . . Malcolm's concern [is] essentially a call for liberational logic, but also for a liberational language. For thinking freely requires a language of freedom."[10] Godwin Ohiwerei describes Malcolm's internationalism when he writes, "people of African descent have not heeded the call of Malcolm X for a close relationship in order to internationalize the plight of Africans on the continent and those in the African diaspora. The continued marginalization of the condition of Black people on the international level calls for the type of leadership that is not ethnic but global in ideology"[11]

James is different from traditional rappers, primarily U.S. rappers, who have referenced Malcolm in their lyrics or sampled his voice in rap songs. James's use is of Malcolm's image as a visual signifier, and this image representation without lyrical reference suggests that James expects his viewers to be familiar with Malcolm's visual iconography, which is a dynamic expectation. This is a standard approach to interpreting what, at first, appears to be an isolated visual representation on an African American iconic figure. However, this visual code flashing is symbolic and meaningful enough to inspire research and analysis based on contemporary Africana theoretical awareness of cultural symbolism and iconography. To make ultimate sense of the coded image in "L'Ombre," modern cyber and digital capabilities enable academic and Internet-based popular study of the phenomenon in two languages—English and French—in order to discern James's personal and/or video team's decisions and expectations regarding using Malcolm's image.

Initially, the strength of Malcolm's appeal seemed to be based on possible linkages between James's national origins and religion. Like Malcolm, James is also a Muslim. In addition, James's Haitian heritage indicates a cultural identity that is attentive to Caribbean versions of Black nationalism surrounding the ongoing pride of Toussaint Louverture, Jean-Jacques Dessalines, and the iconography and heroics of the 1791–1804 Haitian Revolution that ushered in Haiti's early independence. Black Arts poets from the United States proclaimed that death placed Malcolm among such heroes, exclaiming, "Toussaint, Dessalines! Marcus! Patrice!/Behold this man./

Gone. Delivered."[12] Literary scholar Antonio Tillis also historicizes Malcolm's connections to the Caribbean:

> Malcolm's message advocated the unification of Blacks in the Western Hemisphere as he equated the struggles of Blacks in the United States with those of African descent in Central America, South America, and the rest of North America. He further stated that persons of African heritage inhabiting the "Americas" as well as the Caribbean island-nations (or the West Indies) were "Afro-Americans." Indeed, he stressed that such inclusiveness was appropriate because those designated "Afro-American" represented a people bound by the African blood forging through their veins and by the collective struggle to dismantle white oppression for the purpose of Black liberation. Malcolm's broadening of the definition of "Afro-American" created a space for those of African ancestry outside the United States. His inclusion of Caribbean island-nations allowed critics of his sociopolitical thought to include spaces such as the Caribbean islands Hispaniola, home to Haiti and the Dominican Republic.[13]

In examining Malcolm's legacy in globalizing African American thought, Ohiwerei writes specifically about Malcolm's visit to Paris:

> When Malcolm traveled to Paris, he called on the Afro-American community in France and other parts of Europe to unite with the African community—a message that was consistent in his speeches during the later part of his life. . . . He was able to understand that there were people outside the United States with similar problems of subordination. He therefore issued a call for the marginalized peoples of the world to support each other in order to achieve global socioeconomic emancipation.[14]

So, there are multiple routes that are suggestive of the meaning and indications of James's use of Malcolm X. However, after studying multiple versions of James's online biographical sketches, there is a greater similarity between him and Malcolm based on James's 1999–2001 withdrawal from the rap scene and his emergence which indicated a more spiritual and philosophical transformation that has infused his rap art with a depth beyond the profane militancy of his early years with the group Ideal J.

In analyses of Malcolm X's legacy on the international hip-hop scene, global studies of the proliferation of the art form address Malcolm's persona and legacy as represented in Islamic rap, British Asian hip-hop, hip-hop in Italy, and hip-hop in New Zealand.[15] One study, indirectly related to France but notable for its attention to Malcolm X's influence, is the essay "We Are Malcolm X!: Negu Gorriak, Hip-Hop, and the Basque Political Imagery" by Jacqueline Urla. Basque Country includes the French areas of Baxe-Nafarroa,

Lapurdi, and Zuberoa. The French part of Northern Basque Territory is the northern part of Euskal Herria. Though bordering France and using the Basque language instead of French, the ideological approach of the white European Basque language group Negu Gorriak is compatible with James's visual use of Malcolm X in "L'Ombre." Urla notes that "one of the distinctive features of this fiercely antistate, anticapitalist group was the way they drew upon the visual codes and musical forms of nation-conscious rappers in African American hip hop."[16] She couches the group's efforts within terminologies such as "cultural reconversion," "intercultural borrowing," and "cross-cultural borrowing."[17] She writes: "If cultural theorists' love affair with hybridity and transnationalism has taught us anything, it is that meanings do not reside solely in operations of the signs themselves. Rather, they are generated in the interactions that local actors, located in specific historical, cultural, and political circumstances, have with translocal and mass-marketed commodities, images, and processes."[18] Her concern for how "images, and signs of hip-hop acquire the social and political messages they do" is also the central question of James's use of the Malcolm X image in his video for "L'Ombre."[19]

Negu Gorriak has a track named after a slogan from Spike Lee's film *Malcolm X*—"We All Are Malcolm X." Urla suggests that the group's usage of the "nonwhite" is "as a symbol of the militant," and even their usage of the term "Afro-Basque" is a shared appreciation of passion rather than an imitative essentialism.[20] The group inevitably exhibits "a strategic deployment of signifiers" that Urla fully explicates, and as a by-product she introduces possibilities useful in understanding James's signification on Malcolm X's image without direct reference to Malcolm X in the lyrics. In fact, without the video image, listeners would not assume a relationship between Malcolm and "L'Ombre." However, Negu Gorriak borrows "from the iconography of black militancy . . . especially in their identifying symbol the X . . . Negu's visual borrowings transgress boundaries of the urban and the rural, first world and third world, and tradition and modernity to create a new hybridized context in which to articulate the group's concerns and alliances."[21]

Diaspora art studies offer additional angles of interpretation when viewing the aesthetic choices of James's video. Assessing meanings of visual representations and African aesthetics in diaspora art, Kobena Mercer evaluates signs and codes "that connect black people globally by way of an instantly recognizable badge of belonging."[22] This is an accurate description of what transpires when African Americans notice the quick image of a Malcolm X figure in James's "L'Ombre." Viewers struggle for interpretation of the culturally unfamiliar contexts of Black French experience and are forced to admit a "material entanglement of cultural identities"[23] in which Malcolm X is a borrowed international symbol by cultures that take Pan-African or revolutionary license to claim him as both symbol and ancestor.

However, as Ural and others have revealed, particularly in the context of globalized hip-hop, Malcolm's legacy is pervasive and is not exclusively owned by the Black U.S. community from which he emerged. This possibility holds new insight for the assumptions of African American cultural memory studies, adding a globalized and Pan-African context wherein icons and heroic figures are routinely adopted by other cultures that appropriate the figure's meaning in different ways. Mercer substantiates this aspect noting, "The main thread I want to pull out here is not that postcolonial hybridity is a uniform or universal experience for everyone in a given diaspora, but that the two-way process of cultural traffic is now increasingly understood not as special or exceptional but as an ordinary and normal aspect of everyday life."[24] This is an interpretive shift for national communities that expect to find uniform meaning in the appropriation of an image or symbol, whose use could be arbitrary or ornamental rather than reflective of deep structural and collective meaning. This relates to what Mercer defines as "the problem of the visual" which "in turn opens wider perspectives on the complexity of the diaspora's cultural history and highlights dilemmas regarding future possibilities in an era of global media culture."[25]

GLOBALIZING MALCOLM

A host of scholarship that associates Malcolm's legacy with people of African descent beyond U.S. borders, and the globalization of Malcolm's legacy has rich possibilities of germination among African Europeans whose heritages crisscross Africa and the diaspora. For example, Larry Ross examines the extent to which Malcolm appears in Internet sources and writes that "the Italian site Associazione Malcolm X (http://www.malcolmx.it) indicates the global appeal of Malcolm's message."[26] He also summarizes that standard search engine searches ensure that "researchers can find a wealth of information on the life and work of Malcolm X. As a result, they will find that Malcolm's legacy is global."[27] The process that Ross indicates has been invaluable to this study of discerning the meaning of James's use of the Malcolm image; however, Ross's study is not updated to include Malcolm's pervasiveness in European and international rap.

The Internet functions as globalization's primary research vehicle, enabling the transmission of raw data, though not necessarily scholarship. Scholarship on James's art form is elusive, yet an eclectic series of sources contribute to a transnational narrative of cultural exchange.[28] There is an early example of Malcolm's meaning for James in the 1998 song "Hardcore" that he performed with the group Ideal J. There are at least three versions of the music video. One is a classic military combat zone themed visual narrative that shows James and the members of Ideal J trekking across a dusty battle zone in military-green combat attire. As an older song, its lyrics are difficult to locate in the databases that house James's more recent songs. However, in this video, he speaks a quick verse linking the 1960s, Malcolm X, and Tupac. He and Ideal J throw a Black Power fist in the air to emphasize this reference.

In the second, more explicit version of the video "Hardcore," there are English subtitles. This version has profanity and sexually explicit and gruesome images that help emphasize the group's theme that the society of the world is narcissistic, nihilistic, oppressive, and dysfunctional, or *Hardcore*. The images in this version of the video represent a digitized live performance juxtaposed with a generous set of current-event media images of the song's topics, including sequences of heroes and antiheroes mentioned by name in the song. This image shows a sample from one of Malcolm X's speeches (1:39/5:11) with the translation "Hardcore, the violent end of the course of Malcolm X." The third version of the video is a collaboration with African American rapper Method Man, and his English-rap is dubbed over the segments of Ideal J's original lyrics that reference Malcolm. So, while an academic critique is not available, the raw data of the Internet gives clues that can satisfy the inquiry.

Another reference to James's use of Malcolm X appears in the message boards of http://www.rap2k.com, and this conversation links James with the Arab French rapper Médine. A narrative from Médine appeared in *Time* (Europe) in late 2005 as a response to the riots that erupted in France. Médine's observations characterize the Arab, Black, and Asian experiences in France. He says:

People like me—the descendants of immigrants, whether Arab, black or Asian—are turning to our roots and embracing our heritage. . . . But people of my generation are not shy about embracing their heritage and far from seeking invisibility we're standing up to denounce the prejudice and injustice we face. . . . The people who live in projects like those where last week's riots raged are treated as second-class citizens. We have less access to the rights and services of the republic—schools are run down; job opportunities are remote. . . . Before September 11, I would have said this was a kind of residual racism. The problems people had with us were due to our ethnicity, our skin color. Today, with many young people returning to religion as they start searching for their own identities, faith is becoming the difference that's most often pointed out. I'm not just a black guy or an Arab anymore; I'm a Muslim. And that's a code word for alien, someone who's determined not to fit in.[29]

It is no surprise, then, that Médine's 2008 video for "Lecture aléatoire" (trans. Random Reading or Uncertain Perusal) features the hero dynamic of another U.S. hero, Muhammad Ali, as Médine wears an Ali sweatshirt amid a boxing theme that suggests the fight that youth of his culture must wage for freedom and self-expression. A highlight of the video that was the primary consideration of the message boards is Médine's tribute to Kery James in the lyrics and in the video. He sings words of militancy, defiance, honor, and tribute in a Malcolm-esque tone, and likens James to the heroics of Malcolm X. James also appears in approximately 30 seconds of the video (3:50 to 4:19/5:02). It is of note that even though James does not mention Malcolm X by name in "A L'Ombre du Show Business," it is the visual symbolic image in the song's music video that instigates this study. Retracing the visual image leads to a discovery of the artist's—James's—consciousness. The evidence that Malcolm X also appears by name (and not only image as in "L'Ombre") in the artist's previous work and in tribute validates this as a successful inquiry, appropriately reading the signs and codes of transnational cultural aesthetics.

Inevitably, this reading of practices in Black French rap reveals the power of the diaspora's sharing of cultural legacy through visual codes and iconic references in media. It affirms the global appeal and value of Malcolm X as an African American icon and as global inspiration. Returning to the literary dimension of this broad study, U.S. Black Arts movement poets were the first to chronicle Malcolm's legacy in lyric and verse, with the publication of *For Malcolm: Poems on the Life and the Death of Malcolm X* (1969), and they even globalized him in the canon. It is no wonder that diaspora and global rappers also know a similar image like the one Black Arts poets captured regarding Malcolm's relationship to conquering the challenges of hostile urban settings, his international appeal, and his spiritual ascendance and legacy, which survive as his global appeal and power today. The poetic memorials to Malcolm's global identity and appeal stabilize Malcolm's place in not only the literary canon but also in its cross-media formats that expand the implications of the canon to the visual, audio, digital, and cyber. The multidimensionality of the discipline of Africana Studies permits a transcendence in which the literary conversation is extended to account for diverse borrowing, adaptation, genre transition, and global cultural encounters and exchanges that retain the historical genealogy of the culture's creative production and reinforce the discipline's *atmosphere of freedom*.

NOTES

1. Marc D. Perry, "Global Black Self-Fashioning: Hip Hop as Diasporic Space," *Identities: Global Studies in Culture and Power* 15.6 (2008), 635–664.

2. Qtd. in Joanne V. Gabbin, "Furious Flower," in *The Oxford Companion to African American Literature*, edited by Wiliam L. Andrews, Trudier Harris, and Frances Smith Foster (New York: Oxford UP, 1997), 589.

3. Ibid.

4. Andre M. Prévos, "Postcolonial Popular Music in Frnace," in *Global Noise: Rap and Hip-Hop Outside the USA*, edited by Tony Mitchell (Middletown, CT: Wesleyan UP, 2001), 50.

5. Ibid.

6. Felicia McCarren, "Monsiuer Hip-Hop," in *Blackening Europe: The African American Presence*, edited by Heike Raphael (New York: Routledge, 2004), 158.

7. Tony Cokes, "No sell out (overture): I wnt 2 B th ultimate commodity/machine," http://www.vdb.org/titles/no-sell-out [Formerly but now removed from the Internet: "No sell out (overture): I wnt 2 B th ultimate commodity/machine. http://www.vdb.org/smackn.acgi$tapedetail?NOSELLOUT] (Accessed February 28, 2005).

8. Website description of Tony Cokes, "No Sell Out" http://www.vdb.org/titles/no-sell-out (Accessed January 29, 2017).

9. Rap artists and groups including Public Enemy, KRS-I, The Roots, Arrested Development, Tupac Shakur, and DJ Kool have referenced Malcolm in their lyrics and commentary.

10. Maulana Karenga, *Kawaida and Questions of Life and Struggle* (Los Angeles: University of Sankore Press, 2008), 8.

11. Godwin Ohiwerei, "Globalizing African American Political Thought," in *Malcolm X: An Historical Reader*, edited by James L. Conyers and Andrew P. Smallwood (Durham: Carolina Academic Press, 2008), 336.

12. Julia Fields, "Since Malcolm Died," in *For Malcolm: Poems on the Life and Death of Malcolm X*, edited by Dudley Randall and Margaret Burroughs (Detroit: Broadside Press, 1969), 34.

13. Antonio Tillis, "Malcolm X-isms and the Protest Poetry of Blas Jiménez: Liberation By Any Means Necessary," in *Malcolm X: An Historical Reader*, edited by James L. Conyers and Andrew Smallwood (Durham: Carolina Academic Press, 2008), 316.

14. Ohiwerei, "Globalizing," 334.

15. See multiple essays in Tony Mitchell's *Global Noise* including "Islamic HipHop Versus Islamaphobia" by Aki Nawaz and Natacha Atlas Akhenaton.

16. Jacqueline Urla, "We Are All Malcolm X: Negu Gorriak, Hip-Hop, and the Basque Political Imagery," in *Global Noise: Rap and Hip Hop Outside the USA*, edited by Tony Mitchell (Middletown, CT: Wesleyan UP, 2001), 171.

17. Ibid., 173.

18. Ibid.

19. Ibid.

20. Ibid., 180–81.

21. Ibid., 183.

22. Kobena Mercer, "Diasporic Aesthetics and Visual Culture," in *Black Cultural Traffic:Crossorads in Global Performance and Popular Culture*, edited by Harry J. Elam and Kevin Jackson (Ann Arbor: University of Michigan Press, 2005), 143.

23. Ibid.

24. Ibid., 145.

25. Ibid., 153.

26. Larry Ross, "Malcolm X: Internet Resources and Digital Media," in *Malcolm X: An Historical Reader*, edited by James L. Conyers and Andrew P. Smallwood (Durham: Carolina Academic Press, 2008), 264.

27. Ibid., 265.

28. Lyric storehouse websites are helpful because one can locate the full text of the lyrics of "L'Ombre" that permit translations and the ability to examine the lyrics for context and codes related to Malcolm. The video-sharing website "http://youtube.com" and message boards, in particular, written mostly in French, were the most helpful. On YouTube, I was able to locate the version of the video "L'Ombre" that I first witnessed by accident in Paris. There were other versions, including live performances and conversations between James and Aznevour.

29. Médine, "How Much More French Can I Be?" *Time* (Europe), November 6, 2005. http://content.time.com/time/magazine/article/0,9171,1126720,00.html (Accessed January 30, 2017).

Conclusion

An Atmosphere of Freedom

This book illuminates—using James Baldwin's words—the "atmosphere of freedom" and the "transcendence" enabled by what we now frame in Africana Studies critical approaches to literary criticism, literary phenomena, and African American life and experience. The language of "an atmosphere of freedom" and "transcendence" are conceptual treasures from Baldwin's essay "Color," published in *Esquire* in December 1962. His treatise on the "warm and quick and vital" and "rainbow" qualities of Black life that the world overlooks in its easy assumptions has a timelessness as we read it in dutiful survey. It empowers the positioning of this book's ideas which redirect the assumptions about the Africana disciplinary literary enterprise by modeling how professionally trained Africologists (practitioners of centered Africana Studies) think and problem-solve, view knowledge-formation, manage the traditions of the past, and embrace critical and intellectual innovation including providing a holistic understanding of the African-centered past as a resource. Its mix of theoretical, interpretive, anecdotal, and empirical styles of idea formation is intended for academic and lay readers who want to better understand the critical multidimensionality of the discipline.

Describing the literary enterprise of the discipline of Africana Studies as "an atmosphere of freedom" also reflects a generational shift wherein the discipline is responsible for the management and institutionalization of its literary enterprise within the domains of the discipline. This book is a seminal contribution to such stabilization, with the added dimension of indicating Africana phenomenology in literature. Even in the literary enterprise, scholars have the ability to explore the meaning and function of phenomena in cultural and racial worldviews related to people of African descent in a variety of contexts in order to draw conclusions and to apply knowledge for social, political, psychological, and community-based problem solving.

An approach centered on transcendence pays homage to works and efforts that came before it. As a contemporary iteration of the pioneering edited collection of Blackshire-Belay's *Language and Literature in the African American Imagination* (1992), a concluding note benefits from acknowledging that the collection heralded some of the most powerful language announcing the Afrocentric effect on literature, especially with Blackshire-Belay's introduction, "Afrocentricity and Literary Theory: The Maturing Imagination." She writes, "We are transformed by openness to change, by proactive creation by the new, the novel, the useful."[1] She also makes one of the earliest cases for how Africology informs literary practice:

> Including writers from literature, philosophy, linguistics, communication, and Africology, this volume has attempted to combine a broad outline of the issues within the centered structure of the emerging themes in literature and language in the African American community. It is a decidedly Afrocentric project in the sense that it devotes considerable space to theoretical ideas and concepts that explore African Americans as subjects of historical experiences rather than as subsets of other worldviews or perspectives.[2]

A measure of the growth of the Africana literary enterprise since Blackshire-Belay's precursory volume is embedded in the pages of this book as a quantifiable expansion of disciplinary specificity. It also pairs nicely with other self-consciously disciplinary sources such as *Literary Spaces: Introduction to Comparative Black Literature* that frame the comprehensiveness of literary study institutionalized from the domain of Africana Studies.

One of the most pressing objectives for scholars who practice in the Africana literary enterprise is to create theory to sustain and advance the discipline of Africana Studies. If one practices in the discipline, then one should publish in the discipline. Thus, disciplinary specificity is a requirement for institutionalizing Africana literary practices.

A central point at the root of the processes of the Africana literary enterprise is clarifying to what extent the discipline of Africana Studies bears responsibility for acquainting society with the literary canon in a linear curriculum. It certainly contributes and even bears much responsibility, especially in spaces where the English department is not committed to African American literature. The canon is important and the anthologies that convey it, as well as the comprehensive African American literary tradition, are not much conversant with disciplinary parameters of Africana Studies. As an intervention, a transcendent approach in conversation with the canon and the literary tradition meets the need as both a standalone or supplemental volume that instigates many of the shifts in reading and worldview that help place the literature in an Africana context. Traditional English-based literary practices often stop short of teaching Africana Studies disciplinary contexts, even though both enterprises overlap. This is a vital demarcation that underlies this book's necessity to include canon discourse in each chapter.

Defining and expanding the scope of the Africana literary enterprise's specificity is about stabilizing the discipline, reminding readers of the atmosphere of freedom within this disciplinary space, and clarifying the expectation that, in its highest form of practice, while teaching literature we are also responsible for teaching the discipline. This book's audience includes all literary and cultural studies practitioners, many of whom may be surprised by or enlightened by the way the discipline of Africana Studies encourages multidimensionality, or *aggressive interdisciplinarity*, in textual analysis, conceptualization, criticism, effect, and application. The outcomes inspired by this enterprise's atmosphere of freedom are cause for celebration as this book anticipates literary growth on behalf of Africana Studies (anticipating new journals, new courses, more dedicated experts, and robust disciplinary-centered theorization) and with respect to clarifying for collaborating practitioners from other disciplines how Africana literary experts conceptualize our own work within the academy's autonomous and shared spaces.

The discourses on proximity to and redirection away from the canon help to advance these objectives, and at some point practitioners should confer on expectations of scope and domain. For example, mature Africana Studies departments and programs should not be expected to manage merely offerings of introductory and chronological literary traditions. Instead, and optimally, Africana Studies departments are tasked with creating and managing courses that permit the literary enterprise to function as a creative signification on many unified components, including formalist features of aesthetics and writing as well as the discipline's paradigms and priorities. It cannot be taken for granted that one discipline's course meets the standards of another discipline, and healthy cross-listings and clarifying syllabi accommodate the differentials.

One dozen familiar African American texts stabilize this book. The analyses not only treat the texts properly as creative and structured literature, but they also gift to readers a taste of Africana Studies in topics of masculinity, male mortality, Black male studies, Black Lives Matters, humor, Pan-Africanism, transnationalism, cultural negotiation of worldview, the subject place of Africa, cultural mythology, hero dynamics, Black psychology, measures of African worldview, demographics, Ancient African history, early Black studies curricula, the blues, Black liberation theology, cultural conceptualization of God and the afterlife, eulogy, impermanent mortality, Afrofuturism, the Kemetic principle of Maat, gender roles and identity, social and ethical measures of justice, the continuum of Black women's experience, rap and hip-hop, historicizing Broadway's Africana-adjacent performances, and global intersections of performance culture and icons. These topics cover most formally articulated subject areas in Africana Studies, and this expansive list models a central inquiry in Africana literary practices which is, "What do we *do, after* we read?" This question and its answers, many of which this book has attempted to model, are loaded with discipline-based imperatives such as Africana cognitive reading, disciplinary competency, reader-response, applied functionality, dutiful survey, and phenomena pairing, all of which imply a critical, transcendent *process* at work in the Africana literary enterprise.

NOTES

1. Aisha Blackshire-Belay, Introduction to *Language and Literature in the African American Imagination* (Westport, CT: Greenwood Press, 1992), 7.
    2. Ibid., 202.

Bibliography

Adams, Anne. "'Literary Pan-Africanism.' *Africa and Its Significant Others: Forty Years of Intercultural Entanglement.*" Ed. Isabel Hoving, Frans-Willem Korsten, and Ernst van Alphen. New York: Rodopi, 11, 2003.

Adams, Barbara Eleanor. *John Henrik Clarke: Master Teacher.* Brooklyn: A&B Publication Group, 2000.

Adichie, Chimimanda Ngozi. *Americanah.* New York, Alfred A. Knopf, 2013.

Aidoo, Ama Ata. *Dilemma of a Ghost.* Accra: Longman, 1965.

Akbar, Na'im. *Visions for Black Men.* Tallahassee: Mind Productions and Associates, Inc., 1992. viii.

Anderson, Reynaldo and Charles E. Jones, *Afrofuturism 2.0: The Rise of Afro-Blackness.* Lanham, MD: Lexington Books, 2016.

Arblaster, Anthony Arblaster. *Politics in Opera.* London: Verso, 1992.

Armah, Ayi Kwei. *Osiris Rising: A Novel of Africa Past, Present and Future.* Pompenguine, West Africa: Per Ankh, 1995.

Asante, Molefi K. *The Afrocentric Idea.* Philadelphia: Temple University Press, 1998.

———. *Kemet, Afrocentricity and Knowledge.* Trenton: Africa World Press, 1992.

———. "African Betrayals and African Recovery for a New Future." In *Africa in the 21st Century*, edited by Ama Mazama. New York: Routledge, 2007.

———. *An Afrocentric Manifesto: Toward an African Renaissance*, 2007.

Asante, Molefi Kete and Maulana Karenga. *Handbook of Black Studies.* SAGE Publications, 2004.

Assman, Jan. Introduction. *Maat: The Moral Ideal in Ancient Egypt* by Maulana Karenga. Los Angeles: University of Sankore Press, 2006.

Awkward, Michael. "Manhood." *The Oxford Companion to African American Literature.* Ed. William L. Andrews, Frances Smith Foster, and Trudier Harris. New York: Oxford UP, 1997: 475.

Bailey, Constance, "Fight the Power: African American Humor as a Discourse of Resistance. *The Western Journal of Black Studies* 36.4 (2012): 253–263.

Bambara, Toni Cade, ed. *The Black Woman: An Anthology.* New York: New American Library, 1970.

Bell, Bernard W. *The Afro-American Novel and Its Tradition.* Amherst: University of Massachusetts Press, 1987.

————. *The Contemporary African American Novel: Its Folk Roots and Modern Literary Branches.* Amherst: University of Massachusetts Press, 2004.

Belton, Don, Ed. *Speak My Name: Black Men on Masculinity and the American Dream.* New York, Beacon, 1996.

Berrian, Brenda. "The Afro-American-West African Marriage Question: Its Literary and Historical Contexts." *African Literature Today* 15 (1987): 162–59.

Bess-Montgomery, Georgene. *The Spirit and the Word: A Theory of Spirituality in Africana Literary Criticism.* Trenton: Africa World Press, 2008.

Blackshire-Belay, Aisha. *Language and Literature in the African American Imagination.* Westport, CT: Greenwood Press, 1992.

Booker, Christopher B. *I Will Wear No Chain!: A Social History of African-American Males.* New York: Praeger, 2000.

Bourne, St. Clair. *Paul Robeson: Here I Stand.* New York: Eagle Rock Entertainment, 1999.

Bragg, Beauty. *Reading Contemporary African American Literature: Black Women's Popular Fiction, Post-Civil Rights Experience, and the African American Canon.* Lanham, MD: Lexington Books, 2015.

Brooks, Wanda and Susan Browne, "Toward a Culturally Situated Reader Response Theory," *Children's Literature in Education* 43.1 (2012): 74–85.

Brown, Stephanie and Keith Clark. "Melodrama of Beset Black Manhood?: Meditations on African-American Masculinity as Scholarly Topos and Social Menace." *Callaloo* 26.3 (2003): 732–37.

Brown, Sterling A., Arthur P. Davis, and Ulysses Lee. *The Negro Caravan: Writings by American Negroes.* New York: Arno Press, 1969.

Bruce, La Marr Jurelle. "The People Inside My Head, Too": Madness, Black Womanhood, and the Radical Performance of Lauryn Hill." *African American Review* 45.3 (2012): 371–89.

Butler, Octavia. *Parable of the Sower.* New York: Aspect/Warner Books, 1993.

————. *The Parable of the Talents.* New York: Warner Books, 1998.

————. "Science Fiction Writer Octavia Butler on Race, Global Warming and Religion," https://www.democracynow.org/2005/11/11/science_fiction_writer_octavia_butler_on (Accessed 12/13/16).

————. *Wild Seed.* New York: Grand Central Publishing, 2001.

Cannon, Uzzie T. "Tears, Fears, and Queers: Transgendering Black Masculinity in Daniel Black's *Perfect Peace*," *College English Association, CEA Critic* 78.1 (2016): 45–58.

Cappiccie, Amy, Janice Chadha, Muh Bi Lin and Frank Snyder. "Using Critical Race Theory to Analyze How Disney Constructs Diversity: A Construct for the Baccalaureate Human Behavior in the Social Environment Curriculum," *Journal of Teaching in Social Work* 32.1 (2012): 46–61.

Carpio, Glenda R. "Humor in African American Literature," In *A Companion to Afri-cana American Literature*, edited by Gene Andrew Jarrett. 315–331. Malden, MA: Blackwell Publishing, 2010.

Carr, Gregg and Dana A. Williams. "Toward the Theoretical Practice of Conceptual Liberation: Using an Africana Studies Approach to Reading African Literary Texts." In *Contemporary African American Literature: The Living Canon*, edited by Lovalerie King and Shirley Moody-Turner. 302–327. Bloomington: Indiana University Press, 2013.

Cella, Matthew and Allen Neuhauser. "Race and Homicide in America by the Numbers," *US News and World Reports*. September 9, 2016. http://www.usnews.com/news/articles/2016–09–29/race-and-homicide-in-america-by-the-numbers (Accessed 1/03/17).

Childress, Alice and Trudier Harris. *Like One of the Family: Conversations from a Domestic's Life*. 1956. New York: Beacon, 1986.

Christensen, Donna. "Ogling Olga," accessed February 28, 2005. Accessed February 28, 2005. www.cafemo.com/donna/ogling.html/.

Clabough, Casey Howard. "Afrocentric Recolonization: Gayl Jones's 1990s Fiction." *Contemporary Literature* 46.2 (2005): 243–273.

Clarke, John Henrik. "The Boy Who Painted Christ Black." *The Pittsburgh Courier* 29 January 1949: 17.

Coates, Ta-Nehisi. "The Case for Reparations." Accessed December 12, 2016. http://www.theatlantic.com/magazine/archive/2014/06/the-case-for-reparations/361631/.

Cokes, T. (1996). "No sell out (overture): I wnt 2 B th ultimate commod-ity/ machine." Accessed October 2, 2008. http://www.vdb.org/smackn.acgi$tapedetail?NOSELLOUT.

Collins, Julia C. *The Curse of Caste; or The Slave Bride*. 1865. Edited by William L. Andrews and Mitch Kachun. New York: Oxford UP, 2006.

Cone, James. *A Black Theology of Liberation*. 1970. Maryknoll, NY: Orbis Books, 1990.

Crawford, Eileen. "The Bb Burden: The Invisibility of Ma Rainey's Black Bottom." *August Wilson: A Casebook*. Ed. Marilyn Elkins. New York: Garland Publishing, 2000.

Cruse, Harold. "Contemporary Challenges to Black Studies." *The Black Scholar* (1984): 47.

Curry, Tommy. "Michael Brown and the Need for a Genre Study of Black Death and Dying," in *Theory and Event* 17.3 (2014): 4.

———. *The Man-Not: Race, Class, Genre, and the Dilemmas of Black Manhood*. Philadelphia: Temple University Press, 2017.

Dalton, Chantal B. "Teaching Black Literature to Undergraduates: The Problem of a Sense of Perspective." *Black American Literature Forum* 11 (1977): 102.

Dash, Julie. *Daughters of the Dust*. New York: American Playhouse/Geechee Girls, 1991.

Dietzel, Susanne B. "The African American Novel and Popular Culture." *The Cambridge Companion to the African American Novel*. Cambridge, UK: Cambridge UP, 2004.

Douglass, Frederick and William Lloyd Garrison. *Narrative of the Life of Frederick Douglass*. Wortley, near Leeds: Joseph Barke, 1846.

Du Bois, W. E. B. *The Souls of Black Folk*. 1903. New York: New American Library, 1982.

Elam, Harry. "Remembering Africa, Performing Cultural Memory: Lorraine Hansberry, Suzan-Lori Parks, and Djanet Sears." *Signatures of the Past: Cultural Memory in Contemporary Anglophone North American Drama*. Edited by Marc Maufort and Caroline de Wagter. 31–48. Bruxelles: Peter Lang, 2008.

Fabi, M. Giulia. *The Cambridge Companion to the African American Novel*. Edited by Maryemma Graham. 34–49. New York: Cambridge UP, 2004. 34–49.

Franklin, C. W. "Ain't I a Man?": The efficacy of Black masculinities for men's studies in the 1990s. In *The American Black Male: His Present Status and His Future*. Edited by Richard G. Majors and Jacob U. Gordon. 271–83. Chicago: Nelson-Hall, 1994.

Fields, Julia. "The Day Malcolm Died." *For Malcolm: Poems on the Life and Death of Malcolm X*. Eds. Dudley Randall and Margaret Burroughs. Detroit: Broadside Press, 1969. 34.

Gabbin, Joanne V. "Furious Flower." *Oxford Companion to African American Literature*. Edited by William L. Andrews, Frances Smith Foster, and Trudier Harris. 589–591. New York: Oxford UP, 1997.

———. "Malcolm X," *Oxford Companion to African American Literature*. Edited by William Andrews, Frances Smith Foster, and Trudier Harris. 472–74. New York: Oxford UP, 1997.

Garnet, Henry Highland. "(1843) An Address to the Slaves of the United States." Accessed Januray 20, 2017. http://www.blackpast.org/1843-henry-highland-garnet-address-slaves-united-states.

Gates, Henry Louis and Nellie Y. McKay, Eds. *The Norton Anthology of African American Literature, 2nd Edition*. New York: W.W. Norton Company, 2004.

Gordon, Dexter B. "Humor in African American Discourse: Speaking of Oppression." *Journal of Black Studies* 29.2 (1998): 254–76.

Gordon, Michelle. "Somewhat Like War: The Aesthetics of Segregation, Black Liberation, and *A Raisin in the Sun*." *African American Review* 42.1 (2008). 121–33.

Graham, Maryemma, Ed. *The Cambridge Companion to the African American Novel*. Cambridge, UK: Cambridge University Press, 2004.

Grandmaster Flash, Melle Mel, Shannita Williams, Joey Robinson, David McLees, and Rodger Clayton. "The Message." 1982. In The Best of Grandmaster Flash, Melle Mel & The Furious Five: Message from Beat Street. Los Angeles: Rhino, 1994.

Gray, E. S. "The Importance of Visibility: Students' and Teachers' Criteria for Selecting African American Literature." *The Reading Teacher* 62.6 (2009): 472–481.

Green, Tara. *Presenting Oprah Winfrey, Her Films, and African American Literature*. New York: Palgrave Macmillan, 2013.

Greenlee, Sam. *The Spook Who Sat By the Door*. Detroit: Wayne State University Press, 1990.

Guillory, John. *Cultural Capital: The Problem of Literary Canon Formation*. Chicago: University of Chicago Press, 1993.

Guillory, John and Jeffrey Williams. "Toward a Sociology of Literature: An Interview with John Guillory." *Minnesota Review* 61/62 (2004): 95–110.

Haley, Alex. *Roots*. New York: Dell, 1976.

Hansberry, Lorraine. *A Raisin in the Sun*. New York. Penguin Books, 1988.

Harper, Frances Ellen Watkins. *Iola Leroy, or Shadows Uplifted*. 1893. New York: Dover, 2010.

Harper, Philip Brian. *Are We Not Men?: Masculine Anxiety and the Problem of African-American Idenitty*. New York: Oxford UP, 1998.

Harris, Allen C. "African American and Anglo-American Gender Identity: An Empirical Study" in *Journal of Black Psychology* 22.2 (1996): 182–94.

Harrison, Paul Carter. "August Wilson's Blues Poetics," In *August Wilson: Three Plays* by August Wilson. Pittsburgh: University Press of Pittsburgh, 1991.

———. *Drama of Nommo: Black Theatre in the African Continuum*. New York: Grove Press, 1972.

Hawthorne, Nathaniel. *The Scarlet Letter*. Boston: Ticknor, Reed, & Fields, 1850.

Hayes, Floyd. *A Turbulent Voyage: Readings in African American Studies, 3rd Edition*. Lanham, MD: Rowman & Littlefied, 2000.

Hesmondhalgh, D. and Melville, C. "Urban Breakbeat Culture: Repercussions of Hip-Hop in the United Kingdom." In *Global noise: Rap and hip-hop outside the USA*. Edited by Tony Mitchell. 86–119. Middletown, CT: Wesleyan University Press, 2001.

Hill, Lauryn. *MTV Unplugged 2.0* . Columbia, 2002.

Hill, Patricia Liggins, ed. *Call & Response: The Riverside Anthology of the African American Literary Tradition*. Boston: Houghton Mifflin Company, 1998.

Hilliard, Asa. *The Maroon Within Us: Selected Essays on African American Community Socialization*. Baltimore: Black Classic Press, 1995.

Hine, Darlene Clark. "To Be Gifted, Female, and Black." *Women in Africa and the African Diaspora*. 181–92. Washington, D. C.: Howard UP, 1996.

Hollis, Yvette Walker. "Movies and More," Your Interracial e-mag: Love Yourself, Love Each Other." Accessed February 28, 2005. http://newpeople.weblogger.com/movies.

Hudson-Weems, Clenora. *Africana Womanism: Reclaiming Ourselves*. New York: Bedford Publishers, 1994.

Hughes, Langston. "Note on Commercial Theater." In *The Collected Poems of Langston Hughes*. Edited by Arnold Rampersad. New York: Vintage Classics, 1995.

Hurley, Dorothy L. "Seeing White: Children of Color and the Disney Fairy Tale Princess." *The Journal of Negro Education* 74.3 (2005): 221–232.

Hurston, Zora Neale. *Their Eyes Were Watching God*. New York: Harper Perennial, 2006.

Ideal J. *Hardcore* (1998). Accessed October 3, 2008. http://www.youtube.com/watch?v=i2shqSKRiE8

Iji, Edde. "African Cross-Currents and American Echoes: Ego-Identity Crisis in Two Plays." In *Black Cultures and Black Consciousness in Literature*. Ibadan, Nigeria: Heinemann, 1987.

Jackson, George. *Blood In My Eye*. 1972. Baltimore: Black Classic Press, 2002.

Jackson, Lawrence P. *The Indignant Generation: A Narrative History of African-American Writers and Critics.* Princeton: Princeton UP, 2013.

Jackson, Ron L., II and Celnisha I. Dangerfield. "Defining Black Masculinity as Cultural Property: Toward an Identity Negotiation Paradigm." In *Intercultural Communication: A Reader, 13th Edition.* Edited by Larry A. Samovar, Richard E. Porter, and Edwin R. McDaniel. 120–31. Boston: Wadsworth, 2012.

Jamal, Abu Mumia and John Edgar Wideman. *Live from Death Row.* New York: HarperPerennial, 1996.

James, Kery. "A L'Ombre de show business." *L'Ombre de Show business.* Paris: EMI Music, 2008.

Jarrett, Gene Andrew. *A Companion to African American Literature.* Malden, MA: Blackwell Publishing, 2010.

———. *Representing the Race: A New Political History of African American Literature.* New York: New York University Press, 2011.

John, Elton and Time Rice. *Elton John and Tim Rice's Aida,* Walt Disney Theatrical, 2000.

Jones, Gayl. *Liberating Voices: Oral Tradition in African American Literature.* Cambridge: Harvard UP, 1991.

Jones, LeRoi. *Preface to a Twenty Page Suicide Note.* 1961. New York: Marsillo Publishers, 1995.

Kanakaraj, S. "Heritage of an Old African Culture: A Study of Lorraine Hansberry's *A Raisin in the Sun.*" In *Indian Views on American Literature,* edited by A. A. Mutalik-Desai. 100–06. New Delhi, India: Prestige, 1998.

Karenga, Maulana. *Introduction to Black Studies, Third Edition.* Long Beach, CA: University of Sankore Press, 2001.

———. *Introduction to Black Studies, Second Edition.* Los Angeles: University of Sankore Press, 1993.

———. *Kawaida and Questions of Life and Struggle.* Los Angeles: University of Sankore Press, 2008.

———. *Maat, the Moral Ideal in Ancient Egypt.* Los Angeles: University of Sankore Press, 2006.

Kerman, Alfred. *Opera As Drama.* New York, Knopf, 1956.

King, Lovalerie and Shirley Moody-Turner, eds. *Contemporary African American Literature: The Living Canon.* Bloomington: Indiana University Press, 2013.

King, Martin Luther, Jr. "The Drum Major Instinct," *King Encyclopedia, Martin Luther King, Jr. and the Global Struggle.* Accessed January 29, 2017. http://kingencyclopedia.stanford.edu/encyclopedia/documentsentry/doc_the_drum_major_instinct/

Kirk, Keith B. "Eulogy as Mass Mobilization Narrative: Performing Commemorative Discourse in African American Civil Rights Funerals." PhD Dissertation. Northwestern University, 2013.

Knowles, Beyoncé. *Lemonade,* Parkwood Entertainment, 2016. Accessed January 30, 2017. www.beyonce.com/album/lemonade-visual-album/?media_view=songs.

Kunjufu, Jawanza. *HIP-HOP v. Maat: A Psycho/Social Analysis of Values.* Chicago: African American Images, 1993.

———. *State of Emergency: We Must Save African American Males.* Chicago: African American Images, 2003.

Lamming, George. *The Emigrants.* 1954. Ann Arbor: University of Michigan Press, 1994.

Lee, Spike. *Malcolm X.* Warner Brothers, 1992.

Lewis, Derrick C. "Maat, Egyptian Concept Inspires Schools Forum." *Michigan Citizen.* 16 February 1991.

Lindfors, Bernth. "Emerging and Neglected Literatures: Their Place in the Traditional Spectrum of Comparative Literature. *Report, Council on National Literatures* 1 (1974): 4.

Locke, Alain and Alan Rampersad. *The New Negro.* 1925. New York: Touchstone, 1999.

Lorde, Audre. *The Cancer Journals.* Argyle, NY: Argyle/Spinsters Ink., 1980.

M'Baye, Boubacar. *Trickster Comes West: Pan-African Influences in Early Black Diaspora Narratives.* Jackson: University Press of Mississippi, 2009.

Majors, Richard G. and Jacob U. Gordon. *The American Black Male: His Present Status and His Future.* Chicago: Nelson Hall, 1994.

Mane, Youssoupha. "Visiting Humorous Proverbs in African Literary Fiction." *Journal of Pan African Studies* 7.8 (2015): 110–120.

Marable, Manning. *New Black Renaissance: The Souls Anthology of Critical African-American Studies.* New York: Routledge, 2005.

Marsh-Lockett, Carol P. and Elizabeth J. West. *Literary Expressions of African Spirituality.* Lanham, MD: Lexington Books, 2013.

Marshall, Penny. *The Preacher's Wife.* Hollywood: Touchstone Pictures,1996.

Martha and the Vandellas. "Dancin' In the Street." In *Dance Party.* Detroit: Gordy, 1964.

Martin, Denise L. "Maat and Order in African Cosmology: A Conceptual Tool for Understanding Indigenous Knowledge." *Journal of Black Studies* 38.6 (2008): 951–67.

McCarren, Felicia. "Monsieur Hip-Hop." *Blackening Europe: The African American Presence.* In *Global noise: Rap and hip-hop outside the USA.* Edited by Tony Mitchell. 157–50. Middletown, CT: Wesleyan University Press, 2004.

McKay, Claude. *Banjo: A Novel Without a Plot.* 1929. Philadelphia: Harvest Books, 1970.

———. *Home to Harlem,* 1928. Lebanon, NH: Northeastern UP, 1987.

Médine. "How Much More French Can I Be?" *Time* (Europe) November 6, 2005 . Accessed October 3, 2008. http://time.comt/time/printout/0,8816,901051114–1126691,00.html.

———. "Lecture aléatoire." Accessed October 3, 2008. http://youtube.com/watch?v=1-x3kC2ZcQs.

Menken, A. and D. Zippel. *Disney's Hercules.* Milwaukee: Wonderland Music Co. and Walt Disney Music Co., 1997.

Mercer, Kobena. (2005). Diaspora aesthetics and visual culture. *Black cultural traffic: Crossroads in global performance and popular culture.* Edited by Harry J. Elam, Jr. and Kennell Jackson. 141–61. Ann Arbor: University of Michigan Press, 2005.

Miles, Suzanne. "Turning In: The Impact of Inner Resource Training on African American Adolescent Males." PhD Dissertation. Pacifica Graduate Institute, 2012.

Miller, Flournoy and Aubrey Lyles. *Shuffle Along.* 1921.

Miranda, Lin-Manuel and Jeremy McCarter. *Hamilton: The Revolution*. New York: Grand Central Publishing, 2016.

Mitchell, Tony. "Fightin' da Faida: The Italian posses and Hip-Hop in Italy." In *Global Noise: Rap and Hip-Hop Outside the USA*. Edited by Tony Mitchell. 194–221. Middletown, CT: Wesleyan University Press, 2001.

———. "Kia Kaha! (Be Strong): Maori and Pacific Islander Hip-Hop in Aotearoa—New Zealand." In *Global Noise: Rap and Hip-Hop Outside the USA*. Edited by Tony Mitchell 280–305. Middletown, CT: Wesleyan University Press, 2001.

Mizruchi. Susan. "Neighbors, Strangers, Corpses: Death and Sympathy in the Early Writings of W. E. B. Du Bois." *The Souls of Black Folk: Authoritative Texts, Contexts, Criticism*. Edited by Henry Louis Gates, Jr. and Terri Hume Oliver. New York: W. W. Norton & Company, 1999.

Monteiro, Lyra D. "Race-Conscious Casting and the Erasure of the Black Past in Lin-Manuel Miranda's *Hamilton*." *The Public Historian* 38.1 (2016): 89–98.

Morris, David. "Octavia Butler's Evolutionary Movement for the Twenty-First Century." *Utopian Studies: Journal of the Society for Utopian Studies* 19.3. (2015): 270–288.

Morrison, Toni. *Beloved: A Novel*. 1987. New York: Vintage, 2004.

———. *The Bluest Eye*. 1970. New York: Plume, 1994.

———. *Home: A Novel*. New York: Knopf Doubleday, 2012.

———. *Paradise*. New York: A. A. Knopf, 1998.

———. *Song of Solomon*. New York: Knopf, 1977.

———. *Sula*. New York: Penguin, 1973.

———. "Unspeakable Things Unspoken: The Afro-American Presence in American Literature." In *The Norton Anthology of African American Literature*. Edited by Henry Louis Gates and Nellie Y. McKay. 2299–2322. New York: W. W. Norton & Company, 2004.

Munroe, Myles. *Understanding the Purpose and Power of Men: A Book for Men and the Women Who Love Them*. New Kensington, PA: Whitaker House, 2001.

Murray, Carolyn Bennett and Jelani Mandara. "Racial Identity Development in African American Children: Cognitive and Experiential Antecedents. In *Black Children: Social, Educational, and Parental Environments*. Edited by Harriette Pipes-McAdoo. 73–96. Thousand Oaks, CA: SAGE Publications, 2001.

Nadel, Alan. "*Ma Rainey's Black Bottom*: Cutting the Historical Record, Dramatizing a Blues CD." In *The Cambridge Companion to August Wilson*. Edited by Christopher Bigsby. 102–112. New York: Cambridge University Press, 2007.

Nagler, A M. *Misdirection: Opera Production in the Twentieth Century*. Hamden, CT: Archon Books, 1981.

Napier, Wilson. "Madelyn Jablon's *Black Metafiction: Self-Consciousness in African American Literature*." Review of *Black Metafiction: Self-Consciousness in African American Literature* by Madelyn Jablon. (Iowa City: University of Iowa Press, 1996). *MELUS* 23.4 (1998): 216–218.

Nawaz, Aki and Natacha Atlas Akhenaton. "Islamic Hip Hop Versus Islamaphobia." In *Global Noise: Rap and Hip Hop Outside the USA*. Edited by Tony Mitchell. 57–85. Middleton: Wesleyan University Press, 2001.

Nelson, Alondra. *Afrofuturism: A Special Issue of Social Text* (Book 71). Durham: Duke University Press, 2002.

Nickels, Joel. "Claude McKay and Dissident Internationalism." *Cultural Critique* 87 (2014): 1–37.

No author. "Parents Try to 'Sway' Gender of Children." *Telegraph.* 30 Dec 2014. Accessed January 14, 2017. http://www.telegraph.co.uk/news/uknews/11316977/Parents-trying-to-sway-gender-of-children.html.

northup, solomon, Henry Louis Gates, and Ira Berlin. *Twelve Years A Slave.* New York: Penguin, 2012.

Obasi, Ezemenari M., Lisa Y. Flores, Linda James-Myers. "Construction and Initial Validation of the Worldview Analysis Scale." *Journal of Black Studies* 39.6 (2009): 937–961.

Ogle, Patrick. *Facets African American Video Guide.* 1994. Chicago: Academy Chicago Publishers, 2005.

Ohiwerei, Godwin. "Globalizing African American political thought." In *Malcolm X: A Historical Reader.* Edited by James L. Conyers, Jr. and Andrew P. Smallwood. 329–336. Durham: Carolina Academic Press, 2008.

Osborne, Charles. *The Complete Operas of Verdi.* New York: Da Capo Press, Inc., 1997.

Parks, Gordon. *The Learning Tree.* New York: Harper and Row, 1963.

Parks, Suzan-Lori. *In the Blood.* In *The Red Letter Plays.* New York: Theatre Communications Group, 2001.

Parks, Suzan-Lori. *Topdog/Underdog.* New York: Theatre Communications Group, 2001.

Pelzer, Danté L. "Creating a New Narrative: Reframing Black Masculinity for College Men." *Journal of Negro Education* 85.1 (2016): 16–27.

Perkins, Useni Eugene. Introduction to *Countering the Conspiracy to Destroy Black Boys,* by Jawanza Kunjufu. Chicago: African American Images, 1985.

Perry, Marc D. "Global Black Self-Fashioning: Hip Hop as Diasporic Space," in *Identities: Global Studies in Culture and Power* 15.6 (2008): 635–664.

Perry, Tyler, Roger M. Bobb, and Paul Hall. *For Colored Girls.* Tyler Perry Studios, 2010.

Petry, Ann. *The Street.* 1946. New York: Houghton Mifflin, 1974.

Poe, Daryl Zizwe. "Black Studies in the Historically Black Colleges and Universities." In *Handbook of Black Studies.* Edited by Molefi Kete Asante and Maulana Karenga. 204-Thousand Oaks, CA: Sage Press, 2006.

Prévos, Andre J. M. "Postcolonial Popular Music in France." In *Global Noise: Rap and Hip-Hop Outside the USA.* Edited by Tony Mitchell. 39–56. Middletown, CT: Wesleyan University Press, 2001.

Publisher's Weekly. "Editorial Reviews." *Aida: As Told by Leontyne Price* (New York: Gulliver Books, 1990). Accessed January 30, 2017, https://www.amazon.com/AIDA-Leontyne-Price/dp/015200405X/ref=sr_1_2?ie=UTF8&qid=1485829327&sr=8–2&keywords=aida+leontyne+price.

Prisco, Giulio. "Octavia Butler's Fictional Religion of 'Earthseed' Inspires Real Religious Movement." Accessed December 13, 2016. http://ieet.org/index.php/IEET/more/prisco20140620.

Price, Leontyne, "Storyteller's Note," *Aida: As Told By Leontyne Price.* New York: Harcourt Brace Jovanonich, 1990.

Rabison, Rebecca. "Deviance in Disney: Of Crime and the Magic Kingdom." In *Debating Disney: Pedagogical Perspectives on Commercial Cinema.* Edited by

Douglas Brode and Shea T. Brode. 199–209. Lanham, MD: Rowman and Little-field, 2016.

Randall, Dudley and Margaret G. Burroughs. *For Malcolm X: Poems on the Life and Death of Malcolm X*. Detroit: Broadside Press, 1969.

Ransby, Barbara. *Eslanda: The Large and Unconventional Life of Mrs. Robeson*. New Haven: Yale UP, 2013.

Rhodes, Mark Alan. "Placing Paul Robeson in History: Understanding His Philo-sophical Framework." *Journal of Black Studies* 47.3 (2016): 235–257.

Richardson, Marilyn. Preface to *Maria W. Stewart: America's First Black Woman Political Writer* by Maria W. Stewart and Marilyn Richardson. xiii-xvii. Bloom-ington: Indiana UP, 1987.

Riggs, Marlon. *Ethnic Notions*. Berkeley: California Newsreel, 1987.

Robeson, Paul. *Here I Stand*. 1958. Boston: Beacon Press, 1988.

Robinson, Paul. "Is *Aida* an Orientalist Opera?" *Opera, Sex, and Other Vital Matters*. 123–33. Chicago: University of Chicago Press, 2002.

Rushing, Andrea Benton. Introduction to *Women in Africa and the African Diaspora* by Rosalyn Terborg-Penn and Andrea Benton Rushing. ix-xi. Washington, D. C.: Howard UP, 1996.

Sciurba, Katie. ""The Wrong Things About Literature" Invisibility and African American Texts." *Curriculum Inquiry* 41.1 (2011): 126–131.

Seaton, Sandra. "*A Raisin in the Sun*: A Study in Afro-American Culture." *Midwest-ern Miscellany* XX 1992: 40–49.

Selvon, Samuel. *The Lonely Londoners*. 1956. New York: Penguin Books, 2006.

Shange, Ntozake. *for colored girls who have considered suicide/ when the rainbow is enuf: a choreopoem*. 1975. New York: Collier Books, 1989.

Shannon, Sandra D. *The Dramatic Vision of August Wilson*. Washington, DC: How-ard University Press, 1995.

Skloot, Rebecca. *The Immortal Life of Henrietta Lacks*. New York, Broadway Books, 2011.

Soyinka, Wole. "The African World and the Ethnocultural Debate." In *African Cul-ture: Rhythms of Unity*. Edited by Molefi Kete Asante and Kariamu Welsh-Asante. 13–38. Trenton: Africa World Press, 1989.

Stewart, Maria W. "Religion and the Pure Principles of Morality, The Sure Foundation On Which We Must Build." In *Maria Stewart: America's First Black Woman Politi-cal Writer*. Edited by Marilyn Richardson. 28–42. Bloomington: Indiana UP, 1987.

———. "An Address Delivered Before the Afric-American Female Intelligence Society of America." In *Maria Stewart: America's First Black Woman Political Writer*. Edited by Marilyn Richardson. 50–55. Bloomington: Indiana UP, 1987.

———. "Mrs. Stewart's Farewell Address to Her Friends In The City of Boston." In *Maria Stewart: America's First Black Woman Political Writer*. Edited by Marilyn Richardson. 65–74. Bloomington: Indiana UP, 1987.

Tanner, Lisa Renée, Shelley A. Haddock, Toni Schindler Zimmerman, and Lori K. Lund, "Images of Couples and Families in Disney Feature-Length Animated Films." *The American Journal of Family Therapy* 31.5 (2003): 355–373.

Temple, Christel N. "Communicating Race and Culture in the Twenty-first Century: Discourse and the Post-Racial/Post-Cultural Challenge." *Journal of Multicultural Discourses* 5.1 (2010): 45–63.

———. *Literary Pan-Africanism: History, Contexts, and Criticism.* Durham: Carolina Academic Press, 2005.

———. *Literary Spaces: Introduction to Comparative Black Literature.* Durham: Carolina Academic Press, 2007.

———. "The Cosmology of Afrocentric Womanism." *The Western Journal of Black Studies* 36.1 (2012): 23–32.

Terborg-Penn, Rosalyn and Andrea Benton Rushing. *Women of Africa and the Diaspora: A Reader.* Washington, DC: Howard University Press, 1996.

Thomas, Sheree Renée. *Dark Matter: A Century of Speculative Fiction from the African Diaspora.* New York: Aspect-Warner Books, 2000.

Tillis, Antonio. "Malcolm X-isms and the Protest Poetry of Blas Jiménez: Liberation byAny Means Necessary. *Malcolm X: A Historical Reader.* Edited by James L. Conyers, Jr. and Andrew P. Smallwood. 315–328. Durham: Carolina Academic Press, 2008.

Tomassini, Anthony and Jon Caramica. "Exploring 'Hamilton' and Hip-Hop Steeped in Heritage" *The New York Times,* August 27, 2015. Accessed January 2, 2017. http://www.nytimes.com/2015/08/30/theater/exploring-hamilton-and-hip-hop-steeped-in-heritage.html?_r=0.

Touré, Ahati N. *John Henrik Clarke and the Power of Africana History: Africalogical Quest for Decolonization and Sovereignty.* Trenton, NJ: Africa World Press, 2008.

Traister, Bryce. "Academic Viagra: The Rise of American Masculinity Studies. *American Quarterly* 52.2 (2000): 274–304.

Traylor, Eleanor W. "Re-Imagining the Academy: Story and Pedagogy in Contemporary African American Fiction," in *Contemporary African American Fiction: New Critical Essays,* edited by Dana A. Williams. Columbus: The Ohio State University Press, 2009. 160–171.

Tweedy, Clarence W., III. "The Anointed: Countering Dystopia with Faith in Octavia Butler's *Parable of the Sower* and *Parable of the Talents. Americana: The Journal of American Popular Cuture* (1900-Present), 13.1 (2014): 3–3.

Tyler, Tom R., Robert J. Boeckmann, Heather J. Smith, and Yuen J. Huo, *Social Justice in a Diverse Society.* Boulder, CO: Westview Press, 1997.

Urla, James. "We Are All Malcolm X." In *Global Noise: Rap and Hip-Hop Outside the USA.* Edited by Tony Mitchell. 171–193. Middletown, CT: Wesleyan University Press, 2001.

Valkeakari, Tuire. *Religious Idiom and the African American Novel, 1952–1998.* Gainesville: UP of Florida, 2007.

Van Sertima, Ivan. *They Came Before Columbus: The African Presence in Ancient America.* 1976. New York: Random House, 2003.

Walker, Alice. *The Color Purple.* 1982. Mariner Books, 2003.

Walker, David and Peter P. Hinks. *David Walker's Appeal to the Coloured Ctizens of the World.* University Park, PA: Pennsylvania State University Press, 2000.

Walt Disney Pictures ; Walt Disney Animation Studios ; produced by Peter Del Vecho ; original story, Ron Clements, Greg Erb, John Musker, Jason Oremland ; screenplay by Ron Clements & John Musker and Rob Edwards ; directed by Ron Clements, John Musker. *The Princess and the Frog.* Burbank, CA:Walt Disney Studios Home Entertainment, 2010.

Warner, William B. Warner and Clifford Siskin. "Stopping Cultural Studies." *Profession* (2008): 94–107.

Watts, Roderick Watts. "Integrating Social Justice and Psychology." *The Counseling Psychologist* 32.6 (2004): 855–865.

Weidhause, Nathalie. "Beyoncé Feminism and the Contestation of the Black Feminist Body." *Celebrity Studies* 6.1 (2015): 128–131.

Wells, Ida B. *Southern Horrors and Other Writings: The Anti-Lynching Campaign of Ida B. Wells, 1892–1900.* Edited by Jacqueline Jones Royster. New York: Bedford Books, 1997.

Welsh, Kariamu and Molefi Kete Asante. "Myth: The Communication Dimension of the African American Mind" *Journal of Black Studies* 11.4 (1981): 387–95.

West, Dorothy. *The Living Is Easy.* 1948. New York: The Feminist Press, 1987.

Widmer, Kingsley. "The Sociology of Literature?" *Studies in the Novel* 11.1 (1979): 99–105.

Wilkerson, Margaret B. "The Sighted Eyes and Feeling Heart of Lorraine Hansberry." *Black American Literature Forum.* 17.1 (1983): 8–13.

Wilson, Amos N. *Awakening the Natural Genius of Black Children.* 1991. New York: Afrikan World InfoSystems, 2003.

———. *The Falsification of Afrikan Consciousness: Eurocentric History, Psychiatry and the Politics of White Supremacy.* New York: African World InfoSystems, 1993.

Wilson, August. *Fences.* New York: Samuel French, 1986.

———. *Joe Turner's Come and Gone.* New York: Samuel French, 1990.

———. *Ma Rainey's Black Bottom.* New York: Plume, 1985.

———. *The Piano Lesson.* 1987. New York: Theatre Communications Group, 2007.

———. *Radio Golf.* New York: Theatre Communications Group, 2007.

Wilson, Harriet E. and Henry Louis Gates. *Our Nig, or Sketches from the Life of a Free Black*: in a two-story white house, north : showing that slavery's shadows fall even there. 1859. New York: Vintage Books, 2002.

Wilson, Khonsura A. "The Cosmopolitan Creative-Intellectual: The Creative Ideal of Paul Robeson." *Journal of Black Studies* 44.7 (2013): 725–740.

Wolfe, George C. *The Immortal Life of Henrietta Lacks.* Los Angeles: HBO Studios, 2017.

———. "The Last Mama-on-the-Couch-Play." In *The Colored Museum.* New York: Grove Press, 1988.

Wright, Richard. *Native Son.* 1940. New York: HarperPerennial Modern Classics, 2005.

X, Malcolm. *The Autobiography of Malcolm X As Told to Alex Haley.* 1964. New York: Ballantine Books. 1992.

———. *February 1965: The Final Speeches of Malcolm X.* New York: Pathfinder Press, 1992.

Index

About the Author

Christel N. Temple is associate professor and chair of Africana Studies at the University of Pittsburgh.